MW01232229

HISTORIC SMYRNA
An Illustrated History
by Harold Smith

Commissioned by
The Smyrna Historical & Genealogical Society

Historical Publishing Network
A division of Lammert Incorporated
San Antonio, Texas

Powder Springs St.
Harriby St.
Nickjack St. /Sunset Ave.
Southern Grocery
Trolley Depot
King St.
Bank St.
City Hall
Whitfield Grocery
Roswell St.
West Spring St.
Masonic Hall
Smyrna Memorial Cemetery
Drug Store
Railroad Depot
East Spring St.
Concord Rd/Memorial Dr.
D.C. Osborn Gar. & Ser. Station
ATLANTA - MARIETTA
J. L. Reed Home
W&A NC&St.L /L&N RR
Smyrna Hotel
Methodist Parsonage
First Methodist Church
Dr. W. T. Pace Home

Downtown Smyrna, Friday, May 29, 1936.

PHOTOGRAPH COURTESY OF REX PRUITT.

First Edition

Copyright © 2010 Historical Publishing Network

All rights reserved. No part of this book may be reproduced in any form or by any means, electronic or mechanical, including photocopying, without permission in writing from the publisher. All inquiries should be addressed to Historical Publishing Network, 11535 Galm Road, Suite 101, San Antonio, Texas, 78254. Phone (800) 749-9790.

ISBN: 9781935377283

Library of Congress Card Catalog Number: 2010939648

Historic Smyrna: An Illustrated History

author:	Harold Lee Smith
contributing writers for sharing the heritage:	Britt Fayssoux
cover artwork:	Claire C. Curtis, Stacey Jordan

Historical Publishing Network

president:	Ron Lammert
project manager:	Violet Caren
administration:	Donna M. Mata, Melissa G. Quinn
book sales:	Dee Steidle
production:	Colin Hart, Evelyn Hart
	Glenda Tarazon Krouse, Omar Wright

Downtown Smyrna, Thursday, August 6, 2009.

PHOTOGRAPH COURTESY OF JACK COLLINS.

CONTENTS

PREFACE

Extreme Makeover is a term that has become popular, especially in television, radio, newspapers, magazines and other media in recent years. It can mean anything from a facelift, a nose job, a tummy tuck or enhancements of other sundry body parts to making major repairs to a house or commercial building or the complete replacement thereof.

In Smyrna, "The Jonquil City of the South", "Extreme Makeover" means the complete replacement of it's "Downtown" business and government complex. After twenty years the transformation is still taking place. Residences and family owned businesses, shopping centers and other commercial enterprises in operation more than fifty years have been demolished and replaced, or are in the process of being replaced with modern structures.

Vast areas that were previously used for family farms, gardens, pasture land, or just providing green space to enhance the environment have been transformed into office and industrial parks. Hundreds of single and multi-family upscale residences and large subdivisions have been constructed.

One incident that might have accelerated the rush to "Extreme Makeover" happened in July 1988 when a contributing writer for *National Geographic* magazine, in an article entitled "Atlanta on the Rise" referred to Smyrna as "Redneck." Many Smyrna residents took exception to the characterization and demanded an apology. When the apology was slow in coming, an unofficial publicity campaign was conducted throughout the country with a series of news releases directed to the mass media and the Board of Directors and Trustees on the National Geographic Society. Local personalities appeared on radio talk shows locally and in Washington, D.C. The Smyrna City Council even considered a resolution condemning the magazine for the characterization.

Rebuffing the "Redneck" image of the people and the town, the mayor and council took a good look at the old downtown area that might have been partially responsible for the characterization and put their collective minds together. In January 1989 they (mayor and council) asked the Cobb County Legislative delegation to create a Downtown Development Authority for the city through the Georgia General Assembly. The approval came February 23, 1989, and in April the city activated the DDA and started "Building The Dream" of what Smyrna is today—"City of Excellence" 2003-2004 according to the Georgia Municipal Association and *Georgia Trend* magazine.

Of course, it's impossible to publish an in depth, comprehensive history of Smyrna in this one volume but it does give a broad look at some of the people, organizations and events that provided the leadership to make Smyrna one of the most desirable places in metropolitan Atlanta to live, work, and play. This somewhat condensed Smyrna history has been compiled from a variety of sources in the archives of the Smyrna History Museum operated by the Smyrna Historical Society for the City of Smyrna including bound volumes of the *Smyrna Herald, Smyrna Neighbor, the Cobb Chronicle, Vinings Gazette, Marietta Daily Journal, Cobb County Times* and others.

I especially want to dedicate this book to the memory of my late wife, Betty, and acknowledge her for the tremendous amount of research she did that has been incorporated into this history of the city that she loved so much. Her inspiration and encouragement during our 42 years together kept me going, even in those last months, when she was so courageously fighting the cancer that took her life on September 20, 1993. This book would not have been possible without her.

Thanks also to my "almost" lifelong friend, Norma McHann, the Associate Editor of *Lives and Times*, the bi-monthly publication of the Smyrna Historical Society, for about fifteen years of research that has contributed so much to this history. Joan Bennett's outstanding editing, re-editing and proofing, along with her suggestions have greatly enhanced the finished product. I also appreciate Lillie Wood's help in securing photos of some of the city officials and to her husband, City Councilman Pete Wood for the use of information from his monumental work on Smyrna family history *The Paper Boy*.

Throughout the book numerous other sources will be cited and, as always in a work of this kind, unintended mistakes and inaccuracies occur and we apologize for them in advance and ask your indulgence. Your corrections will be appreciated.

Harold Smith

CHAPTER I

WHAT'S IN A NAME?

❖

Excerpt from an 1860 map
of Georgia.

PHOTOGRAPH COURTESY OF PARKER M. LOWRY.

On a warm June day in 1872, a group of around twenty ladies and gentlemen were making ready for a trip from Marietta to Smyrna to attend a Saturday evening meeting of the Smyrna Lodge of Good Templars. (an organization promoting temperance). They had planned to ride the train for the ten-mile trip, but a schedule change on the railroad required that they make other arrangements. The "other arrangements" turned out to be a wagon drawn by two mules.

The wagonload of folks arrived in Smyrna about dark. On their arrival they were greeted by Mr. Davenport (possibly W. L.) and the ladies and gentlemen enjoyed supper by moonlight on a "carpet of green", the company of each other, fun and fellowship and the temperance meeting that was the purpose of the trip in the first place.

The unknown writer of that *Marietta Journal* article on June 15, 1872, went on to say there were speeches by Reverend W. A. Roberts of Marietta, Mr. Dozier of Atlanta and Dr. Bell of Smyrna. "The meeting was largely attended and much good will result from it", the writer predicted. The significance of that particular article was not the trip or the meeting, but that the narrative included a brief description of Smyrna as it existed just two months before its first incorporation on August 23, 1872…only seven years after the conclusion of the War Between the States.

The article went on to say, "Smyrna is one of the best openings for a large town in the state. Surrounded by a vast area of unoccupied territory where fine edifices could be built with the greatest convenience, only requiring the expenditures of a little greenbacks. A splendid depot, a frame church, a brick schoolhouse, and a framed store house and dwelling constitute its present size. A gushing spring of pure water edges the growth of timbers at the base of a gently sloping hill."

❖

Above: Smyrna Methodist Church, 1882, located on the west side of Concord Road, now Memorial Drive—a one block long street in front of Smyrna Memorial Cemetery. A portion of this building still exists and is used for commercial purposes at the rear of the original Gautschy House—now the Honeybee Boutique.

Right: Yankee Civil War General Neal Dow.

That was downtown Smyrna. Possibly the framed church shown here is the one that replaced the one referred to in the newspaper article. According to the 150-year history of the Methodist Church, *But Thou Art Rich*, this one was dedicated on August 24, 1882. It was located on Concord Road. At the time Concord was the short street in front of the Smyrna Memorial Cemetery, now referred to as Memorial Drive, and the building is believed to have been located on the property with the cemetery. The brick schoolhouse was the Smyrna Boy's Academy

In the outlying areas there were some houses and farms but even then the people were few and far between. It makes one wonder why the town fathers would think about incorporating such an isolated, unoccupied area. Eight years later, when the first U. S. Census of Smyrna was taken in 1880, there were still only fifty-one families in the town.

It could have had something to do with the end of the military occupation of the area by Union forces after the reconstruction period ended. Unfortunately, the real reasons for incorporating the town at that particular time have been lost to history. Anyone who might have had personal knowledge of it has long since died, and all official city records that might have shed some light on it were lost in a fire in the early 1920s.

There was a brief reference in the *Marietta Journal* to the incorporation in August 1872 but no other comments or details were given.

One theory attributed to the late Kennesaw Mountain National Park Superintendent, B. C. Yates, is that during the construction period of the W & A Railroad, the area was known as Neal Dow. Official federal maps of the Smyrna area before and during the War Between the States confirm this.

Dow was said to be a friend of engineer Stephen Harriman Long who laid out the W & A Railroad that runs through the middle of the town. The name Neal Dow was distasteful to the residents, according to Mr. Yates, of Smyrna, because he was an abolitionist and a Yankee military officer. The Smyrna folks, according to Mr. Yates, didn't want the town named for Dow and at the first opportunity they had after the restoration of the civil rights to the former Confederate States following the war, they took it. Thus it was incorporated by the Georgia Legislature with the Biblical name "Smyrna."

In addition, the area that is now Smyrna had also formerly been known as Varner's Station and Ruff's Station or Siding during and after the construction of the W & A Railroad. The Varners were landowners on the north side.

Buffalo Fish Town was another name given to the area when the Indians lived here. As soon as the white settlers started buying land and moving in the early days of the 1830s it was established as a non-denominational religious campground called by the Biblical name "Smyrna" after one of the churches established in Asia by the Apostle Paul in the first century A.D.

The interpretation that Smyrna was the site of Buffalo Fish Town was that of Sarah Gober Temple in Cobb County's premier history, written in the early 1930s, *The First Hundred Years*. She based her opinion on George White's *Historical Collections of Georgia*, written in 1849 and 1851. She quoted White as saying "Buffalo Fish Town was upon the plantation now owned by Mrs. Varner."

Solon Zackery Ruff's first wife was Susan Volumnia Varner. She died giving birth to Martin V. Ruff on September 18, 1858. They were the ancestors of many Ruff family members who still live in Smyrna and Cobb County.

Mrs. Temple went on to say that since Smyrna was originally known as Varner's Station, she assumed that the Varner plantation referred to by Mr. White was located in the area that is now Smyrna. In the earlier edition of his *Historical Collections*, he placed Buffalo Fish Town as "16 miles southwest of Marietta".

Regardless of the former names, shortly after the unwelcomed military rule and its associated hardships and the civil restrictions of the reconstruction period had ended, the name "Town of Smyrna" was officially incorporated in the charter that was granted by the Georgia Legislature on August 23, 1872.

The Charter provided:

1. The Town of Smyrna could sue and be sued and have a common seal as a body corporate.
2. The boundaries for the town extended one mile in every direction from the Smyrna Academy.
3. An intendant and four aldermen were named to hold office until an official election could be held on the first Saturday in July 1873.
4. The intendant and aldermen were given the power to make all rules and ordinances necessary for the peace, welfare, and prosperity of the town, but couldn't imprison anyone for more than twenty-four hours, nor could they fine anyone more than five dollars.
5. They had the authority to impose ad valorem taxes on all species of property, but the aggregate amount of taxes from "the entire citizenship" could not exceed fifty dollars for any one year.
6. Finally, this initial charter gave the town leadership control over "spirituous or malt liquors" and prohibited the manufacture or selling of them without authorization from the town.

The Act named John C. Moore as the first intendant (mayor) and E. D. L. Mobley, W. R. Beel (misspelled-should have been Bell), W. L. Davenport and G. P. Daniel as the aldermen.

But the development of the area had actually started some seventy-two years before the town fathers decided to be incorporated. The area had its beginnings in controversy and land disputes much like the annexation controversies between the Cobb municipalities and the Cobb County government in the past few years.

The difference is that in the early 1800s the disputes were between the Cherokee and Creek Indians, the State of Georgia and the government of the United States. The area that is now Smyrna was sparsely occupied by Indians who were here when DeSoto marched into what is now Georgia looking for gold and other treasures for the Spanish king. Too, both the Cherokee and Creek Indians, at one time or the other, claimed the territory where the City of Smyrna is now located.

Traditional history says the Cherokees won the land from the Creeks in a game of ball-play, or stick-ball. The ball for this game was made from a deer hide, and sticks, about two feet long that had an animal skin netting on one end—similar to lacrosse. The game is said to have taken place at what is now the city of Ball Ground in Cherokee County.

The dividing line between the Cherokee Nation and the Creeks was of no particular consequence until the Sate of Georgia decided it wanted the land. In a series of treaties the Georgia government had acquired all of the lands previously owned by the Indians, except the portion in the northwest section occupied by the Cherokees.

The land, now normally considered to be in the "Smyrna area", if not in the corporate limits, was located in the Cherokee territory and was sparsely settled at the time. On February 27, 1819, the Cherokees ceded a large portion of the northwestern territory to Georgia that eventually became parts of Cherokee, Dawson, Habersham, Hall, Lumpkin, Towns, Union and White counties.

This did not, however, resolve the problems dealing with the Indians because the Cherokee nation was developing its own government, alphabet, and newspaper and they had every intention of occupying the remainder of its northwest Georgia land permanently.

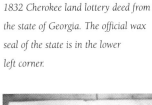

❖

1832 Cherokee land lottery deed from the state of Georgia. The official wax seal of the state is in the lower left corner.

Since the dividing line between the Cherokees and the Creeks had been in question, the State of Georgia claimed the area south of the Etowah River as its own, contending that the disputed area had actually belonged to the Creeks and that the land was ceded to the State of Georgia on January 22, 1918, in a treaty that also included the land south of the Ocmulgee and Altamaha Rivers. That area now comprises Coffee, Appling and Irwin counties.

These cessions, along with another of January 8, 1821, and usually referred to as the Indian Springs Cession, led to the formation of Dooly, Houston, Monroe, Fayette and Henry counties. DeKalb County was carved out of a portion of Henry and Fayette counties in 1822. This set the stage for the Georgia legislature to extend its jurisdiction into the area once considered Indian territory.

The Indian Springs treaty had also led to the distribution of the land through the fifth of Georgia's eight land lotteries. Legislation passed May 15, 1821, provided that the area previously mentioned should be divided into nine-mile square districts and land lots of 202 half-acres and distributed by means of a lottery. This still left the southern portion of the Cherokee Nation in dispute and this included the land that is now Smyrna.

The State of Georgia had urged the federal government to remove the Indians from the state for years to no avail. When the Cherokee Nation adopted its constitution in 1827, and established the capitol in what is now Calhoun Georgia (Gordon County), and proposed its own newspaper, *The Phoenix*, Georgia retaliated quickly. On the day after Christmas 1827 the General Assembly passed legislation extending criminal jurisdiction into the Cherokee Nation by adding that territory to Carroll and DeKalb counties.

In the meantime, gold had been discovered in Dahlonega and hundreds of Georgians were flowing into the area in search of the precious metal. A year later on December 20, 1829, the General Assembly passed additional legislation that placed the entire Cherokee Nation under Georgia law and divided the territory among several counties. They followed this up during the session of the legislature in 1831 by removing the land from the previous counties and making one large county called Cherokee.

That legislation provided that the land be distributed by means of a lottery and that all white, adult males who had lived in Georgia for the past four years were eligible for the drawings. Others who were eligible to participate were widows of

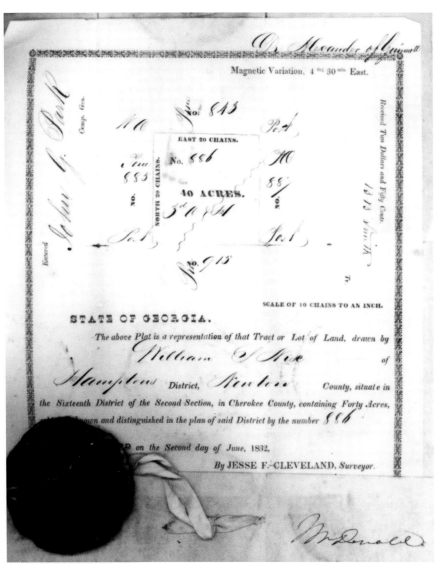

soldiers, orphans, physically handicapped persons, veterans, and their descendants.

The legislation also provided that the person whose name was drawn could obtain fee simple title to the land lot by payment of $10 into the treasury of the State of Georgia. In December 1833 the Legislature reduced the amount to $5.

Originally the person had five years in which to pay the money, but the deadline was extended several times. However, on December 21, 1843, the General Assembly approved legislation setting the final deadline to October 1, 1844. Any lots not accepted and paid for by that date were forfeited and reverted to the state.

Forfeited lots could be obtained by any citizen of the state by paying a certain amount of money for the lot of their choice on the schedule as follows:

Between	October 1, 1844	and November 1, 1844	$2,000
Between	November 1, 1844	and December 1, 1844	$1,500
Between	December 1, 1844	and January 1, 1845	$1,000
Between	January 1, 1845	and May 1, 1845	$500
Between	May 1, 1845	and July 1, 1845	$250
Between	July 1, 1845	and September 1, 1845	$100
Between	September 1, 1845	and January 1, 1846	$25
After	January 1, 1846		$5

Following the awarding of the granted lots, settlers started coming into the area to check out the lots to determine if they wanted to pay the price. Some left disappointed. Others brought their families, their worldly goods—lock, stock, and barrel—and started making a new life in the wilderness. Many of those who received the gold lots sold them, sight unseen.

Some of the people did not pay for their land right away although they did possess it. Others paid the fee without ever moving in and later sold the lot. For this reason it is impossible to tell who did and who did not move into what is today Cobb County.

Another thing that makes it virtually impossible to determine who actually settled in Cobb County is that most Probate Court wills and estate files, as well as Superior Court records of property transfers, sales, etc., prior to the War Between the States, were destroyed in the chaos of that conflict, and only those transactions and deeds that were "re-recorded" by the property owners after the war are part of the permanent records. The Georgia Department of Archives in Morrow, Georgia, does have some estate files.

Although there have been some stories over the years that the courthouse records were removed and carried to a safe place before the Union soldiers arrived to destroy and burn the Cobb County Courthouse, there are no substantiating records to confirm it. In a 1984 interview with Probate Court Clerk Vernon Duncan, he said none of the records that were supposedly "saved" have ever shown up anywhere and long-time Superior Court Clerks Ty Lee Terry and Jack Graham said the same thing about records for the Cobb Superior Court.

During the renovation of Glover Park in Marietta in 1985, the news media reported that a wooden tunnel under the park, said to have existed prior to the War Between the States, was believed to contain the long-lost courthouse records, but none were ever found.

The most accurate and readily available records as to who took possession of the lots are located in the office of the Surveyor General of the State of Georgia that is located in the State Archives building. When dates and lot numbers are referred to in this history, for the most part that's where the information was obtained from original records.

By the spring and summer of 1832, the surveyors were hard at work dividing the territory into "gold" lots of 40 acres and "land" lots of 160 acres. The drawings began in October, 1832 and the winners were announced at the state capitol in Milledgeville and a list sent to each of the counties.

But even before the surveyors finished their work, when the white men and women started coming into the area, their first priority was to construct shelters in which to live. The first structures were made of logs from forests of pine, dogwood, hickory, chestnut, sycamore and walnut. Mrs. Temple in her *The First One Hundred Years*, published in 1936, stated that the first structures were lean-to types, with just a

An exhibit featuring replicas of Sequoyah, the creator of the Cherokee Indian alphabet, and other Cherokee Indian leaders, was featured at Cumberland Mall in 1981.

top, a back and two sides. The front was open but it was said to afford protection against the elements and wild animals.

But the lean-to's were quickly replaced with the more substantial one-room log cabins, that more than likely had a dirt floor. Mud packed between the logs kept the cold winter winds out, and hinged solid wood "windows" would swing open to allow cooling breezes in. Unfortunately, none of the early log cabins in the Smyrna area are known to have survived, perhaps because of the war, or simply because the residents of the area demolished them to make room for more substantial buildings.

The second priority of these pioneers was to clear sufficient land to enable them to raise enough fruits and vegetables to provide food for the family, the animals that were used in farming, and the animals and fowl that were used for food.

Who the earliest pioneers of the Smyrna area were is still somewhat of a mystery and controversy. Descendants of some of the pioneer families tend to place their ancestors here earlier than available records confirm. Mrs. Temple, in her *First Hundred Years*, speculated as to when many of Cobb's first families actually arrived. Even with her extensive research, later records have emerged that indicated some of them arrived much later than first thought and some earlier.

A number of people who came into the newly-organized Cobb County had previously been residents of DeKalb County, and as mentioned earlier, for a short while, the area now known as "Smyrna" and vicinity, was a part of the Indian land that became DeKalb.

As those settlers arrived, one of the first things they did was to establish houses of worship. Early in 1832, even before Cobb County was created by the legislature, members of the Nancies (original spelling in church minutes of July 3, 1824) Creek Baptist Church in DeKalb County, including my great-great-great-grandparents, Greenville and Nancy Barnett Henderson, great-great-grandparents William A. and Martha Henderson Conn, and Mr. and Mrs. J. W. Lord, were asked by some settlers who had already come to this area, for help in establishing a church here. The Nancies Creek minutes read as follows:

"March 3, 1832: Third: Item—The church read a petition from several on the west side of the Chattahoochee River desiring to become a Constitution. Laid over until next meeting."

"April 1, 1832: Item—Called for reference and took up the reference on the petition of the Brethern (original spelling) at Nickajack. Brethern requesting to become an arm of this church. The request granted."

The outgrowth of that brief discussion led to the organization of the Concord Baptist Church —the first church of any kind to be established in what became Cobb County.

The first conference minutes for the Concord Baptist Church were recorded on October 13, 1832, two months before the establishment of Cobb County in December 1832.

Another important event in the early beginning of the church occurred on April 13, 1833. "The church agreed to call Brothers Solomon Peak, J. Reeves, Mitchell Bennett and some of the most experienced members of the Nancies Creek Church as helpers to examine it, and if found fit, to be constituted into a church." It was officially sanctioned by the Nancies Creek mother church two months later on June 8, 1833, thus establishing the area that is now Smyrna with a traditional religious background.

The traditional history of the church says the first meeting place was a log schoolhouse located near what is now the Crossings Shopping Center at the intersection of South Cobb Drive and Concord Road.

Buildings number 2, 3 and 4 were constructed on the property on Fowler Road where the Concord Baptist Cemetery is located which is presently owned by the Cobb County government. This building was moved piece by piece and reassembled at the present location on Floyd Road where Concord Road deadends.

Seventeen members who had worshiped in the log cabin school building for the first few months of the church's existence are considered the charter members: Roberts and Sarah Carter, (land lot 480), Benjamin and Rachel Collins, Mary Cox, Stephen Dale, James L. and Nancy Davis (land lot 768), Jane Harris, Mrs. Sarah Hinkle, Martin and Mary Ingram, Lucinda Malone, Margaret and Nathan Poole, Franky Reed (land lot 815), Rebecca (Mrs. Daniel) Reed, (land lot 342). These families formed the nucleus of the community. Reverend Thornton Burke was their first pastor.

In May 1833 the congregation constructed its church building near Nickajack Creek in the area that later became Mill Grove, the Concord Woolen Mill, the Daniel/Ruff Grist Mill, the Concord Baptist Cemetery and a thriving residential community.

COBB COUNTY CREATED

In December 1832, the Legislature divided Cherokee County, created the year before, into a number of counties, including Cobb. They named it for Thomas Welch Cobb of Lexington and Greensboro, Georgia. He was a lawyer, a United States Representative and a U. S. Senator. He died on February 1, 1830, two years before the establishment of Cobb County.

Before the land lottery and the creation of Cobb County, the white settlers had started moving into the area on a somewhat limited basis but, for the most part, in spite of some of the traditional history which indicates earlier settlement and development of the area, the district surveyors found little more than wilderness when they arrived in the spring of 1832.

W. F. Vanlandingham, a district surveyor for the State of Georgia, surveyed the 17th District third section of Cherokee in which Smyrna is located. The notes he made in his field book are unsurpassed in establishing the condition of the land, the improvements made by the Indians, the approximate number of acres in cultivation or cleared, and the relative value of the land with improvements. He also noted the type of vegetation and trees growing in the area. In addition, the notes established the names of Indian occupants at the time the county was organized in 1832.

Many historians have indicated settlements other than the ones recorded by Vanlandingham, but they were not specific as to where the settlements were located and the timeframe in which the Indians occupied the territory.

Cobb County archeologist Larry Myers, in an interview in 1983, stated that there are indications of an earlier Indian civilization in the area of what is Pretty Branch Drive but insufficient excavations and investigations and modern development have prevented learning much about the former occupants. Since the encroachment of the white man started some years

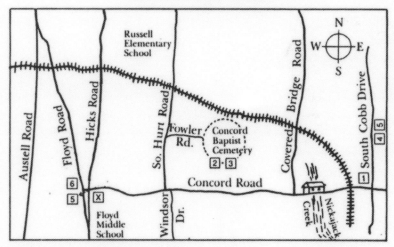

CONCORD BAPTIST CHURCH HOUSE LOCATIONS

Bldg. No. 1 The first meeting house, a log cabin schoolhouse, utilized in 1832.

Bldg. No. 2 Erected in May, 1833. The church was constituted the following month.

Bldg. No. 3 Completed in 1842, enlarged in 1853, and perhaps modified again in 1860. This building was rendered useless after the Civil War.

Bldg. No. 4 Built in 1866 in three months time. Another building was completed in 1883.

Bldg. No. 5 Completed in 1889. In 1909 was moved piece by piece to Floyd Road at which location it still stands.

Bldg. No. 6 Educational Building - started in 1961 and completed in 1965.
The present sanctuary - started in 1969 and completed in 1970.

Also noted on the map above is the pastorium, which is designated by an "X" at the intersection of Concord Road and Hicks Road. This house was purchased in 1964.

Right: Map showing Indian settlements in the early 1800's in the area that is now Cobb County.

Opposite, clockwise starting from the top left:

A portion of the west wall of the Concord Woolen Mill along Nickajack Creek that has fallen since this photo was made in February 1983. Other ruins of the factory that replaced the homes of the Cherokee Indians have been stabilized with supports in the shape of the original buildings and have been made part of Heritage Park.
PHOTOGRAPH COURTESY OF HAROLD SMITH.

The print shop at New Echota, the Capitol of the Cherokee Nation, near Calhoun, Georgia, where the Cherokee newspaper, The Phoenix was published. We have been unable to identify any Cherokee log cabins or other buildings in Cobb County that survived since the 1830s.
PHOTOGRAPH COURTESY OF HAROLD SMITH.

Typical log home of the Cherokees in the 1820s. This one is located in New Echota near Calhoun, Georgia.
PHOTOGRAPH COURTESY OF HAROLD SMITH.

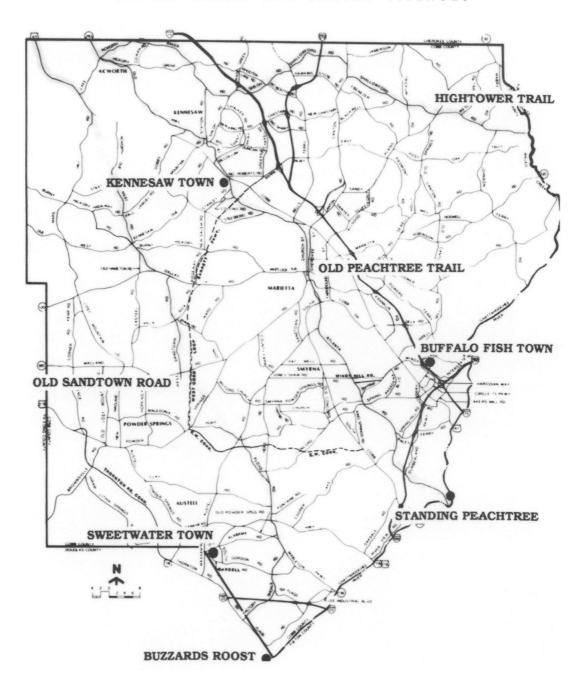

earlier, it is possible that many of the Indian families started leaving voluntarily long before the forced removal in 1838.

As mentioned earlier, when Mr. Vanlandingham surveyed the land he found only a relatively few Cherokee Indians in and around the land that is now closely associated with Smyrna, as noted in his field book dated June 15, 1832:

An Indian woman named Nana occupied lots 15 and 57. There were approximately 3 or 4 acres in cultivation. One acre on land lot 57 was planted in peach trees. Improvements on the land were assessed at $30.

An Indian woman named Naja occupied the area that is now Walnut Way, White Oak Lane and Shay Drive She had approximately 4-5 acres in cultivation and three log cabins on it worth $30 according to the assessment by the surveyor.

Cicada Nickajack is, no doubt, the person for whom the creek that flows through a large portion of south Cobb county was named, and at the time of the survey occupied the 160-acre tract that makes up land lots 124, 125, 164 and 165. Presently the property is bounded on the north by Church Road, on the southwest by Harris and Hurt Roads, on the south by Lakeshore and

Right: Many of the fortunate draws sold their land without ever looking at it. The Silver Comet Trail, a part of Heritage Park, is now located on the former railroad bed of the Seaboard Air Line Railroad right of way that has been converted a walking and bike trail. The photograph taken August 14, 1989, shows the dismantling of the railroad. The bridge over the trail was replaced with a fabricated steel and concrete bridge in May 2009.

Below: Entrance signs to some of the subdivisions located in the area of the former Indian territory near the Concord Bridge Historic District.

Opposite, top: Map of Smyrna and South Cobb County showing development on former Indian lands. All that remains of the Cherokee heritage in the Smyrna area today are a few names like Nickajack, Okema, Noses, Chattahoochee, Alatoona. Perhaps a few other Cherokee Indians still occupied several of the land lots, shown in the photo, in the spring and summer of 1832 when Cherokee County was surveyed by the state of Georgia for implementing the Cherokee Gold and Land Lottery.

Opposite, bottom: Smyrna city limits 1872-2009, the large circle represents the original city limits—one mile in every direction from the Boy's Academy. The city was reduced to one-half mile in every direction in an 1897 Charter Change and remained there until 1951 when the Belmont Hills area and property on the southwest border were added. Most of the other additions since that time were voluntarily annexed into the city by developers and other property owners wanting city services.

MAP COURTESY OF CLARENCE BLALOCK, CITY OF SMYRNA.

Plantation Drives and on the east by Old Concord Road and Nickajack Creek. Eight to ten acres were in cultivation and two log cabins were located on the property. It was valued at $35.

The fortunate draws in the Cherokee Land Lottery who paid for the 40-acre lots were Simeon G. Glenn of Jasper County, LL 124, Eberneza Jackson of Chatham County, 125, Hollis Cooley of Jasper County, 164 and John Crafts of Washington County, 165.

An Indian family named Chulow occupied land lot 190 at the time the survey was made. The property was noted to have a fine stream, a comfortable log cabin and ten acres of cleared land. The value of the improvements was said to be $40. The land lot was drawn for Lewis Barton of Habersham County and he paid for it on January 7, 1833. He was not listed as a resident of Cobb County when the first U. S. Census was done in 1834. A portion of land lot 190 is where the Concord Covered Bridge, the Daniell/Ruff Mill,

the ruins of the Concord Woolen Mill, Heritage Park, part of the Silver Comet Trail, the site of Cobb County's first Historic District and several mid and late-1800s houses are now located.

An Indian named Telurkirka occupied the adjoining land lot 191. The writing in the journal was bad and the improvements on the property could not be determined but it was valued at $30. The fortunate draw was James J. Turner from Henry County. He paid for the lot on December 25, 1838.

David Lockett was the fortunate draw for land lot 242 but William Barber actually took title when he paid for it on October 25, 1837. Land lot 243 was drawn by Garland Goff of Marion County and he paid for the lot on March 17, 1837. These three lots became part of the home land of the Ruff estate and is currently owned by the Harold and Janice Ivester family.

Portions of those lots and other nearby land later became the location for the Daniell/Ruff

Grist Mill and Concord Woolen Mill operations, the home of Cobb County State Senator John Gann and a post office called Mill Grove that was established on September 28, 1837 with its Postmaster Alexander McLarty.

Others that settled in the area were the Daniell, Griffith, Ruff, Love, Reed, Rice and other families, as well as the people who founded the Concord Baptist Church.

These properties currently make up several subdivisions including Deerwood, developed by the Bennett family in the 1970s and '80s; Norton Place (now Heritage Mill) developed by Dr. Benny and Nell Norton in the 1980s, Bentley Place, Patricia Place, and others in the 2000s.

Old Chulow possessed land lot 260 at the time of the survey and Thomas I. McCleskey was the fortunate draw for that land and paid for it on July 9, 1835. It contained a log cabin and had approximately 4 or 5 acres of cleared land worth $30.

An Indian named Tatagarka, the son of Walking Stick, was the occupant of land lot 317. There was a log cabin and about six acres of cleared land. The value of the improvements was set at $25. Eli Pritchett, of Coweta County paid for the land on January 30, 1836, but the fortunate drawer for this land lot was Revolutionary Soldier, Robert Henry, from Muscogee County.

An Indian named Wawneta was the occupant of land lot 318 containing a cabin and four or five cleared acres with a value of $20. The lottery winner for this lot was Julius Holmes of Bibb County. Land lot 319 contained a log cabin and four cleared acres and the value was $25. However, the handwriting in the journal was illegible and the name of the Indian could not be determined.

The four previously mentioned land lots 260, 317, 318 and 319 form an inverted L-shape that straddles Nickajack Creek and the East-West Connector partly between Concord Road and Fontaine Road. It includes a portion of an industrial tract of land adjoining the Seaboard Coast Line Railroad that was annexed into the city of Smyrna. Other development on that property includes the Anne Place subdivision, Castlebar Court, Saint Ann Court, Warrior Place, Peace Circle, Settendown Trail, Broken Arrow Court, the George W. Thompson, Sr., Park. Other nearby development has occurred along the East-West Connector/Concord Road,

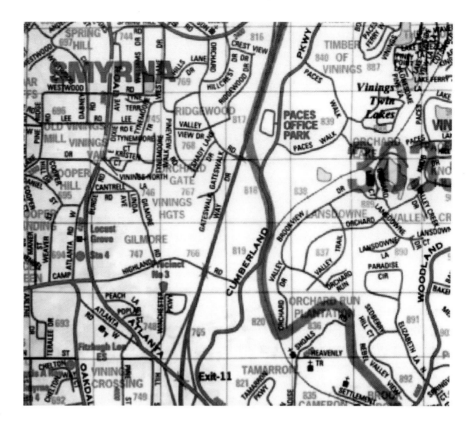

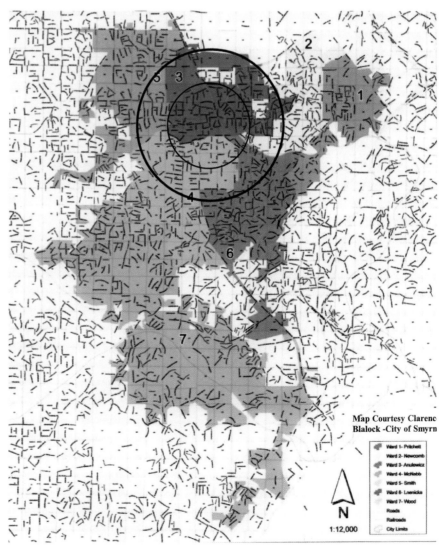

Map Courtesy Clarence Blalock -City of Smyrna

Ward 1- Pritchett
Ward 2- Newcomb
Ward 3- Anulewicz
Ward 4- McNabb
Ward 5- Smith
Ward 6- Lnenicka
Ward 7- Wood
Roads
Railroads
City Limits

1:12,000

Looking north towards Smyrna from the intersection of South Cobb Drive and U. S. Interstate 285. The first intersection north of I-285 is Oakdale Road. A quarter below the top of this photograph the light strip with considerable development on it is the East-West Connector that runs from the intersection of Atlanta Road and Cumberland Boulevard and joins with Barrett Parkway at the Dallas Highway in Marietta. Kennesaw Mountain in the background. The Smyrna city limits encompass over 2,000 acres of the land on the left beginning at I-285 and includes all of the Highlands Office and Industrial Park, a number of subdivisions on Oakdale Road on the west side of South Cobb Drive and the 13-acre River Line Park that cannot be seen in this photo and extends to Veterans Memorial Highway (Old Bankhead Highway in Mableton). Also located in the area is the huge Vinings Estates with over 400 houses with price ranges from $300,000 to $2 million. It is in the Smyrna city limits but has a Mableton, Georgia, 30126 address. City fathers have asked the postal service to change it to Smyrna. One of the twenty-seven Confederate Shoupades constructed to defend Atlanta during the War Between the States has been preserved in River Line Park.

PHOTOGRAPH COURTESY OF JACK COLLINS.

such as Heritage Park, Silver Comet Trail, Woodbridge, Heritage Mill (formerly Norton Place), Concord Walk, Deerwood, Hampshire Place, Patricia Place, Vinings Estate, Bentley Park and others.

There was a log cabin and 5-6 acres of cleared land on land lot 334 that William Reavis drew in the lottery. He was from Monroe County and paid for the land on August 15, 1837. The name of the Indian occupying the land could not be determined. The land later became part of the J. L. Dodgen estate on which a post office was located and which currently is in the vicinity of Nowlin Drive, a portion of North Cooper Lake Road, the site of the abandoned city of Smyrna Bohannon Creek Sewage Treatment Plant and landfill. It is currently being developed into an approximately 30 acre city park. Other housing developments are taking place in the area also.

The name of the Indian occupying land lot 339 could not be determined because of bad writing in the journal but there were three or four acres of cleared land valued at $10. The land covers what is now the intersection of North Cooper Lake, Concord, Hurt, and South Sherwood Roads.

An Indian named Wookana occupied land lot 391. It contained a log cabin and had eight acres in cultivation. The assessed value was $25. The land later became part of the J. L. Dodgen estate.

Land lot 402 that adjoins 391 contained a log cabin and had five or six acres of cleared land and the value placed on it was $20. It was also owned by Indian Nickajack.

An Indian named Talatangue owned land lot 546 with a log cabin and eight acres of cleared land valued at $30.

Land lots 690, 691, 750 and 751 were in possession of Indian Killis. There were three log cabins and a corn crib on the property and approximately 15 to 20 acres were in cultivation. The property was valued at $50. These land lots are located in the vicinity of present day South Cobb Drive, Oakdale Road and Church Road. For land lot 753 the field book notation said "An Indian improvement which has become the property of the State of Georgia by reason of the former owners evacuation to Arkansas. It has been rented out to a state agent named Phillips. The value of the property is $50." The land is presently divided diagonally by South Cobb Drive just north of Interstate 285 and contains dozens of commercial establishments, the entrance to the 1,000-acre Highlands Office Park that contains hundreds of large and small businesses. Much of that area is within the city limits of Smyrna including Highlands Park.

Land lots 754 and 755 were in possession of an Indian named Crawfish but the surveyor noted in the field book, "Elizabeth Elliott, a halfbreed has a title to the two lots valued at $20".

A man named Killin Morre had possession of 756 and 757, but Elizabeth Elliott had title to the two lots by legal transfer also. Improvements were worth $20.

The lots just mentioned stretch from the intersection of South Cobb Drive and Oakdale Road to the Chattahoochee River. They include Riverview Road, Maner Road, the Elmwood subdivision and a variety of business establishments, Riverview Cemetery and other development between I-285 and the Chattahoochee River.

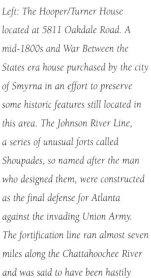

❖

Left: The Hooper/Turner House
located at 5811 Oakdale Road. A
mid-1800s and War Between the
States era house purchased by the city
of Smyrna in an effort to preserve
some historic features still located in
this area. The Johnson River Line,
a series of unusual forts called
Shoupades, so named after the man
who designed them, were constructed
as the final defense for Atlanta
against the invading Union Army.
The fortification line ran almost seven
miles along the Chattahoochee River
and was said to have been hastily
constructed by a thousand slaves.

Below: South Cobb Drive just north of
I-285. The vertical sign on the left is
located at the entrance to Smyrna's
1,000 acre Highlands Office and
Industrial Part that provides
headquarters and branch offices for
some of the nation's large
corporations. Prior to 1832 this area
was occupied by Cherokee Indians.

The last lot relative to today's Smyrna area is land lot 891. It was occupied by an Indian named Viskohajka (spelling?) who had a log cabin and 8 to 10 acres of cleared land. It was valued at $30. The streets in that area are North Elizabeth Lane, Rebel Valley, Sedberry and Hill Court.

As far as it can be determined through known existing official sources the lots named above were the only ones in the Smyrna area that were occupied by Cherokee Indians at the time the surveying was done in 1832. The "Gold" lots of 40 acres and "Land" lots of 160 acres were created with the numbers that are still in use today to identify the location of property.

The surveyor's journal that provided the information on district 17 also contained information for 21 land lots numbered from 1101 to 1234 in district 16 that is mostly located in Marietta and East Cobb. The information on those are not included in this book. However, we are including the 160-acre tract that make up lots 1174, 1175, 1202 and 1203. That land was occupied by a "Colonel Rice" who lived on the property that contained an "excellent limestone spring". The value of the property was $40. These land lots are included because of the significance of the name Rice to the development and operation of the Concord Woolen Mills in the last half of the nineteenth century and descendants who still live and work in the area today.

According to the field notes few Indians were left in the Smyrna area, even in 1832, when the survey was made. The Cherokees continued their struggles to retain their lands through the federal courts, but by 1835 some Indian leaders came to the realization that the troubles would end only with removal and that a treaty under the best possible terms was necessary.

In December 1835 a group of about three hundred Cherokees signed "The Treaty of New Echota" which was ratified by the United States Senate and signed by President Andrew Jackson on May 23, 1836. By the end of 1838 all of the Indians had left voluntarily or were removed by force by the federal government.

The city also owns the pre-War Hooper/Turner house that was part of the Johnston River Line and is said to have been used as a field hospital.

City council has also asked the United States Census Bureau to adjust the enumeration district in the 2010 census to include the citizens in that 30126 area to be counted in Smynra.

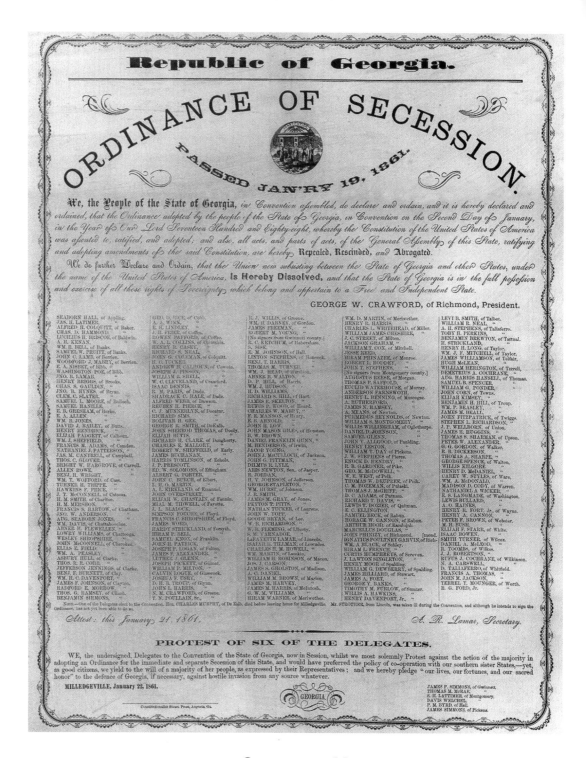

PROTEST OF SIX OF THE DELEGATES.

WE, the undersigned, Delegates to the Convention of the State of Georgia, now in Session, whilst we most solemnly Protest against the action of the majority in adopting an Ordinance for the immediate and separate Secession of this State, and would have preferred the policy of co-operation with our southern sister States,—yet, as good citizens, we yield to the will of a majority of her people, as expressed by their Representatives ; and we hereby pledge "our lives, our fortunes, and our sacred honor" to the defence of Georgia, if necessary, against hostile invasion from any source whatever.

MILLEDGEVILLE, January 22, 1861.

PHOTOGRAPH COURTESY OF TONY DOYLE.

CHAPTER II

FROM CHEROKEES TO WAR BETWEEN THE STATES AND BEYOND

The creation of Cobb from Cherokee lands by an act of the Georgia Legislature was passed on December 3, 1832. The distribution of the land by way of the lottery to the pioneers, eager to occupy the land, set the stage for developing Smyrna and the other villages, towns and cities that make up the dynamic metropolis it is today.

While pioneer families continued to come into Cobb County to claim their newly won land and start their new lives, sixteen months after the county was organized there were only 1,576 people in this vast wasteland. The first official census of the county was certified on March 4, 1834. It is, perhaps, the most accurate record of residency in Cobb during those early days. The census was completed in March 1834 by Ferdinand Jett. That census listed a total of 275 residences in the entire county and a total of 1,576 persons in those households.

This information has been arranged alphabetically, rather than in the order in which it was conducted for ease in locating a particular name. Please see the list on page 20. The number at the beginning of each line did not appear in the original census but was put in by the author. The number in the first column is what numerical order the census was conducted. and recorded by Mr. Jett. The number following the name is the number of people in the household. He certified the census as follows:

"I Ferdinand Jett, do hereby certify that I have taken the number and census of the whole population, who are citizens of Cobb County, to the best of my skill and information, which number is one thousand, five hundred and seventy six, this 4th day of March, 1834".

The names in bold type are the people who were closely associated with Smyrna in the early formative years. This determination has been made through a variety of records including minutes of the Maloney's Spring Primitive Baptist Church, the Collins Spring Primitive Church, and the Concord Baptist Church.

The 1834 census had been authorized by the Georgia Legislature on December 21, 1833, when the following legislation was passed. "It shall be the duty of the justice of the inferior courts, which have been created since last session, to appoint one "fit and proper" person to take a full and accurate census on or before April 1 the next." Just before the end of the year the Georgia Legislature passed House Bill No. 51 on December 19, 1834, incorporating the Village of Marietta.

The name Robert Daniell, (or any other Daniell) who was instrumental in or associated with developing Cobb County's first "industrial complex" on Nickajack Creek, did not appear in the 1834 census and was still listed as a resident of Clarke County in the 1850 U. S. Census. However, his brother-in-law, William Barber, who had married Robert's sister Rachel, was listed in the 1834 census. Like the Daniell family, some of the Barber family members had obtained land in the lottery and moved to Cobb from Clarke County Georgia where they had operated Barber's Mill near Bogart.

William Barber acquired at least 13 of the 40-acre "Gold" lots totaling some 520 acres in the 1832 lottery and other land purchases later. Judge James. Jordan Daniell (1877-1973) a son of Robert Daniell, and a former Judge of the Court of the Ordinary for Cobb County for sixteen years, speculated that William and some of the other Barber family members, who had also received land in the lottery, were the first of the family members to move to Cobb. They found it to be a desirable place to develop what eventually became the Daniell/Ruff Mills complex in the late 1840s in what is now the Concord Covered Bridge Historic District. In his writings Judge Daniel seemed to feel that Robert Daniell was enticed by his brother-in-law and sister to come to Nickajack before he actually moved from Clarke County. George White, in his 1849 *Statistics of Georgia,* reported the existence of Nickajack Factory and a saw mill operation in the area.

❖

Above: James Jordan (J. J.) Daniell, January 15, 1877, to March 21, 1973. He was Cobb County Court of Ordinary judge for sixteen years. Judge Daniell was one of a three member advisory board that governed the county. Daniell was the son of Cobb pioneer Robert Daniell, owner-operator of the Concord Woolen Mill along with Martin L. Ruff. In 1951 after Judge Daniell retired as Ordinary, he became executive director of the Cobb Chamber of Commerce. J. J. Daniell Middle School is named after him.

Below: These names are not part of the official census shown on page 20, but are names that were known to be in Cobb County in 1834 included in the count but not by name. The following names and the dates they joined the church were taken from the minutes of the Concord Baptist Church.

Carter, Sarah	June 8, 1833	Haynes, Malinda	September 13, 1834
Collins, Rachel	June 8, 1833	Hinkle, Sarah	June 8, 1834
Cox, Mary	June 8, 1833	Ingram, Mary	June 8, 1834
Davison, James L.	June 8, 1833	Malone, Lucinda	June 8, 1834
Davison, Nancy	June 8, 1833	Reed, Frankie	June 8, 1834
Ellis, Nancy	August 13, 1834	Reed, Rebecca	June 8, 1834
Harris, Jane	June 8, 1833		

No.	Name	No.	No.	Name	No.	No.	Name	No.	No.	Name	No.
3	Adams, Martin,	4	56	Dales, Stephen	5	125	Hunter, James	3	267	**Power, James**	2
260	Akins, John	9	108	**Davenport, Thomas**	5	44	Ingram, Martin	8	250	**Power, Samuel A.**	3
233	Akins, Thomas	8	186	Davis, Garry	9	96	James, John	4	58	Price, William	9
206	Anderson, Charles	2	187	Davis, James	7	112	Jefries, John	12	179	Pritchard, John	4
271	Anderson, James	6		L. (Davison?)	7	192	Jett, Ferdinand	10	135	Pruitt, John	4
65	Arnold, Elizabeth H.	5	254	Davis, Jesse	5	122	Johnston, Archibald	1	217	Pucket, Alexander	5
150	Austin, David G.	6	183	Davis, John S.	6	97	Johnson, Josiah	7	189	Quinton, Joseph	7
149	Austin, John	5	131	Davis, Jonathan. R. S.	8	223	Jowet, Gabriel	9	52	**Reid, Daniel (Reed)**	12
147	Austin, Nacissa	8	23	Davis, William M.	6	109	Kemp, Ira	3	49	**Rice, William**	3
239	**Baber, B. A.**	5	204	Delk, David	2	194	Kemp, Wiley	4	262	Richards, John	8
275	**Baber, George**	6	153	Dobbs, Martin	4	101	Kimbari, John	6	171	Roper (Raper), Joseph	8
240	**Baber, James**	2	118	Dobbins, William	8	273	Kuirttey, Lemma	5	121	Rowe, John	6
57	Baggett, Rural	10	245	Dougherty, James	7	154	Leathus, Abraham	6	133	Rowell, James	7
80	Baker, Absalom	3	181	Dozier, John	2	165	Linsey, John	9	6	Runnels, Gallant	8
216	Baker, D. C.	5	185	Dudley, Daniel	4	71	Long, Charles	5	83	Rush, James	3
79	Baker, William	12	205	Dukes, Mozes	2		Low, John C.	6	182	Sanders, B. B.	10
70	**Barber, Richard**	2	103	Duncan, Will W.	8	18	Lowry, John W.	8	90	Samson, William	10
53	**Barber, William**	12	156	**Dunn, Henry**	3	2	Luther, Josiah	3	61	Shaw, Haley	8
94	**Barnes, Martha**	7	207	**Dunn, William**	9	29	Malone, Robert	9	107	Shumate, Joseph D.	8
272	Beavers, Mary	5	261	Edwards, Alfred	4	35	Malone, William B.	8	51	**Simpson, Dicey**	6
32	Belk, Warner A.	1	204	Ellington, David B.	4	14	**Maloney, Samuel**	4	277	**Simpson, Leonard**	7
172	**Bell, George**		45	Ellis, Silas	3	16	**Maloney, William P.**	4	228	Sims, John	8
236	Berry, James	9	27	Ellsberry, Linsey	11	110	**Maloney, William W.**	7	72	Smith, Abaslom	4
139	Benson, William B.	4	265	Fielder, George	7	208	Martin, Austin	5	268	Smith, Bradley	3
117	Blackstock, Wilson	?	98	**Gober, G. W.**	10	92	Martin, John	6	173	Smith, Gideon	3
62	Blocker, Redding	8	111	Glenn, John	8	249	Martin, Larkin	6	196	Smith, Stephen	2
66	Bolton, John	5	211	Glover, Richard	5	248	Martin, Nathan	5	198	Smith, Stephen	2
212	Booth, Margaret	2	178	Goddard, John	5	215	Martin, Robert	3	258	Stancel, Elijah	4
193	Bredwell, Henry	5	225	Goggins, Elihu	4	213	Martin, Tandy K.	5	143	Stewart, George	4
234	Brockman, John B.	7	244	Goss, Riley	6	4	Massey, Josiah	8	138	Stewart, James	5
50	Brogdin, David	1	93	Gour, Notley	6	114	May, Daniel	7	124	Stewart, Robert	7
253	Butler, George	8	151	Gray, Isasc	3	136	Maway, George H.	3	89	Stinson, Frances	1
41	Camp, Abner	7	222	Gregory, Jackson	5	270	Mays, Edward	6	120	Stroud, A. G. W.	2
161	**Camp John T.**	6	238	Griffin, Solomon	6	123	Meadows, Jacob	4	115	Stroud, John	7
175	Canada, David	7	190	Grizzell, James	5	7	Mills, Enoch R.	4	191	**Tait, William**	3
162	Canada, William	4	163	Guess, Nathaniel	13	140	Minor, Robert H.	3	5	Thompson, John	8
1	Carlile, William	7	188	Guess, William	9	73	Moore, Joel	9	19	Thrasher, Jesse	8
170	Carnes, Green	6	148	Gurley, Elizabeth	3	25	**Moore, John**	13	214	Treadaway, Hezekaih	4
168	Carnes, James	7	77	Hacket, Oliver	7	176	Morris, Josiah	9	36	Trout, Gideon	11
174	Carnes, Joseph	2	106	Harmon, Samuel	12	166	Morris, Moses	6	78	Tucker, John	8
169	Carnes, Lydia	9	91	**Harper, George**	5	76	Morris, William	9	81	Tucker, Nelson	1
160	Caruth, Robert	9	63	Harris, Archibald	5	167	Morris, William	3	201	Wadkins, Davis	2
33	**Carter, Robert**	9	10	Harris, Charles	9	88	Mulligan, Berry	6	02	Wadkins, Jesse	4
34	Chastain, Joseph	8	64	Harris, Ester	4	132	Mullins, Ausburn	9	255	Wallace, Elizabeth	2
37	Clark, Caleb	6	95	Harris, James	3	130	Mullins, Buda	3	55	Wallace, Peter	7
100	Clay, James	7	15	Harris, James	3	129	Mullins, Burgi	8	74	Waller, James B.	1
85	Clay, John	10	39	Harris, William	7	11	Mullins, John D.	2	226	Watson, Robert	5
84	Clay, Silas H.	2	99	Harris, William	5	152	Mullins, Samuel	4	209	Web, Clinton	4
266	Coleman, John	4	12	Harvel, Riley (Harrell?)	8	57	Murdock, Joseph A.	6	87	Wells, John A.	5
219	Coleman, Renne	3	180	Hawk, Thompson	8	59	**Muriner, John C.**	8	113	West, Thomas C.	3
237	Coleman, Renne	7	60	Haynes, Ephram	5	21	McAfee, James T.	4	42	**Whitfield, Elizabeth**	2
218	Coleman, Richard	4	28	Herndon, Benjamin	6	227	McDonald, Joseph	5	82	Whitehead, Gideon	2
184	**Collins, Charles**	4	8	Henderson, James	9	67	**McDowell, Robert**	4	48	Whitehead, Thomas, Jr.	4
264	**Collins, James**	7	247	Henderson, Mahaffy	3	177	McKenzie, John	9	134	Williams, Briant	6
158	**Collins, John**	8	31	Henry, George	1	17	McLain, Silas	6	142	Williams, Elijah	2
30	**Conn, Samuel**	9	120	Henson, Isaac	5	126	Nesbit, Jeremiah	2	137	Williams, William	4
104	Copeland, Thomas	?	210	Hestalir, James	8	195	**Pace, Abraham**	9	241	Williford, John M.	13
220	**Cox, Robert**	3	257	Hicks, Henry	8	26	**Pace, John**	11	153	Wilson, William	6
69	**Cox, Willis**	3	116	**Hill, John**	5	197	**Pace, John**	5	144	Winfra, Jesse	10
68	Crenshaw, Nathaniel	8	128	**Hill, Joshua**	9	252	Paxton, Martin R.	4	275	Winter, George W.	9
200	Crow, Jacob	11	224	**Hill, William**	7	276	Pearce, Elizabeth	4	75	Wolf, Mary	2
40	Croxton, Elijah	2	159	Hollins, Benjamin	3	229	Pearce, Mastin	7	242	Womack, Bird	5
243	Cudd, John	11	141	Hollaway,	4	55	Pearce, William	3	235	Womack, Thomas	5
19	Cupp, Henry, Jr.	3	146	Hollaway, Samuel	4	51	Pollard, James W.	4	246	Worthy, William	4
13	Cupp, Henry, Sr.	4	27	Hornbuckle, R. B.	4	251	Pope, Micajah	6	256	York, William	8
20	Cupp, Michael	4	43	Hubbard, John	4	145	Porterfield, Nelson	3			
259	Cupp, Thomas	4	164	Hulbut, Samuel	9	46	Powell, Lewis R.	9			

In the meantime, while Concord and Mill Grove were developing along Nickajack Creek, the state of Georgia was making more decisions that would have a major effect on Smyrna's future. The idea for a railroad from Chattanooga, Tennessee, to Terminus had been discussed for years. The state had also discussed the possibility of making the Chattahoochee navigable for commercial purposes. However, it wasn't until December 21, 1836, that legislation passed authorizing construction of the Western and Atlantic Railroad. That act set in motion the eventual construction of the state-owned railroad that still runs through the heart of Smyrna today.

The route of the railroad from Chattanooga to Terminus, (changed to Marthasville and eventually Atlanta) followed or paralleled some of the old Indian trails and roads. Stephen Harriman Long was hired as the engineer to undertake plotting the route and building the Western and Atlantic Railroad.

Construction planning and work for the W & A started on July 4, 1837. The first trip from Marthasville to Marietta was made on Christmas day, December 25, 1842. It probably was not as important a date as the July 4, 1864, when the Battle of Smyrna Campground was fought during the War Between the States but the construction of the railroad had a profound effect on the future of the area. It helped to establish a permanent location for the town between Marietta, the county seat of Cobb and Marthasville (changed to Atlanta in 1847).

Originally, the city limits of Smyrna and Atlanta were separated by approximately fifteen miles. Today, on Smyrna's south side in the area of I-285 and South Cobb Drive, and Atlanta's north edge that runs along the Chattahoochee, the city limits are less than one mile apart.

On the north, Smyrna and the Marietta city limits have both expanded and currently join in several places near the intersection of Windy Hill Road and Roswell Street and along U. S. 41 (Cobb Parkway).

The community at Mill Grove and Concord had been the main focus of activity in the southern part of the county but now the construction of the W & A Railroad was bringing new people and new jobs into a different area more and more of the fortunate draw winners in the Cherokee Land Lottery found it easier to get to their new land. As they settled in and started building homes near the railroad, they found that the nearest place of worship was about three miles west—in the Mill Grove and Concord area. The W & A brought in some of the people who established the Smyrna Campground.

Opposite: The first official census of Cobb County, certified on March 4, 1834.

Above: Located in the heart of the city, the grave marker shown is that of Betty and Harold Smith, co-founders of the Smyrna Historical Society and the Smyrna Museum. Betty died September 20, 1993. Shortly before she died, Betty, Smyrna Public Relations Director Kathy Barton and Keep Smyrna Clean and Beautiful activist Sue Brissey developed the slogan that is on the Smith family marker. The inscription says: "Our message for Smyrna: Challenge the present, vision the future, reflect the past, cherish the heritage." The slogan has been used on a number of the city's news releases, brochures and documents.

Left: Historical markers in Smyrna Memorial Cemetery showing burial place of Smyrna's first mayor.

One of the oldest historic features in the city is the Smyrna Memorial Cemetery said to have been established in 1838 by the Methodist Church. The city accepted ownership of the cemetery from the church in 1959 and took responsibility for its upkeep.

Smyrna's first Mayor, John C. Moore and one of the city's first councilmen, Dr. W. R. Bell, October 30, 1826, to July 3, 1876, and other city leaders are buried at Smyrna Memorial Cemetery.

Traditional history says the new people coming into town as a result of the railroad construction established a brush arbor non-denomination worship center that became known throughout Georgia as "Smyrna Campground", named for one of the churches established by the Apostle Paul in Asia Minor. It was located in land lot 522 at the intersection of what is now the southeast corner of Church and King Streets. This property was eventually acquired by the Smyrna Methodist Church through gift or purchase. Over the years, according to their 150-year history *But Thou Art Rich,* published in 1990, the location was the site of several brush arbors, the Smyrna Methodist Campground and five Smyrna Methodist Church facilities.

The somewhat questionable date, according to their history, of the founding of today's Smyrna First United Methodist has been placed at 1838. Some people who are said to have donated the property for the church apparently did not own the land at the time. In a deposition February 2, 1915, in an effort to "recreate" a deed that had been destroyed by federal troops during the War Between the States, J. P. Bowie said "about 1846 the trustees of the Methodist Episcopal Church-South purchased from Hardy Pace a lot of land number five hundred and twenty-two in the 17th district and second section of Cobb County containing forty acres, more or less". The Smyrna Memorial Cemetery is located within that forty acres.

In 1994 the City of Smyrna authorized the establishment of the Smyrna Cemetery Association to work it into the downtown redevelopment program. Mayor Bacon and members of the council appointed the five original board members: Nancy Hancock, Chairperson, Jim Wooten, Charlotte Bryan, Bobby Landers and James Mixon. Jean Bennett was named secretary. City council members who made up the original

Historical Review Committee were Bill Scoggins, chairman, Jim Hawkins and Pete Wood. In the next few months John Woodyard and Harold Smith were added. The association initiated a program to install a new rock wall and a wrought iron fence around it, a new landscape and beautification plan, a memorial walk where individuals could purchase bricks to honor their loved ones, and several historical markers telling the history of the cemetery.

Another major project was an archeological survey to determine if there were any unmarked graves. The survey revealed 243 marked graves and 395 unmarked graves. The Cemetery Association secured marble numbered markers for each of them and documented their location.

By 1840 many of the family names that are familiar today were beginning to arrive in what is today's "metropolitan Smyrna". Cobb County had grown to a population of 7,538 and a goodly number of them were in the southern part of the county.

The earliest settling of these areas can almost be traced by the dates that U.S. post offices were established. The very first post office in the county was the Cobb Courthouse Post Office, established on September 23, 1833. The first one in the Smyrna area was Mill Grove, September 28, 1837. It was located in the area of the Daniell/Ruff Grist Mill. Alexander McLarty was the postmaster. Three other postmasters served at Mill Grove: John H. Walker, December 19, 1838, Samuel Burdine, May 8, 1839, until January 5, 1867, when the post office was discontinued. It was re-established on July 1, 1869, with Hartwell A. Baldwin as postmaster. The Mill Grove post office was discontinued forever on April 3, 1870.

Another post office in the vicinity of today's Smyrna was at Boltonville (Log Cabin, Collins Spring, Carmichaels area) and was established December 22, 1842, with James A. Collins as postmaster. Henry Y. Dean became the postmaster June 19, 1845, and the name of that post office was changed to High Bridge on March 2, 1846, with Bushrod Pace the postmaster. It was changed back to Boltonville November 13, 1849. Another familiar name associated with Smyrna Methodist Church was Joseph V. Stanback. He served as postmaster for the Boltonville post office from March 8, 1855, until February 20, 1857.

Joe Chaney's Arm

Many years ago before Joe Chaney's body was laid to rest in the New Smyrna Cemetery on Hawthorne St., his right arm was laid to rest at this approximate location in this cemetery.

He lost his arm when a shotgun discharged and severed the limb while he was removing the gun from the back of a wagon to shoot a water moccasin in a creek on Spring Road. The arm was buried here and Mr. Chaney often visited the severed member and placed flowers on the grave. He was born Feb. 22, 1875 and died May 14, 1954.

Boltonville was one of the train stops reported in the 1854 Phelps' Travel Guide of Railroad, Canal, Stage, and Steamboat Routes in the U.S. Smyrna was later added to the stops on the W & A Route. The schedule was donated to the Smyrna Museum by former resident and relative of Smyrna's Swain family, Bill Dennis, and his wife Betty.

There was a post office named Paces Ferry established on December 2, 1839, that was changed to Cross Roads in DeKalb County. It was discontinued March 2, 1846. The postmaster was none other than the well known, by this time, Pinkney Randall who is believed to be one of the original founders of the Smyrna Methodist Church, along with Asbury Hargrove and the Bowie family.

On May 25, 1852, Martin L. Ruff was postmaster for the "Neal Dow" post office, one of the names Smyrna was called in the early days. He served until replaced by William S. Tweedall June 24, 1856. Isaac R. Teat became postmaster on January 28, 1858, at Neal Dow. Furman R. Robert served as postmaster from August 27, 1858, until the post office was discontinued in November 1858.

The census of 1845, conducted by the state of Georgia, gave Cobb County 10,518 inhabitants, of which 1,474 were slaves. In the 1850 U.S. Census, Cobb County had a total of 11,571 free persons. That number included 2 free colored females and one free male. There were 5,872 free white males and 5,696 free white females. This was the first census when a separate census of

the slaves was conducted. The slave schedule was enumerated again in the 1860 census. That year there were 2,272 slaves in the county. In all of Cobb County there were 931 farms and 10 manufacturing operations of various kinds

In the meantime, two additional churches were organized on Smyrna's outskirts. About one mile north of today's Smyrna the Maloney's Spring Primitive Baptist Church was constituted on September 12, 1851. The charter members of the church were: John and Elizabeth Walraven, Mason Ragsdale, Iti Margaret and Mary Prewett, and Margaret White. Isaac R. Teat was the pastor and Mason Ragsdale was the clerk.

On the south side in the area that is now the intersection of I-285 and Atlanta Road, the Collins Springs Primitive Baptist Church was chartered around 1856. Unfortunately the original church and all its records were destroyed during the War Between the States and minutes from the church are only available since 1866, the year the church was rebuilt. In 2008 the building was sold to the Atlanta Freethought Society.

The adjoining Collins Springs Cemetery is owned by the Collins Springs Cemetery Association, Inc. Many of Cobb's early pioneers are buried there including Alfred Maner who was a justice of the peace and the state representative from Cobb when the creation of Fulton County was authorized by the Georgia General Assembly in 1853 from part of DeKalb County. In 1923 the state eliminated Campbell

◆

This building was located on the east side of Log Cabin Drive just south of present-day I-285 and Atlanta Road. It was operated by the family of Jimmy Carmichael who was general manager of the Bell Bomber Plant in Cobb County 1942-1945 during World War II. The family also had their residence and a blacksmith shop on the property. The buildings were demolished in the early 2000s to make way for mixed use of single family residences, townhouses and multi-family housing. Jimmy Carmichael won the popular vote for governor of Georgia in the late 1940s but lost the election because of the county unity system of voting.
PHOTOGRAPH COURTESY OF VIRGINIA CARMICHAEL AND THE SMYRNA MUSEUM.

and Milton Counties and the Roswell District of Cobb and added the land to Fulton.

In addition to the churches providing for the spiritual life of many of the citizens they also provided a lot of the social activities including picnics, hay rides, fish frys and a variety of other games and activities.

The I-285 and Atlanta Road intersection is a quarter mile north of the Collins Springs Church and Cemetery and it is, perhaps, the southern boundary of the mid-1800s Oakdale and Gilmore communities. Easy access from Atlanta via the W & A Railroad and later by the Atlanta Northern Railway Interurban Trolley brought many prominent Atlanta business people and families to the area. They purchased large tracts of inexpensive land and established weekend retreats and summer homes. Like Smyrna, Oakdale and Gilmore, until the late 1930s, had the old Dixie Highway (U.S. 41) running right through the middle. The traffic heading south helped provide business for grocery stores, service stations, doctors' offices, barber shops, and garages and other small business.

Groundbreaking ceremonies for West Village at the intersection of I-285 and Atlanta Road took place in 2005. Two years later it was awarded the "2007 Development of Excellence" by the Atlanta Regional Commission and the Livable Communities Coalition. The development replaced 46 homes and/or businesses on 44 acres in the Oakdale community. In ceremonies sponsored by the Cobb Chamber of Commerce in December 2007, the Smyrna/Vinings *Bright Side* newspaper quoted Woody Snell, a partner with the Pacific Group, as saying "West Village has brought the Smyrna community together with a variety of places to shop, eat and live. We offer something for everyone in a classic neighborhood environment." The first phase includes 105,650 square feet of retail space, 115 townhouses, 120 condominiums and 292 for-lease-condos and 23 single-family residences. An additional 400 condos will be constructed in eight-story buildings as the market demands according to Mr. Snell. Sale prices start at approximately $200,000, for the condos, $400,000 for the town houses and $600,000 for the single family, detached residences.

❖

Left: Map shows the route of the Western and Atlantic Railroad through Smyrna.
PHOTOGRAPH COURTESY OF MELINDA JOLLEY MORTON.

Right: Train schedule from the 1854 Phelps Travel Guide was donated to the Smyrna Museum by former Smyrna resident Bill Dennis and his wife.

(439) F'M ATLANTA TO CHATTANOOGA, Tenn. Western and Atlantic RR.		
Boltonville	8	
Marietta	12	20
Noonday	6	26
Acworth	9	35
Alatoona	5	40
Cartersville	9	49
Cassville	5	54
Kingston	6	60
Adairsville	10	70
Oothkaloga	10	80
Resaca	5	85
Dalton	15	100
Tunnel	8	108
Ringold	8	116
Chickamauga	13	129
CHATTANOOGA ..	11	140

The Fitzhugh Lee School is located near the "heart' of old Oakdale.

The Oakdale community developed mainly around the one room Locust Grove School that was established in 1896 that later became known as Fitzhugh Lee School, and the nearby Locust Grove Baptist Church founded in 1910. It was an outgrowth of a community Sunday school organized in 1909 by Mr. and Mr. W. N. Nichols that was held each Sunday afternoon at the Locust Grove School.

Within a short time the need for a church, in addition to the sunday school, was realized and Mr. and Mrs. Nichols, J. E. Brown, William Berry, and Charlie, Joe and Rube Brown worked out some financial arrangements. Charlie Brown donated the property on which the church was to be located and a $300 gift from the Georgia Baptist Convention Home Mission Board made it possible to hold the first meeting of the Locust Grove Baptist Church on July 10, 1910. Its members and others in the community have played a key role in the development of Oakdale and the south Cobb area in its ninety-nine years.

But back to the story and the conditions of the Smyrna area near the end of the 1850s. Robert Daniel and Martin Ruff, who had become partners in the saw mill and woolen mill operations on Nickajack Creek, acquired land in the middle of Smyrna and constructed the town's first brick building. It is believed to have been finished in 1849 and in operation as the Smyrna Boy's Academy in 1850.

The 1850 census of Cobb showed the following employed at the Concord Woolen Mill: William I. Brown, male age 17, machine operator; John N. Brown, male age 15, machine operator; Sarah A. Brown, female age 13, machine operator; John Herberts, male age 34, overseer. Elizabeth Williams, female, age 27, weaver; Elizabeth Lindley, female age 27, weaver; Martha Williamson, female age 50, weaver, and others.

The 1851 tax digest of Cobb County showed that Martin Ruff owned two slaves and 695 acres of land in Cobb County. In 2009 the current owners of the miller's house and the Daniell/Ruff Grist Mill, Robert and Pat Burns Roach, discovered a list of the slaves that were owned by the Ruffs attached to a shelf in a closet in the house. The slaves listed were: Matilda Ruff, age 40, a black female washer woman; Calvin Ruff, age 17, a black male farm hand, Yeuda Ruff, age 11, a black female and Rhoda Ruff, age 7, a black female.

Another land deal that unknowingly played somewhat of a part in Smyrna's participation in the War Between the States was recorded on page 274, of Cobb County Deed Book A, dated December 25, 1854: "Pickney H. Randall sold to

Left: Collins Spring Primitive Baptist Church was destroyed during the War Between the States and was rebuilt in 1866. The first marked burial in the adjoining cemetery is that of Charlie M. Maner, the sixteen-year old son of Mr. and Mrs. W. G. Maner, who died July 21, 1857. The church building is located in the area of the original Boltonville post office. The building is currently owned by the Atlanta Free Thought Society.

Right: Homecoming Day, October 21, 1945. Locust Grove Baptist Church celebrating a debt-free building. W. A. Anderson was pastor at the time. This congregation moved to a new location on Fontaine Road several years ago. St. Benedict's Episcopal Church, a new congregation, purchased the building in 2007 and at an open house celebration May 31, 2008, announced plans for rehabilitating and renovating it for worship and an educational center.

❖

The I-285 and Atlanta Road Intersection.

PHOTOGRAPH COURTESY OF JACK COLLINS.

Alexander Eaton of Cobb County for $500, a lot and mill and water rights formerly deeded to M. L. Ruff, including privileges in original deed from E. T. Hutson. Witnessed by John H. Boling by mark X, and Alfred Maner, Justice of the Peace." The house constructed on that property became the headquarters of Confederate Lieutenant General John B. Hood during the Battle of Smyrna Campground and Ruff's Mill.

Every new year brought improvements and growth to the area but going into the 1860s, differences between the north and south were becoming more pronounced. Marcus C. Thayer III and Darren D. Wheeler, in their *A Southern View on the War Between the States* cited six major reasons for the war for southern independence that involved regional differences: "Cultural Differences—the people of the South were primarily of Celtic descent. The people of the North were primarily of Danish and Saxon descent. The Population Shift—the population of the North and South were basically even when the constitution was ratified. Over the next seventy years most of the 800 percent increase in population was in the North. This increased their number of representatives in the U. S. House. Thayer and Wheeler pointed out that by 1860 twenty-one new states had entered the union but only nine of them were in the South. That gave the North the advantage in the Senate and total control of the congress. Economic Issues—by the 1850s Gross National Product of the country was driven by Southern

exports (cotton, tobacco and sugar) and by 1860 seventy-five percent (3/4) of the total federal budget was financed by Southern agricultural exports. The northern-controlled House and Senate passed restrictive tariffs that Southerners viewed as discriminatory and in which money was leaving the South and going to the North to fuel the Northern industrial revolution. State's Rights—the South felt they should be governed locally and that the federal government was an agent of the states, to be used to the advantage of all of the states. Independence—each Southern state believed that they were sovereign and independent and were only part of the Union because they had voluntarily agreed to enter into that Union. Slavery—by the mid 1800s, most of the Northern states had done away with slavery because they found it was not profitable in their new industrial society. The Northern industrialists simply sold their slaves to the Southerners. That enabled the Northern slave owners to recuperate their investment in the slaves. There was no mass emancipation of the slaves owned by Northerners."

Those were some of the conditions that fueled the coming conflict. It's interesting to note that Abraham Lincoln's Emancipation Proclamation did not apply to the Northern states and when it was written the Southern States had already seceded from the Union.

The Secession Ordinance passed on January 19, 1861. According to the *New Georgia Encyclopedia* it was publicly signed by Georgia politicians in a ceremony on January 19, 1861. However, two days earlier, delegates to a convention in Milledgeville voted, 208 to 89, for the state to secede from the Union.

The delegates who signed the document for Cobb County were Elisha Hamilton Lindley from Smyrna, George D. Rice and Albert Allen Winn.

The hardships that were created by the recruitment of the South's young men to fight for the Confederate forces, and some of them to die and/or be impaired for life, had a devastating effect on the South. Smyrna and Cobb County citizens were not subjected to the actual fighting and battles until early 1864. But, for the most part, the war, with its variety of names, for Georgia started with the signing of that document.

CHAPTER III

SMYRNA IN THE WAR BETWEEN THE STATES

Southerners have several names for the "War": The War for Southern Independence, The War of Northern Aggression, The War for States' Rights, The Uncivil War, *The Invasion of the Southern States and War of 1861-1865* and possibly others. No matter what it was called, there is no doubt "The War" was devastating to the South and especially so for Georgia during and the years immediately following the war. The southern states did have representation again in the federal government, but in a dispute over "states rights", the North-dominated Congress passed the so-called "Reconstruction Act", declaring the southern states to be outside the indivisible Union. U. S. troops re-entered the South and implemented U. S. military rule.

In the meantime, the Fourteenth Amendment to the U. S. Constitution was proposed, taking some powers from the states and transferring them to the federal government. Twenty-eight of the thirty-seven states were needed to ratify the amendment, but only twenty-two voted for it. Twelve of the southern states voted against it. After the implementation of the Reconstruction Act, the southern states were required to ratify the amendment as the price of readmission to the Union. Otherwise, they would remain under military rule. The state of Georgia was the last of the former Confederate states to be readmitted to the Union in 1878.

Late 1830s-1840s, Daniell/Ruff's Grist Mill was on property now owned by Robert and Pat Burns Roche at 10 Concord Road. The grist mill was in operation until 1920-1921. Located near the north end of the double "S" curve in Nickajack Creek that surrounds the miller's house. This scene is the creek winding south under the covered bridge, behind the miller's house and then northwest for another curve southwest that finds its way to the woolen mill.
PHOTOGRAPH COURTESY OF HAROLD SMITH.

In regards to the effects of "The War" on the South, Kennesaw Professor of History, Tom Scott, concluded, in his *Outline History of Concord Covered Bridge Area for the Heritage Park Project of Robert and Company*, that: "As a result of the Civil War the South went from being the wealthiest part of the country to the poorest. Not until World War II, three-fourths of a century later, would the region make significant progress in narrowing the economic gap with the North. As late as 1940 per capita Georgia income was only 57 percent of the national average. It is debatable why the South remained poor for so long.

How residents of Smyrna and other citizens in Cobb County responded to the impact of "The War" may be summed up in the undated note in the minutes of the Maloney's Spring Primitive Baptist Church. The note was written between the service on May 14, 1864, and the next time the church met on July 16, 1865, a little over a year after the Battle of Smyrna Camp Ground and Ruff's Mill.

Because of the difficulty of reading the minutes it is transcribed here, and I quote: "After the meeting in May, and before the next meeting in June, the Armies fell back upon this section of the county and most of the members of the church, together with the pastor, took refuge in other sections of the country, and, so remained until the next spring and summer, when in the providence of God, we were again permitted to return to our homes. And, although most of us have lost all our earthly goods and property, yet we feel that we have abundant reason to thank the Lord that it is no worse. The first conference meeting after our return was held on the 15th of July, 1865 as the next minutes will show. signed by Thomas H. Moore, clerk".

As shown in the minutes of the Maloney's Spring Primitive Baptist Church, many Smyrna citizens left the area, as the troops and fighting got near, and didn't return until the war was over.

The battles in the area were over in a few days. Smyrna native, James W. Nash, did extensive research on the Battle of Smyrna Campground and wrote an article he named "Two Days at Smyrna: Sherman and Johnston above the River Line."

The two days were July 3 and 4, 1864. The other battle in the immediate area was at the Daniell-Ruff's Mill complex that included the Concord Woolen Mill, a grist mill, a saw mill and a small village for the workers.

Another Smyrna native, Sadie Robinson McDowell, recounted some memories of her grandmother, Sarah Jane Brown Cannon, March 23, 1847-April 30, 1890. She lived on Church Street during the war with her parents. The house was on land where Smyrna Elementary School was eventually constructed—land currently owned by the Smyrna First Baptist Church. Mrs. McDowell said that signs of the breastworks and trenches could still be seen on the playground when she attended school there.

Sarah Jane's parents were expecting their sixth child when her father was killed in the war. Their oldest son, David was called into service and he was also killed and buried in Virginia. As the fighting drew closer to Smyrna, Sarah Jane's mother took the other children to her brother's plantation in South Carolina.

While they were waiting for the one train a day going from Rome to Atlanta via Smyrna, to South Carolina, they could hear the sounds of cannons and fighting towards Marietta. All the homes and buildings in the area were destroyed.

James Nash described the Smyrna lines of fortifications as: "along the Roswell Road just north and east of town (generally south of where Dobbins A. F. Base is now located) and west of Rottenwood Creek, then across the railroad tracks (W & A) and the road just south of the train siding known as Ruff's Station." The line apparently crossed the road just north of town and faced west for a short distance along the higher ground parallel to the road in the area of the old Smyrna School (mentioned by Mrs. McDowell) Finally, the line headed southwest out the Concord Road towards Nickajack Creek and out King Springs Road towards Johnston's headquarters.

❖

Above: Sarah Jane Brown Cannon.

Below: Copy of the minutes of the Maloney's Spring Primitive Baptist Church shortly after the end of the War Between the States.

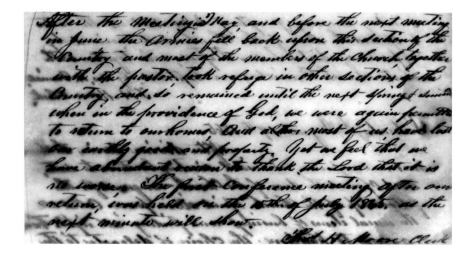

Jack Gibson, another Smyrna resident and War Between the States scholar, described some of the Battle of Smyrna Camp ground as follows: "Early on the morning of July 4, the Federals made first contact with picket lines of the main Confederate force about 8/10 of a mile north of Smyrna Campground across the railroad from present-day Belmont Hills Shopping Center. A number of Confederate skimiersers and pickets were overrun and captured or killed. The action slowed General Howard's overall advance and gave him a clue that something ominous was in front of him.

About 11:30 a.m. Sherman rode forward to Howard's position by the railroad to see what the slowdown problem was. Howard tried to convince Sherman that a large force of some sort lay just ahead. Sherman insisted 'you are mistaken, there is no force in the front of you.' Gibson went on to say that Howard's response was, 'Well, General, let's see.' "Howard pressed his troops forward at once. The 75th Illinois Infantry Regiment of Grose's Brigade led the charge across a large corn field.

They drove back the remaining Confederate pickets and took a number of prisoners. Then suddenly they were met by a 'sheet of lead' that came from infantry men in the hidden works to their front. Unseen batteries hurled shot after shot into their lines. They had met Major General Patrick Cleburn's famous division at the main Smyrna line. The artillery fire apparently came from several gun emplacements along the line and from a large fort."

Gibson, described the fort as follows: "It had a commanding view of the wagon roads, railroad, and all the terrain to the north. The fort is best described in the words of a reporter from the *New York Tribune* who was traveling with Sherman's troops." He said, "On the Marietta Road proper is a cleared space of some twenty acres, where, on a rise of land, they have a regular fort, septagon in shape, one hundred feet in diameter in the inside with embrasures for seven guns, commanding every point on the compass." Then he states that the fort is about 250 yards in front of the main line. Later, he (the reporter) said "On the road, the work is particularly strong, and has embrasures for seven guns on one side, and four on the other, sweeping the road." The walls, according to Gibson's research, were at least fifteen feet thick as that was the accepted thickness of dirt to stop a typical cannonball at close range. This large artillery studded fort, and the extensive fortifications along the Smyrna Line, made the overall Confederate position quite strong.

All this was quite a fourth of July surprise for General Sherman, The Federal attack was repulsed with heavy losses, including the death of the commander of the 75th Illinois. Many of the surviving Federal assault troops were forced to seek whatever cover they could find in front of the Confederate works as they were totally exposed if they tried to retire.

Both Jim Nash and Jack Gibson concluded, from their research, that General Sherman's opinion of the Battle of Smyrna Campground was that it was "a noisy but not desperate battle." Gibson's research indicated that the Federal losses were 370 killed and wounded and the Confederates were approximately 100 killed and wounded. In checking official records of The Union and Confederate Armies, Jim Nash said that the Federal IV Corps reported that it had suffered 130 killed and wounded that day and had taken 90 prisoners, mostly Confederate skirmishers out in front of the lines.

A story about General William Tecumseh Sherman that is well known to Civil War buffs, is one that he related in his William T. Sherman's *Personal Narrative of His March Through Georgia* as edited by Mills Lane. Sherman tells of how he came closest to getting killed during the entire war at Smyrna Campground. He is quoted as saying "It was here that General Noyes lost his leg. I came very near being shot myself while reconoitring in the second story of a house on our picket-line, which was struck several times by cannon-shot and perfectly riddled with musket-balls." The local version is that while there, one bullet whizzed close to his head. and the general suffered a complete demolishment of his hat. The true story might never be known. However, if General William Tecumseh Sherman could return to Smyrna today, he would be very proud that someone thought enough of him to name a street in one of the city's many subdivisions— Creatwood. But they used his middle name for the honor and his namesake is a very short Tecumseh Trail.

❖

Top: John Henry Cantrell, March 16, 1846-November 11, 1936, CSA, Company E, 14th Georgia Infantry.

Above: J. Gid Morris, July 20, 1847-November 12, 1936, CSA, Company B, 2nd Georgia Regiment, Wheelers Calvary, Smyrna mayor, 1925-1926.

Below: Martin Van Buren Ridling, June 15, 1841-February 16, 1913. Wounded at Chancellorsville May 3, 1863. Great grandfather of Harold Smith. Inscription on tombstone reads: Served four years in the Civil War. Sleep on Ridling and take thy rest. God calls away when he sees best.

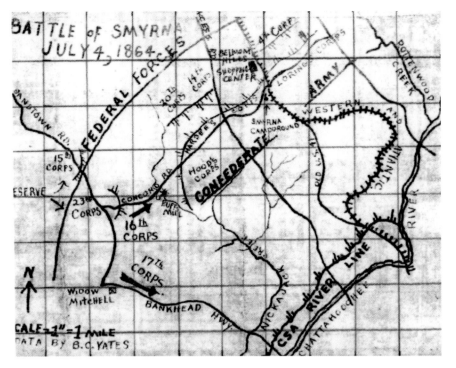

The Presbyterians purchased the Boy's Academy for a place of worship in 1874 and in 1884 the First Baptist Church was allowed to organize and share it with the Presbyterians until the Baptist constructed their own building. In 1905 the Presbyterians sold it to the Smyrna Board of Education for $1,600 and in 1923 it was sold to the Nelms Lodge number 323 of Free and Accepted Masons. The Lodge demolished it in 1954 and replaced it with a similar looking building that housed a variety of businesses over the years including the Smyrna Post Office. The building was demolished in 1998 to make room for the Market Village.

But back to the war! Like the Battle of Smyrna Campground, the Battle of Ruff's Mill, three miles southwest of the town, was a very short one. For the most part, it took place July 5, 1864.

The assembled Confederate forces in the area were General Joseph E. Johnston's Army of the Tennessee consisting of Lieutenant General John B. Hood's Corps and Major General Carter L. Stevenson's Division.

The four brigades were Cumming's, Brown's, Reynolds, and Pettus' and were made up of soldiers from Georgia, Tennessee, North Carolina, Virginia, and Alabama.

Federal units present at Ruff's Mill were: Major General William T. Sherman's Military Division of the Mississippi; Major General James B. McPherson, Union Army of the Tennessee; Fifteenth Army Corps of Major General John A. Logan; Second Division, Fifteenth Army Corps, Major General Morgan L. Smith; Second Brigade under Brigadier General Joseph A. Lightburn. The solders were from Indiana, Ohio, and Illinois. The order to proceed to Ruff's Mill came from General James B. Mason on July 2, 1864: "Major General G. M. Dodge, will commence moving his command from the left at McPherson as Major General F. P. Blair's troops have filed out and will march by the most practicable route, selected by his staff officers today to The Sandtown Road (now Floyd) and there follow Major General Blair's command down to where the road branches off to the Ruff's Mill on the Nickajack Creek, and take up a good position near Ruff's Mill".

By the evening of July 2nd they had reached the vicinity of the Moss House, located at the intersection of Sandtown (Floyd) and Concord Roads where they spent the night erecting breastworks.

At 8:30 a.m. on July 3, two regiments from Brigadier General Joseph A. Lightburn's second brigade was sent east along Concord Road on a reconnaissance toward Nickajack Creek. The 30th and 53rd Ohio Infantry Regiments marched astride the road in heavy skirmish formations.

At approximately 10:00 a.m. when Lightburn's two regiments crested a small ridge and entered open farm fields near John Gann's Home, they were spotted and engaged by Confederate General Stevenson's pickets and artillery.

John Gann acquired land lot number 47 on December 12, 1834, in the 1832 lottery and the house is believed to have been constructed in the early 1840s. He acquired land lot 117 from James W. Hill.

As soon as former State Senator John Gann heard that the Federal troops were advancing from Kennesaw Mountain toward the Chattahoochee River, on their way to Atlanta, he sent his children, livestock and slaves to refuge at his birthplace in Clarke County. This information was in a research report by Alice (Mrs. Gordon) Ruckart, who lived in the miller's house from 1976 until the present owners purchased it in the 1980s. The miller's house was constructed about 1850.

Mrs. Ruckart went on to say that John Gann and his wife stayed in the house until they heard the first shots fired, then they headed for Ruff's Station (Smyrna) but were turned back by Union soldiers who, under command of Brigadier General Fuller, were waging battle with the Confederate soldiers at the nearby Ruff's Mill at Nickajack Creek. The information apparently came from an article in the *Atlanta Journal* on

July 6, 1959, that included an interview with two Gann grandsons. They said John Gann and his wife had to billet fifteen Yankee officers. Mrs. Gann, according to the grandsons, had to cook, wash, and iron clothes for the soldiers and Mr. Gann was forced to shine boots, chop wood and do other menial chores. There was some indication that the soldiers started to burn the house down but spared it because they found a Masonic apron in the attic. Some research indicated that the Daniell-Ruff Grist Mill was not destroyed because a Yankee sympathizer was the mill operator at the time.

In the meantime, the battle resumed. Official records show John K. Duke, of the 43rd Ohio Infantry reported: "July 3rd was a Sunday. After two months of such campaigning what would the soldier not have given for one quiet day of rest

Opposite, top: Map of Battle of Smyrna prepared by B. C. Yates for the Smyrna Herald.

Opposite, middle: Typical fortifications on the Confederate Line in the Smyrna area.

Opposite, bottom: Inside view of an earthen fort in Atlanta—similar to the ones at Smyrna.

PHOTOGRAPH COURTESY OF JACK GIBSON.

Above: General Joseph E. Johnston, Commander of the Army of Tennessee C. S. A.

Bottom, left: Smyrna Boy's Academy, it was the only building left standing in downtown after the war. It was originally constructed in 1849 as a Boy's Academy by Robert Daniell and Martin L. Ruff. For several weeks after the start of the War Between the States the building was used as a place for training Confederate soldiers. During and after the battles in the area it was used as a hospital for both Confederate and Union troops.

Bottom, right: The exact date of construction of Ruff's Grist Mill is unknown but a 1847 Georgia map shows there was a settlement in the area known as Mill Grove and a post office was established there on September. 28, 1837. Martin L. Ruff purchased land lots 118, 119, 171, 190, 191 and 242 from Lacy H. Griffin on May 17, 1856 and the property was believed to contain a bridge, a miller's house and a grist mill.

and a square meal at mother's table. We moved one mile in advance of our works and then the shot and shells were too much for us and we retreated half a mile to escape the shelling."

Several eyewitness accounts of the action on the 3rd and 4th of July were quoted in a preservation study entitled *Fireworks Were Plenty*, by Douglas R. Cubbison and P.E.A.C.H. (Protect Endangered Areas of Cobb's History) in connection with the construction of the long-proposed East-West Connector) Brigadier General John W. Fuller provided a detailed description of the attack: "On the following morning July 4, the 1st Brigade was ordered to drive the enemy (Confederates) from a position they held on the opposite bank.

We crossed the stream at the mill, and as soon as we reached the hill beyond, the 39th Ohio and 64th Illinois were deployed in line, and the 27th Ohio and 18th Missouri were formed in column on either flank. The Rebels were soon encountered, and after a sharp skirmish fell back to a strong line of works, where they were found to be in force. During the skirmish, and while ascertaining the position of their line, we lost 30 or 40 men.

After forming our lines within 200 or 300 yards of the enemy, we constructed continuous rifle pits for the infantry, and also placed a battery in position to command his works."

Major Charles H. Smith of the 27th Ohio Infantry described their conditions: "The position of the men at the time were most fatiguing. They had marched so far all the morning hours, and since before noon had been lying upon the ground in battle line without food, expecting every moment to execute the forward movement. They were greatly fatigued, and began to be impatient and were quite out of humor, embittered and desperate at the delay." Private George H. Cadman of the 39th Ohio Infantry noted, "we were roasted." Private John J. McKee recorded, "it was hot as an oven." The Major General's description of the attack was, "On the following morning, July 4, the First Brigade was ordered to drive the enemy from a position he held on the opposite bank. We crossed the stream at the mill, and as soon as we reached the hill beyond General Morgan L. Smith was heard to remark that more men would be lost by sunstroke than by bullets." As the regiments were moving into line, they were exposed to Confederate fire. The acting Major of the 35th New Jersey, Captain Charles A. Angel, was struck and killed. Private Benjamin F. Sweet of the 27th Ohio Infantry wrote: "When the bugle blew 'forward', it was the stillest time I ever heard. Our line advanced a hundred yards. The bugle blew 'double quick' and the whole army hollered. The very trees trembled with the sound. The enemy fired one volley and left as fine a line of works as I have every seen. For fifty yards in front the works the trees had been cut on one side and left hanging on the stump, the tops straight from the works and limbs sharpened. We lost 39 men from the one volley which they fired. The 39th lost about the same number. We were only a few minutes making the charge, but were soon relieved, and every man glad he was still alive."

Included in the report of Major Charles Smith of the 27th Ohio was this account: "Both the enemy (Confederates) and our own troops heard the bugle sound at the same time, and the enemy being prepared, poured upon the charging column heavy volleys of musketry fire. Their bullets struck the ground everywhere.

Below: Masonic Hall, Smyrna.
PHOTOGRAPH COURTESY OF ELIZABETH ANDERSON AND THE SMYRNA MUSEUM.

Bottom: John Gann acquired land lot number 47 on December 12, 1834 in the 1832 lottery and the house is believed to have been constructed in the early 1840s. Gann also acquired lot 117 from James W. Hill.

Our loss in killed and wounded in this engagement was over one hundred and forty men in the two regiments. The 39th Ohio lost its brave Colonel, E. F. Noyes, whose wound caused the amputation of his leg. General Sprague said that the charge was the wedge that cleaned out the Rebel Works for a distance of six miles. Johnston's Rebel army retreated to the Chattahoochee and crossed over that night."

The *Fireworks Were Plenty* report continued: "On the night of the 4th Confederate Lieutenant General Hood's report indicated that the Federal troops were turning his left, and that his own forces were insufficient to defeat their design or hold them back. Confederate General Morgan L. Smith, reported that the Federal cavalry was pressing on him in such force that he would be compelled to abandon the ground he had been holding and retire before morning to General Shoupe's line of redoubts. As the position in question covered a very important route to Atlanta, and was nearer the main body of our army to that place, the necessity of abandoning it involved the taking of a new line. The three corps were accordingly brought to the entrenched just prepared by General Shoupe." The morning of July 5th revealed the Rebel trenches to be empty. The Battle of Ruff's Mill was over.

During the battle temporary field hospitals were established at the Ruff and Gann homes and the miller's house.

Confederate Lieutenant General John B. Hood directed his troops from the home of Alexander Eaton that was located on what is now King Springs Road near the intersection of Reed Road. Several subdivisions, Griffin Middle School, The Assembly of God Church, King Springs Elementary, Ryan Park, St. Thomas Catholic Church, Faith United Methodist Church and other structures are located on land that was previously the Eaton property.

Rufus Alexander Eaton, June 24, 1858-May 22, 1942, a son of Alexander, was six years old at the time of the battle and he said he saw Confederate General Joseph E. Johnston at the Eaton house also.

Rufus constructed a house similar to his father's about one mile east from the original homeplace on the same King Springs Road. It was demolished in the 1950s to make way for a new subdivision called the Bennett homes, for the name of the developer that had just annexed the property into the city limits of Smyrna. The streets involved in that development include Pinedale, Oakdale and Oakview Drive, Pinehurst Drive and Circle, Daniel Drive, Hayes Drive and Cliffwood Circle. The original farm consisted of more than 200 acres.

The home of Rufus Alexander Eaton, Jr., and Myrtice Parnell Eaton, parents of Gerald Eaton, Smyrna Historical Society member and museum volunteer, is still located on the northwest corner of King Springs Road and Oakdale Drive.

Exactly how many Smyrna and Cobb County people served in the military during the War Between the States is not known. However, on July 26-28, 1904, a reunion of Company A, of the 9th Georgia Battalion Artillery of the Confederate States of America was held in Smyrna. When the long roll of 150 names was called by Sergeant Joe Daniell, 21 men answered to their names.

Left: The Martin L. Ruff House located at 86 Concord Road, was constructed in the 1850s. Mr. Ruff was born in 1807 and died in 1877. His wife, Judith, died in 1887. Their son, Solon Z. Ruff, was killed in the war. The house was used as a field hospital during the war and it remained in the Ruff family until 1943 when an English couple, Ian and Jenny Milroy purchased it. They sold it to Harold and Janice Ivester in 1976 and one of the children and family live there now (2009).

Right: The miller's house constructed c. 1850 is located on Concord Road between and slightly south of the grist mill and the Concord covered bridge. It is currently owned and occupied by Dr. Bob and Pat Burns Roche.

Above: This was the home of Rufus A. Eaton, son of Alexander, whose house similiar to this one was used for General Hood's headquarters.

Right: The State of Georgia erected a historical marker indicating the significance of the house in the war. Because of major development in the area in the 1950, '60s and '70s, the marker was moved from its original location to the east side of South Cobb Drive on the property of the former Smyrna Hospital that is now Emory-Adventist Hospital at Smyrna.

Below: Alexander Eaton's older son, Joseph W., served in Company I, 7th Georgia Regiment and was captured in Virginia. He was paroled on April 10, 1865.

The list of 150 names of the Company had been compiled some 25 years after the end of the war when a few of the surviving members met and did it from their memory. The Battalion was organized as the 9th Georgia Artillery. Company A was organized in Atlanta. Company B was from Buckhead, Company C from Columbus, Company D from Gwinnett, and Company E was formerly part of Company A but it was divided because of the numbers.

The battalion tendered their services to the Confederate Government instead of the State of Georgia, consequently, there was considerable delay in going to Virginia.

Of the original 150, 71 of them were known to be dead.

As a result of the reunion a new organization was formed: "The Survivor's Association of Company A 9th Georgia Battalion Artillery."

They decided to have their reunion in July, and the next one was scheduled "in the

beautiful grove just across the railroad from Mr. E. Legg's home, one mile and a quarter from Smyrna."

Officers elected for the next year were: Captain W. R. McEntire, Adjutant John W. Woodruff, Quartermaster T. E. Legg, Quartermaster Sergeant E. D. L. Mobley and Joe Daniell, Commissary.

Charter members at Smyrna on July 27, 1904, were: T. R. Ashworth, James Boling, G. M. Daniell, J. G. Daniell, G. B. Eidson, Albert Fambrough, Ed Gann, John F. Gramblin, William Hawes, John Humphries, Tom Hooper, J. D. King, T. E. Legg, E. D. L. Mobley, and Tom McCauley.

Editors Note: Information on the reunion is from "Lives and Times, Volume 12, No. 4, July-August, 1997."

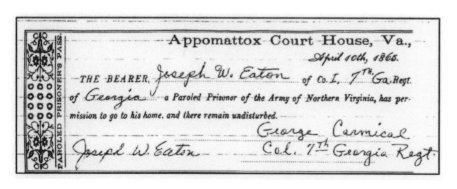

Collins Springs Cemetery

Argo, Francis M.
Born: February 14, 1829
Died: April 17, 1908

Bolling, James J.
Born: February 29, 1841
Died: August 18, 1911

Brown, Wiley
Born: October 30, 1837
Died: March 26, 1903

Carrell, William W.
Born: August 28, 1811
Died: April 15, 1891

Gordon, John B.
Born: August 4, 1833
Died: September 4, 1898

Hill, Andrew T.
Born: August 27, 1836
Died: August 30, 1899

Lee, Henry J.
Born: May 7, 1840
Died: October 17, 1895

Jordan, James
Born: April 7, 1818
Died: June 26, 1904

Lee, William J.
Born: 1829
Died: 1911

Maloney, John H.
Born: December 1, 1828
Died: November 18, 1916

Maner, William E.
Born: April 1, ?
Died: November 10, 1904

Maloney's Spring Cemetery

Anderson, George W.
Born: August 5, 1844
Died: March 6, 1923

Barber, Jacob Brown
Born: September 7, 1832, Clarke County, Georgia
Died: March 5, 1912

Burgess, Andrew J.
Born: October 4, 1840
Died: April 24, 1914

Chadwick, Wesley W.
Born: April 11, 1818
Died: July 29, 1899

Clayton, Floyd E.
Born: ?
Died: July 19, 1924

Griggs, John H.
Born: May 11, 1846, Georgia
Died: August 7, 1920

Hamby, Benajah Judson "Judge"
Born: July 11, 1836, Walton County, Georgia
Died: July 5, 1917

Hamby, Micajah Leonard
Born: October 15, 1834, Walton County, Georgia
Died: April 3, 1909, Confederate Soldiers
Home, Atlanta, Georgia

Martin, Jesse W.
Born: January 2, 1841, Madison County, Georgia
Died: May 24, 1920

Owens, J. W.
Born: July 19, 1839
Died: May 19, 1914

Pace, J. T.
Born: November 2, 1842
Died: December 5, 1923

Maloney's Spring Cemetery

Polston, John D.
Born: October 8, 1830
Died: January 21, 1907

Reed, Isaac A.
Born: December 8, 1847, Georgia
Died: May 4, 1915

Stephens, Henry Patrick
Born: February 19, 1844, Cobb County, Georgia
Died: 1923

Wylie, James Lee
Born: December 20, 1834
Died: 1916

Federal soldier buried in Maloney's Spring Cemetery:

Fortner, Levi Franklin
Born: April 24. 1838, Wilkes County, North Carolina
Died: April 18, 1922

Confederate soldiers buried in the
Gann Family Cemetery

Gann, Alexander
Born: December 25, 1845
Died: November 4, 1912

Gann, Henry
Born: February 28, 1816
Died: February 24, 1914

Williford, Benjamin
Company F, CSA
No dates

Williford, Jeptha
Company A, 9th Georgia, CSA
No dates

Summers, John*
Born: 1762
Died: 1848

*Revolutionary

Smyrna Memorial Cemetery

Alexander, William M.
Born: January 14, 1846
Died: April 7, 1889

Brown, Marshall H.
Company A, 9th Georgia, CSA
No dates

Copeland, William R.
Born: February. 17, 1826
Died: September 26, 1899

Eaton, Joseph W.
Born: November 1, 1839
Died: October 29, 1926

Fambrough, Albert J.
Company A, Georgia Light Artillery, CSA
No dates

Gann, Edmond
Born: April 4, 1843
Died: June 15, 1915

Hamby, Tandy Kay
Born: January 23, 1844
Died: July 18, 1896

Ireland, John Calvin
Born: April 25, 1845
Died: August 21, 1919

Segars, Dick
Company A, 9th Georgia Light Artillery
No dates

Turner, John V.
Born: March 6, 1844
Died: August 9, 1919

Whitfield, Thomas P.
Born: June 20, 1836
Died: March 3, 1903

Edison Family Cemetery

Eidson, Giles Brantley
Born: 1824
Died: June 29, 1908

Bethel Baptist Cemetery

Grizzard, Joseph
Born: January 22, 1845
Died: April 30, 1907

Ashworth, John
Born: May 12, 1822
Died: August 12, 1917

Mitchell, Henry
Born: January 2, 1833
Died: September 12, 1912

Concord Baptist Cemetery

Gann, Francis Franklin
Born: August 10, 1834
Died: November 18, 1917

Moss, James C.
Born: June 12, 1837
Died: April 13, 1880

Hargrove Family Cemetery

Hargrove, Francis A.
Born: December 22, 1843
Died: September 19, 1917

Hargrove, James P.
Born: January 23, 1836
Died: November 29, 1863

Reeves, William F. M.
Born: June 1836
Died: May 30, 1916

Milford Baptist Church

Alexander, Smith
Born: 1809
Died ?

Blair, William Byrd
Born: November 18, 1849
Died: November 3, 1931

Brown, J. W.
Born: ?
Died: March 8, 1890

Gann, Henry Thomas "Rattler"
Born: March 14, 1830
Died: June 16, 1909

Lowe, Aaron
Born: ?
Died ?

Morris, I. J.
Born: April 7, 1847
Died: October 22, 1914

Reed, Joshua Hopkins
Born: October 10, 1825
Died: September 25, 1906

Seay, Isaac B.
Born: April 6, 1840
Died: April, 3, 1934

Shaw, H. C.
Born: June 25, 1844
Died: January 14, 1926

Smith, John S.
Born: June 27, 1824
Died: June 17, 1913

New Smyrna Cemetery

Cantrell, John Henry
Born: 1846
Died: 1936

Fleming, John Newton
Born: February 24, 1833
Died: April 10, 1913

Fuller, Jones A.
Born: December 3, 183?
Died: April 12, 1917

Leonard, Thomas C.
Born: June 6, 1839
Died: June 29, 1917

McCravy, Archibal Perry
Born: January 9, 1836
Died: September 12, 1912

Ruff Family Cemetery

Reed, John L.
Born: 1846
Died: 1920

Ruff, Henry Clay
Born: April 2, 1845
Died: September 7, 1907

Miller Family Cemetery

Blair, S. W.
Born: May 5, 1845
Died: July 22, 1909

Osborne Family Cemetery

Conn, William E.
Born: October 10, 1837
Died: April 26, 1862

CHAPTER IV

SMYRNA—AFTER THE WAR

Campbell Road in 1895 was at grade with the Western & Atlantic Railroad. The train would stop for passengers at Argyle, the name of the Campbell plantation, named after their ancestral home in Scotland. The Richard Orme Campbell family brought several land lots in the area of the present day Campbell Middle School, Campbell Road, Argyle Estates subdivision and much of the property reaching to Spring Road. The inset in the upper right corner is Mrs. Harriet Campbell with her bicycle and her infant child, Isolene, in a carriage standing at the top of the steps at the Argyle stop. The Argyle house and other outbuildings are behind the trees. The photograph was donated to the Smyrna Museum by Gretna Poole, the last operator/owner of Aunt Fanny's Cabin before it was purchased by Frank Johnson at an auction.

B. C. Yates, the long-time superintendent of the Kennesaw Mountain National Park, in his history of Cobb described the conditions like this when the soldiers returned: "It was not the home they had left. Slaves were freed; Confederate money and bonds were worthless; credit and capital were not to be had. Men had to work hard with their hands to eat; by federal law all men who had fought in the Southern armies or worked for the Confederate government, were deprived of the vote. Slaves and carpetbaggers were in control. They spent tax money that property owners had to work hard for to pay. Nor was Georgia even a state, it was a Military district under rule of a minority supported by the military." That's what the families that left Smyrna during the war to escape the ravages and hardships of the actual fighting and battles faced when they came back home. They had taken refuge with relatives and friends in other parts of the state where there was no military action. Many returned home to find nothing was left. The houses, barns, farm equipment, and everything that could not be taken or used by the conquering military units that swept through the area, were destroyed. The soldiers who had served were able to return home only after signing a pledge of loyalty to the Union. Many of them came back with missing limbs and shattered bodies. Some had been in horrible, crowded prisons in the North until the end of the war. But they were thankful that peace had come after four long years.

But the war had not quenched their spirits the people were ready to rebuild. In "downtown" Smyrna. On May 2, 1870, Smyrna got its first post office named "Smyrna." There had been one before in the same area but it had been named "Neal Dow." Four postmasters served in that one beginning on May 25, 1852. Martin L. Ruff was the first one and served until June 24, 1856, when William S. Tweedall was appointed. He served until January 28, 1858, until Isaac R. Teat was appointed. Mr. Teat served until Furman R. Robert replaced him on August 27, 1858, and then the Neal Dow post office was discontinued on November 4, 1858.

Thomas P. Whitfield, W. N. Pace and John Stone opened grocery stores in the "starting to rebuild" town and W. J. Eidson had a general merchandise store.

G. B.'s Place, a popular "fast food" restaurant from 1937 until 1974 owned by G. B. Williams, was located at the rear of this building facing East Spring Street. It, too, was demolished in the redevelopment and road widening program of the 1980s and '90s. Nearby Williams Park was dedicated to his memory on April 25, 2004.

The Whitfield grocery store was located several hundred feet north of this building and the John Stone Grocery Store, with the post office, was located on the west side of Atlanta Road and Nickajack (Sunset Avenue) Street. This building was replaced with Dr. W. C. Mitchell's Medical Building in 1948.

John Stone, December 7, 1848, to January 10, 1953, in addition to operating the grocery store, was the Smyrna postmaster from March 15, 1887, to July 11, 1895. He eventually got into politics and was elected as the Judge of the Ordinary. One of the duties of that office was to be responsible for the operation of the Cobb County's Alms (Poor) House.

Traditional Smyrna history says that "Stone Creek" was named for him. His wife was Lavenia Payne Stone, March 1, 1850, to October 10, 1932. They had two daughters: Mary Ruby and Maude Elizabeth. Eventually the family moved to Marietta.

Another business enterprise that had opened in town was operated by Joseph W. Oglesby. He described himself as a "gin maker" and manufactured "Oglesby Gin." He lived on the land that became Belmont Farm that was visited by people from all over the country when it was flourishing in the early 1900s.

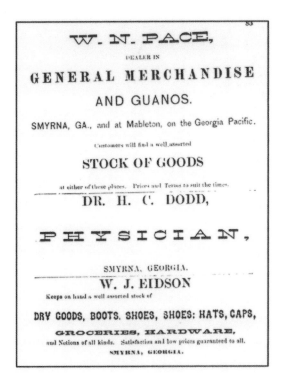

The downtown commercial area of Smyrna was growing slowly after the town officially incorporated in August 1872 with its city limits "one mile in every direction from the

Left: This advertisement appeared on page 83 of the city directory of Marietta, Acworth, Smyrna and Cobb County for 1883-1884.

Below: The W. N. Pace Grocery Store, 1914, was located on the northeast corner of the intersection of Atlanta Road and East Spring Street. The man on the far right with the line pointing to him is the only one that has been identified. He is Wesley Robinson. The man in the middle of the photograph is believed to be Dr. William Tatum Pace, whose drug store was on the southeast corner of this same intersection directly across Spring street. This building, that backed up to the W & A Railroad tracks, was demolished to make way for a service station eventually operated by C. J. and Jerry Fouts. The City of Smyrna installed and dedicated a bronze plaque and garden to C. J. on this site on May 25, 2006, for his long service to the city through a variety of civic and service organizations including the original Smyrna Downtown Development Authority. Mr. Fouts died less than a month later on June 13, 2006. Ralph Grady purchased the property and operated his Smyrna Radiator and Auto Repair Garage there until it was demolished in the downtown redevelopment program.

destroyed also. It was rebuilt as a covered bridge after the war and today is the centerpiece of the Concord Covered Bridge Historic District—the first historic district in Cobb County.

The dam on the north side of the bridge created a lake on Nickjack Creek that helped provide the water power for operating the gristmill as well as the woolen mill that by this time had become known as the Concord Manufacturing Company.

Robert Daniel and Martin Ruff rebuilt the woolen mill. On March 2, 1869, the *Marietta Journal* reported: "One of the greatest enterprises that Southern ingenuity and capital has brought into existence is the Concord Manufacturing Company situated on Nickajack Creek. Construction began last fall and is near completion. The machinery from New York is being received and skillful and efficient machinists are engaged in putting it up ready for operation".

"This woolen factory will have in process 32 looms and 600 spindles that will give constant employment to 52 operators, besides other laborers whose service will be needed."

In 1872 Ruff and Daniell sold the woolen factory to three Atlanta businessmen: Zachariah A. Rice, James H. Porter, and Seymour B Love. Rice's son Parker came to work as bookkeeper. By 1873 the factory was producing "40 different kinds of jeans and cashmeres." Seymour B. Love and Parker M. Rice, along with a large number of members of the Ruff family and their descendants, became a very large part of the political, social and business life of Smyrna.

Love Street was named for the S. B. Love family. It originally started at its intersection with Atlanta Road and followed the route of the present-day Concord Road past King Street and deadended at Dunton Street at its intersection with Medlin Street. Former Smyrna Mayor, J. M. "Hoot" Gibson lived at 222 Medlin Street.

In a road-widening project in the 1970s, the name of the portion of Love Street from Atlanta Road to King Street was changed to Concord Road. Today, Love Street goes from the intersection of Concord Road and King Street for about a quarter mile to the dead end that has been the site of multi-family housing since Mayor Gibson sold his property when the Medlin Street Apartments were constructed in the 1960s. The name has changed several times

Smyrna Boy's Academy. However, the town had been unable to attain the status of "a large town…of fine edifices built with the greatest convenience" that was the hope of the article writer in the *Marietta Journal* of June 15, 1872.

There were still only two churches in "downtown" Smyrna—the Methodist and the Presbyterian. There were three Baptist Churches in the Smyrna suburbs: Maloney's Spring, 1852, on the north side, Collins Springs, 1856, on the south and Concord, 1832, on the west side.

In the meantime, on the west side, the Concord Woolen Mill was coming back to life after the devastation of the War. The Union Army destroyed the woolen mill July 4, 1864, during the Battle of Ruff's Mill. It had been manufacturing uniforms for the Confederate Army. The flat bridge over Nickajack Creek was

and is currently known as "Mitchell Park Apartment Homes".

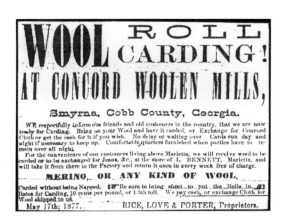

Many of Smyrna's elected officials and their families lived on Love Street: City Councilman and Mayor George Kreeger, State Representative and Cobb County Superior Court Judge George Kreeger, Jr., Councilman and Mayor Pat Edwards, Councilman G. C. Green, Councilman Glenn Yarbrough, Councilman and Mayor P. F. Brinkley.

Other prominent families of Love Street were: Claude Hamrick and his wife Laura Alice, who was the daughter of G. C. and Lena Mae Gann Green, and their two daughters Laura Ellen and Claudia; Reverend John Knight and his wife Bonnie lived in the Smyrna Presbyterian manse

with their two daughters Grace and Mary; Mrs. Corrine Hosch, a teacher and counselor for Smyrna High and Campbell High Schools; Mr. and Mrs. T. P. Holleman and their three children, Melvin, Irene and Harold. Melvin, who was born on Love Street, still lives there. He is a long-time member of the Smyrna Historical Society and a volunteer at the Smyrna Museum.

Shortly after Rice, Love and Porter purchased the Concord Woolen Mill, a tragic event occurred and was reported in the *Marietta Journal* on January 15, 1874, as follows: "A child was crushed to death last Saturday at Ruff's Grist Mill which resulted in the death of a little three-year-old son of Mr. John Reed. Little Zolliecofer, December 30, 1870 to January 10, 1874, had wandered unnoticed to the upper story of the mill and while there its clothes got caught in two cogs that are almost on the level with the floor and the revolving machinery drew the body of the child within its crushing iron jaws and then forcing the body through a very small opening closed in upon by upright shafting. The mill stopped and Mr. Bose Waters, the miller, being on the first floor was puzzled to know the cause and several times he tried to put the mill in motion but it refused to budge. So he ascended to the upper floor and to his horror

Opposite, starting from the top:

John Stone Grocery Store at the intersection of Sunset Avenue and Atlanta Road.

John M. Stone.

Bronze plaque and garden area dedicated to C. J. Fouts, May 26, 2006, on former site of Fouts Brothers Service Station and the W. N. Pace General Store.

Above: Concord Bridge and dam looking northeast from the Mableton side of the bridge, c. 1940.
PHOTOGRAPH COURTESY PARKER LOWRY.

Left: Advertisement for Concord Woolen Mills.

found the child stripped of its clothing, bleeding, gashed and lifeless wedged in among the machinery. It was extricated from the position but the vital spark was extinguished and its soul had winged its way back to the God who gave it. Mrs. Reed had given birth to a new child, Schale Reed, January 10, 1874, to March 13, 1877, on that day and when the sad intelligence of the horrible death of her child was conveyed to her the agony she experienced was heart rending in the extreme".

With the coming of the new owners many improvements were made to the facilities and additional people were hired.

The mill superintendent's death was reported in the May 22, 1879, issue of the *Marietta Journal*. "The sudden death of James Earnshaw, July 2, 1822 to May 20, 1879, superintendent at Concord Woolen Mills has cast a gloom over this community." His wife Lucy worked there in the 1880s. Their daughter, Mary, married John W. Ruff. William Dailey followed Earnshaw as superintendent.

Some Smyrna area families had more than one person working at the mill at the same time: George and Josiah Daniell; John and Nathaniel Sherman; Artemus and Narcisas Dobbs; Mary, Jane and Millie Hurst (all seamstresses) and John and Julia Kendley. At one time it was thought that 200 people might eventually be working in the mill. That never happened, but the mill did provide more jobs in Smyrna in the late 1800s than any other commercial endeavor.

During the 1880s and '90s the factory produced a variety of goods that won numerous prizes for excellence in quality and design at exhibitions and trade shows throughout the country.

In October 1889 tragedy struck the plant again when a fire consumed most of the building. By January 1890 restoration was underway, but tragedy struck again on June 10, 1890, when Martin L. Ruff, Jr., who was rebuilding the factory died of pneumonia.

The 1860 U. S. Census showed that Martin L. Ruff owned 9 slaves, 5 females and 4 males. Two of the former slaves who continued to work on the Ruff farm for the family were shown in the 1880 census as Silvia, age 30, and Horace Anderson, age 53, they were referred to as Uncle Horace and Aunt Silvia.

A new machine called the "Wright Spinner" was installed in the rebuilt factory. It was believed to be the only one in the South. The new looms were the latest, improved Gilbert pattern. For the new spinner, an engine was installed to supplement their power.

On December 20, 1894, John W. Rice bought interest in his father's estate (Z. A. Rice had died intestate) from his sister Mary Lou Stocks.

The factory had purchased a dynamo by 1895 that was said to be of great importance in lighting up the building in the evenings and on cloudy days where it could operate 24 hours a day.

Left: The superintendent's house was located just south of the present-day Concord Road between Nickajack Creek and the Seaboard Airline Railroad bed that is today the Silver Comet Trail.

PHOTOGRAPH COURTESY OF PARKER LOWRY, A DESCENDANT OF THE RICE AND RUFF FAMILIES.

Right: Horace and Silvia Anderson, former slaves of the Ruff family who continued to live with them after the war. Referred to as Uncle Horace and Aunt Silvia. They are shown in the yard of the Ruff family farmhouse.

PHOTOGRAPH COURTESY OF PARKER LOWRY.

But the past glory of the woolen factory was not to continue. Rice, Love and Porter operated the mill through the early 1900s but competition from "cotton mills' and other factors led to the demise of the enterprise.

Robert Daniell, who had sold his interest in the mill operation in 1872, had established quite a reputation as a farmer. He was one of the original builders and owners of one of Cobb County's first industrial complexes and had turned to farming after the sale. He was known as a very progressive farmer using machines and methods far ahead of his time and he was the first farmer in Cobb County to raise 100 bushels of corn on an acre of land. He had purchased 500 acres from Chamealous Bennett on January 15, 1852.

His home was located on the north side of Concord Road near the present-day intersection of Havilon Way. He married his first wife, Naomi Burnett, on August 11, 1836, and they had nine children. She died in November 1862 and was the first person to be buried in the Daniell family cemetery located at the intersection of Havilon Way and Cloudland Drive. A marker near the entrance to the cemetery is inscribed: "This property 300 feet square deeded by Robert Daniell revised plat book number 1, page 80 to the white citizens within one-and-a-half-miles of same for cemetery purposes." Margaret Fleming was his second wife. Robert

was almost thirty years her senior when they married. They had seven children.

In the 1880s Smyrna finally had a Baptist Church and it was in the middle of town. In fact, it was in the building the original city limits were drawn from—the Smyrna Boy's Academy—but by this time the Presbyterians had purchased the building. They allowed the Smyrna Baptist Church (eventually Smyrna First Baptist) to organize a new congregation in their building on August 30, 1884, with four charter members: T. E. and Amanda Legg and Benson and Fanny Bell. The charter minister was Reverend J. A. McMurray. The church met once a month: usually services were on a Saturday and Sunday.

The congregation grew quickly and by May 1886 they had constructed their own building on Atlanta Road. It was a white frame building very similar to the one the Methodist Church had built in 1882.

The churches provided a lot of the social activity in the 1800s. For example, the *Marietta Journal* reported in their June 28, 1889 edition, a Sunday School outing at King's Spring "The Methodist Sunday School gave a picnic last Saturday, the other school being invited and participating. The amusements were swinging, jumping the rope, playing croquet, marbles, etc. The good ladies of Smyrna know how to make a picnic occasion or any other occasion pleasant." And on May 11, 1899, the *Marietta Journal* reported: "a party of young people from this place wasted the day last Saturday at Terrell's Mill—fishing. They caught nothing but colds and received a good jolting in going to and returning from the mill. Three of our young

Left: Smyrna First Baptist Church constructed in 1886 on Atlanta Road near present day Second Baptist Church.

PHOTOGRAPH COURTESY OF MARY TERRY.

Right: The Robert Daniell home was built c. 1872. It was located on Concord Road near Havilon Way that leads to the Daniell Family Cemetery. Left to right: Ed Dewees, a neighbor, Jessie, Jennie, Mary, Mrs. Fanny Daniell, Putman and Pliney Frank Daniell, c. 1885.

Taylor Brawner House

Smyrna Community Development Department & Cultural Center

Photo by Jack Collins August 2009

ladies appropriated a young man's bicycle and indulged in the art of cycling. I am told it was a sight for men and little fishes! They sometimes rode the wheel and sometimes it rode them, and they tore up the earth for a block around."

One of the greatest changes that had taken place in the town of Smyrna was that people from Atlanta and other places, with lots of money, had started buying large tracts of cheap land in unincorporated Cobb County between Smyrna and the river. Apparently, as a result, the town officials decided to reduce the town limits from one mile to one-half mile and petitioned the legislature to give Smyrna a new charter and on December 8, 1897, the Legislature approved the request in House Bill 201. The city limits did not change again until 1951. The new charter also added an alderman from the original four to five council members to be elected in January of each year.

Possibly one of the reasons for the reduction in the city limits was that it eliminated the need for providing municipal services to the new people who were moving into the area—people like the Crowes, Rays, Eubanks, Andersons, Taylors, Campbells and others. The first letter in each of the first five family names listed above were used to create the name "Creatwood"

which designated the area on the edge of the original Smyrna city limits that was eliminated when the charter was changed. The Taylor family brought the "jonquils" to the city. The Crowe family brought the Creatwood Dairy and the Guernsey Jug. The Ray family brought family members who were cornerstones of the churches and civic organizations. The Campbell family brought Argyle and Aunt Fanny's Restaurant.

Steven and Mary Taylor bought 80 acres in the area that had been known as Bowie Woods for many years. They constructed a residence that eventually became known as the Taylor/Brawner House. It is located on Atlanta Road on the southern edge of the Smyrna city limits when the deed was recorded in October of 1896. About a year later the city of Smyrna reduced the city limits and removed them from the city.

The Taylors lived in the house only about eleven years and then moved to Spokane, Washington, to live with their only son, Maxie. However, several years before moving to Spokane Maxie had sent his parents a bag of jonquil bulbs that seemed to flourish in the red Georgia soil. The Taylors shared the bulbs with their friends and neighbors and soon the town had thousands of the beautiful yellow blooms in the early Spring.

SMYRNA'S BRAWNER PARK DEDICATED APRIL 18, 2009

In the late 1920s and '30s U. S. 41 was the only paved street in the city and the population was just a few hundred. In the early spring Smyrna's residential yards and right-of-ways became a mass of yellow. Thousands of jonquils bloomed profusely for several weeks and attracted the attention of the tourists traveling back to their homes in the mid-west and Canada after having spent the winter in Florida or the tourists heading south. The jonquils were popular with the tourists and other motorists driving through town.

Some of Smyrna's young boys gathered up bunches of the jonquils and sold them on the side of the road for ten or fifteen cents a bunch. Mr. and Mrs. Parker M. Rice had, perhaps, the largest yard of jonquils in the city Their house was located on the southwest corner of King

and Church Streets where the Carmichael Funeral Home is located now. Their grandson, Parker Lowry, was one of the boys who sold jonquils and he had to split his profits with his grandmother. Melvin Holleman was another of the youngsters who sold them. Both are volunteers at the Smyrna Museum and long-time members of the Historical Society.

Unknowingly, the Taylor family had introduced the city to the beautiful floral image that distinguished Smyrna from dozens of other villages and towns along U. S. 41. (Atlanta Road) and had given the city its nickname although it didn't occur until many years later.

At this point, the history. gets a little controversial when it comes to saying who was the first single source for the name "Jonquil City of the South," For a number of years some members of Smyrna's Business Men's organization claimed they were the first but the ladies have a different story. They say the incident that first caused the city to be referred to as "The Jonquil City of the South", according to traditional history, occurred on June 24, 1928, in Toronto, Canada. When Grover Cleveland Green and his wife Lena Mae and Horace and Evelyn Mulkey, among others, were attending a convention there, one of the delegates, who had traveled on U. S. 41, through Georgia, asked Mrs. Green the name of the little town north of Atlanta that has all the pretty yellow flowers. Mrs. Green is said to have responded, "that's Smyrna, Georgia, the Jonquil City of the South."

Opposite, clockwise starting from top:

Brawner Hospital, after complete restoration by the City of Symrna, April 2009. The hospital was originally constructed in 1910.
PHOTOGRAPH COURTESY OF HAROLD SMITH.

Painting used for designing Smyrna's jonquil logo.
PAINTING COURTESY OF FANNY COBB.

The Taylor/Brawner House.
PHOTOGRAPH COURTESY OF MELVIN POTTS.

Smyrna's Brawner Park dedicated April 18, 2009.
PHOTOGRAPH COURTESY OF JACK COLLINS.

Below: Jonquils in full bloom at the home of Mr. and Mrs. Parker M. Rice, present location of Carmichael Funeral Home.
PHOTOGRAPH COURTESY OF ELIZABETH ANDERSON.

Nine years later on September 21, 1937, eighteen Smyrna ladies met at the Woman's Club building to organize a garden club and the name suggested and adopted was The Jonquil Garden Club. It is probably the longest lasting of the garden clubs in the Smyrna area that is still active. Oddly enough, Mrs. G. C. Green, the person who is credited with originating the jonquil city name was not a charter member of the club.

The beautiful jonquil image has been incorporated into the official logo of the city. The administrative services building and the community center are topped with towers that feature stained glass reproductions of the jonquil. The original design that has been modified several times was adopted from a painting by Smyrna artist, Fanny Cobb.

The Taylor family had disposed of some of their land in 1907 when they moved to Spokane and in 1908 they sold the remaining 80 acres to Dr. James Brawner who established one of the first facilities in the state of Georgia for treating patients with alcohol, drug and mental problems. It remained an important part of Smyrna's economy until the late 1990s. In a brief history of the Taylor/Brawner house, Mike Terry, the financial director and historian of the Taylor/Brawner Foundation stated, "After opening in 1910, the hospital quickly became a world class facility for the treatment of mental afflictions and drug dependency. It operated until the late 1990s and at that time was the oldest operating privately owned hospital in the nation."

The city of Smyrna acquired the Taylor/Brawner house, the Brawner Hospital and twelve acres of land that contained a total of thirteen buildings in August, 2001 for 2.9 million dollars. The buildings included residences for some employees of the hospital, several large treatment facilities, a small building used for training nurses, an administrative building, a large detached dining hall, an indoor swimming pool and exercise facilities.

The city offered the Taylor/Brawner to the Smyrna Historical and Genealogical Society but an investigative committee of the Society determined and recommended that it probably could be best handled through an independent organization set up especially for the purpose of restoring the building. The Taylor/Brawner House Foundation was incorporated under the laws of the State of Georgia as a Domestic Nonprofit Corporation on October 27, 2004, by the Secretary of State. Almost five hundred thousand dollars was raised and spent on the restoration of the house. It has become one of the main features of the city of Smyrna's 20-million dollar Brawner Center complex that houses several departments of the city and a park facility for public use.

The founding officers and board members of the foundation are: Lillie Wood, president; Nancy Thomsen, secretary; Mike Terry, vice president, historian and financial director; Harold Smith, director-at-large; Barbara Kincaid, director-gifts; Randy Jordan, construction superintendent; Mickie Higgins, vice president fund raising; Susan Drinnon, vice president communications; Marion Campbell, director restoration, Ed Whittington, director newsletter and website; Geri Brooks, director membership; Sandy Sands, director of fundraising; Jan Campbell, director of grounds; Jacque Landers, director of interior; Nancy McGee, director historic registry.

Another of the Atlanta residents (West End) whose land was removed from the city limits in the 1897 charter amendment was Dr. Walter A. Crowe, an Atlanta surgeon. He had purchased 180 acres of the Bowie Woods in 1892 and constructed a house on the property for the family to use for weekend retreats.

Arthur Crowe, Jr., presenting a program to the Smyrna Historical Society in the 1990s, said the family would ride to Smyrna on the railroad train called the "Short Dog." It traveled on the W & A tracks from Atlanta to the North Georgia Mountains. The conductor would stop for passengers along the track and let them off at their place of choice. The family would also ride

❖

Above: Dr. Walter A. Crowe.

Below: left to right: Grover Cleveland and Lena Mae Green, Evelyn and Horace Mulkey at the Government House in Toronto, Canada, June 24, 1928.

PHOTOGRAPH COURTESY OF THE MULKEY ESTATE.

Left: The Guernsey Jug, Atlanta Road, c. 1950.

PHOTOGRAPH COURTESY OF DAN HOPWOOD.

Below: Menu from The Guernsey Jug, c. 1940s.

PHOTOGRAPH COURTESY OF ARTHUR CROWE, JR.

the same train back home after the weekend in the "country." When the Atlanta Northern Railway, an electric trolley, came to Smyrna in 1905 the Crowe family traveled on it.

The Creatwood Farms operation was established in 1896. The northern property line of the Crowe family land adjoined the Taylor family's southern border.

Dr. Crowe purchased additional acreage and most of the 250 acres was devoted to pastures, woodland and hay crops for the Guernsey cattle at the dairy.

Dr. Crowe retired from his medical practice in 1920 and moved the family to Smyrna permanently. He never cared for farming but his son Arthur Crowe, Sr., was a landscape architect and loved to farm. He started the Creatwood Dairy and Guernsey Jug Restaurant that were popular with the tourist trade on U. S. 41, the old Dixie Highway. The "Jug" was billed as a "Roadside Market of the Creatwood Farm Dairy developed primarily for the sale of products from the dairy, as well as an attractive place for the motoring public to stop for food and refreshments.

Arthur Crowe, Sr., also started an outdoor advertising business (billboards) and a landscaping company but after the end of World War 11 the Bell Bomber Plant closed down. The Atlanta Northern Railway discontinued the trolley line, and the large dairies were buying the smaller ones. The entire Creatwood operation was discontinued by the end of 1947. However, the family retained ownership of the property and rented the residences including the building that had housed The Jug.

In the mid 1990s Arthur Crowe, Jr., and his sister sold the property to John Weiland Homes for the construction of an upscale subdivision known as Heritage of Vinings. The Guernsey Jug building was moved from its original location to the north end of the property and made into a clubhouse for the subdivision complete with a swimming pool and other recreation facilities. That way the historic building became a permanent landmark in Smyrna. The other structures on the property were demolished.

Unfortunately some of those properties that were de-annexed in 1897 didn't come back into the city until the 1960s, '70s and '80s.

For the most part, at the end of the nineteenth century, Smyrna was still an agricultural area and most of the citizens were involved in farming. During the spring of 1889 the *Marietta Journal* reported: "Old fashioned diversified farming is coming to the front. Daniel Reed has corn, cotton, wheat, oats, rye, sorghum, millet, melons, sweet and Irish potatoes. Reverend A. G. Dempsey was said to have cotton six inches high in late May and John Reed's corn was two and a half feet high.

The late 1800s had brought all kinds of changes to Smyrna. They were now incorporated, they had a "money order" post office and telegraph. There were a few telephones in town and electric lights had been installed in some of the public buildings. Plans were underway for the electric railroad to start construction in the near future and a new family, Ed L. Wight, had moved into the area with big plans to start the Belmont Farms. Smyrna was ready for the twentieth century.

The 1880 United States Census was the first one after Smyrna was incorporated as a town and at the time there were only fifty-one residences.

Note: Although the actual census contains the color, gender, age and names of all the people living in the household, only the name and relationship to the head of the house are being listed here.

1. Stone, John M., 31, grocer, wife Lavenia; daughter Maude; daughter unnamed infant, brother-in-law James J. Payne; servant, Julia Harden.
2. Hill, Thomas J., 40, school teacher, wife Jennie; son Herbert; Ann E. Hill, sister-in-law.
3. Oglesby, James J., 41, gin maker, wife Annie; son Ernest J.; daughter Telemon; daughter Julia; son James V.; son Albert; son Julius K.; son, not named.
4. Anderson, Horace, 53, works on farm, wife Silvey.
5. Mable, Joel, 35, school teacher, wife Elizabeth; daughter Lizzie; daughter Susie; daughter Lollie; daughter Lella, son Mautry F.
6. Fambrough, Albert J., 35, farmer, wife Sarah E., Laura M., Sarah M.
7. Owens, John W., 41, railroad track hand, wife Julia; son James; son Robert E.; son Arthur Q.; son John.
8. Whitfield, Thomas P., 45, clerk in store, wife Savannah; son Thomas W.; daughter Claude; daughter unnamed; boarder Henry Dodd.
9. Bell, Benson A., 31, railroad agent; wife Fannie; daughter Elena; daughter Fannie; daughter Nellie; son Benson A.
10. Not listed
11. Snow, Samson, 26, works on farm, wife Lucendia; son George; son Elisha; Dooley Jackson, wife Susan.
12. Foster, Nickleboro, 22, works on farm, wife Martha (?) C.; son John H.; daughter Laura; Glozie R., Joseph C., 21, works in wood shop, wife Sarah E; daughter Marthe F.; boarder David Cook.
14. Flemming, John N., 47, farmer, wife Hilda H.; son Charles A.; son William R.; son Monroe; son Albert F.; son Robert; daughter Mary; son Harvey; daughter Minnie; son John; daughter Saluda.
15. Fleming, Pliny R., 34, farmer, wife Mary; son Virgil; son Grady.
16. Evans, Joshua, 40, works on farm, wife Fanny; boarder Sally Moore.
17. Hardy, Spencer, 54, works on farm, wife Jennie; daughter Gracie.
18. Crawford, William, 32, farmer, wife Easter; son John F.; daughter Emma J.
19. Wright, Francis, 65, wife Jane L.
20. Thomas, Hannah, 30, washer woman, son Henry G.; daughter Mary J.; son Wesley; son Chesley; daughter Nannie (or Annie).
21. Bell, Margaret, 52, keeping house, daughter Narcissus; daughter Julia; daughter Chester M.; daughter Margaret J.
22. Cates, Thomas, 35, laborer, son John; daughter Nancy; daughter Nettie.
23. Ash, Martha, 25, works on farm, son Willie; son Henry.
24. Landmon, William H., 44, works on farm, wife Mollie; son James; daughter Carrie L.; daughter Sallie W.; daughter Frannie S.
25. Dempsey, Rubin P., 25, railroad flagman, wife Mattie; son Samuel; son Willis A.
26. Connally, William E., 37, physician, wife Emma; son William P.; son Ralph P.; son Maury; daughter Lotta.
27. Pace, William N., 32, grocer, wife Elizabeth; daughter Hattie B.; boarder Oswell Boyd.

Author's Note: The information recorded here is taken from copies of microfilm originals of the United States Census. Some of the handwriting is difficult to read and the spelling and actual names may be different from what is shown here. If you are aware of misinterpreted information in the names, or the spelling please notify the author.

This was the first official United States Census taken of the Village of Smyrna after its incorporation in 1872. At that time the city limits were one mile in every direction from the Smyrna Boy's Academy that was constructed in c. 1849-1950.

STATISTICS

Calculated by the author: Not census taker K. K. Harden.

White Males 103   White Females 115
Black Males 20   Black Females   17
Mulatto Males 2   Mulatto Females 1

28. Mobley, Ephriam D., 45, real estate agent, wife Rowena; son Carlos H.; daughter Bessie M.; daughter Rowena Q.; daughter Avis; son Stuart W.; father Ephriam W.; sister-in-law Elizabeth Hale.

29. Reed, John L., 33, farmer, wife Nannie A.; daughter Alma; daughter Cora; boarder Charles R. Turner; servant Broughton Jenkins.

30. Tanner, George, 25, works on farm, servant Nancy.

31. Moore, John C., 46, railroad conductor, wife Rebecca; son George; son Richard; daughter Hattie; daughter Eleanor; son John; son Thomas G.; daughter Jerrie.

32. Brown, Julia, 54, son William; daughter Fannie.

33. Long, David C., 35, works in blacksmith shop, wife Susan; son Thomas W.; daughter Mary Ann; daughter Rebecca; son John D.; daughter Silvey W.; daughter Ella Q.; boarder Ben F. Mitchell.

34. Burroughs, Henry, 63, wife Isabella; daughter Fannie; daughter Josephine; son James J.

35. Hembrey, Wilburn, 28, works on farm, wife Mary.

36. Sluder, Sanford, 22, works on farm, wife Sarah J.; daughter Sillie; son Samuel.

37. Dempsey, Alvin G., 48, minister, wife Martha E.; son Robert A.; daughter Mary M.; son Beddoe P.; daughter Sarah M.; daughter Raaomah D.; son William S., daughter Emma L.

38. White, Abraham, 60, farmer, wife Elizabeth J, Talulah H.; daughter Savina F.; son Tomas P., son James R.; daughter Jo; daughter Ella C.; daughter Minnie P.

39. Dempsey, Lazarus, 90, farmer, daughter Rena C.; daughter Mary M.

40. Copeland, William R., 67, wife Caroline.

41. Daniell, Jerry, 40, works on farm, wife Emma; son Isaac; son Wyley.

42. Broughton, Samuel, 26, works on farm, wife Mattie; brother Davis; son Ira R.

43. Pritchett, Ann R., 54, keeping house, son Frank A.; son John; daughter Nannie.

44. Harden, William, 58, physician, wife Sallie; son Arthur M.; daughter Corrie L.; son Robert R.; daughter Jessie L.; son William P.; daughter Claude; daughter Florine.

45. Dunn, Ishmael, 43, railroad conductor, wife Carrie L.; son Willis S.; son James H.; daughter Saura; daughter Lee C.; daughter Mattie L.; daughter May L.

46. King, Hiram, 62, farmer, wife Martha C.; granddaughter Jessie L. Grish.

47. Medlin, Warren H., 37, works on farm, wife Louisa C.; daughter Maggie; daughter Nora L.; son Edgar F.; son Willie F.; daughter Lizzie; son Harry W.

48. Holbrook, Jessie E., 49, peddler, wife Mary L., daughter Mary M.; daughter Hannorah, daughter Jessie L.

49. McDonald, James H., 33, farmer, wife Mary E.; daughter Dora; son James C.; son Charles M.; mother-in-law Martha Cook.

50. Whitfield, Thomas W., 63, farmer, wife Eliza L.; son Charles E. Pearson; John F.; wife Vandilsa.

51. Pierson, John F., 29, works on farm, wife Van.

Post Offices played a part in the early development on Smyrna and the surrounding territory.

Mill Grove: This was located in the area of the Concord Woolen Mill and the Daniell/Ruff Mill and Concord Covered Bridge Historic District area on Nickajack Creek.

Alexander McLarty	September 28, 1837, to December 19, 1838
John H. Walker	December 19, 1838, to May 8, 1839
Samuel Burdine	May 8, 1839 to January 5, 1867, discontinued
Hartwell A. Baldwin	Re-established July 1, 1869, discontinued April 21, 1870

Cross Roads: Formerly Paces Ferry in DeKalb County.

Hardy Pace	April 16, 1839, to December 2, 1839[+]
Pickney Randall	December 2, 1839, to March 2, 1846, discontinued
Tillman G. McAfee*	Re-established as Vinings Station, October 2, 1868

[+]Harold Glore, *Cobb County History.*
*Franklin Garrett, *Atlanta and Environs.*

Boltonville and High Bridge: This post office was established December 22, 1842. It was located in the general vicinity of what is now South Atlanta Road and Interstate 285 and known as Carmichaels, Log Cabin and Collins Springs. On March 2, 1846, the name was changed to "High Bridge" referring to the recently completed W & A Railroad bridge spanning the Chattahoochee River at what later became Bolton on the Fulton County side of the river. It was changed back to Boltonville November 13, 1849. It was discontinued on June 22, 1866, but reestablished two months later on August 20. The postmasters for the post office were:

James A. Collins	December 22, 1842
Henry Y. Dean	June 19, 1845
Bushrod Pace	March 2, 1846 (High Bridge)
James A. Collins	January 22, 1853
Joseph V. Stanback	May 20, 1853
James M. Lowe	December 29, 1854
Joseph V. Stanback	March 8, 1855
Clark Howell	Febraury 20, 1857
Sylvester Marion	July 20, 1859
Benjamin Mauldin	August 20, 1866
Thomas Moore	February 21, 1872 (now in Fulton County)

Neal Dow: One of the early names given to the Smyrna area when the railroad was being constructed.

Martin L. Ruff	September 24, 1852, to June 24, 1856
William S. Tweedall	June 24, 1856

Cicada: This post office was established July 13, 1882, and was located in the J. L. Dodgen & Son General Store at Dodgen Mill which was located on Nickajack Creek. The area served was in the southwest area in the vicinity of present day Cooper Lake Road. The two postmasters were:

Warren A. Dodgen	July 13, 1882, to January 15, 1886
Thomas B. Dodgen	January 15, 1886, to November 11, 1886

Cicada Nickajack was the name of the Cherokee Indian who had lived in the area and for which the creek was named.

Nickajack: Established June 21, 1888, and basically served the area around the Concord Woolen Mills and the Covered Bridge area. Its only postmaster was Parker M. Rice. The post continued in operation until May 31, 1909.

Isaac R. Teat	January 28, 1858, to August 27, 1858
Furman R. Robert	August 27, 1858, to November 4, 1858, discontinued

Smyrna: Site of present downtown Smyrna intersection of Atlanta Road and East and West Spring Streets at the Market Village and various other nearby locations.

Benson A. Bell	May 2, 1870, to January 4, 1872
Wilson L. Davenport	January 4, 1872, to March 6, 1872
Wade White	March 6, 1872, to March 15, 1887
John M. Stone	March 15, 1887, to July 11, 1895
Sam J. Ireland	July 11, 1895, to January14, 1902
Alma Reed	January14, 1902, to October 19, 1908, married Henry Konigsmark
Alma Konigsmark	October 19, 1908, to January 16, 1916
Jesse R. Deavoirs	January 15, 1916, to April 17, 1922
William V. Cobb	April 17, 1922, to July 14, 1933
Zeland T. Wills	July 14, 1933, to January 30, 1934
Arthur B. Caldwell	January 30, 1934, to July 31, 1944
Zeland T. Wills	July 31, 1944, to April 8, 1966
Walter T. Gillespie	April 8, 1966, to August 11, 1967
C. Austin Atkins	August 11, 1967, to March 12, 1976
W. Daniel Honea	March 12, 1976, to July 31, 1976
Leman C. Parks	July 31, 1976, to March 24, 1990
Clarence Robinson	March 24, 1990, to December 30, 2000
Wesley Newsome	December 30, 2000, to November 30, 2002
A. Max Bacon	November 30, 2002, to June 10, 2006
Leann T. Theriault	June 10, 2006, to present

Gilmore: Located in the area of Atlanta Road at its intersection with Gilmore Road, just north of the Oakdale Community

G. M. McKinnon	September 18, 1889, to ?

❖

Postmaster Zeland Wills, 1933. This post office, located on Atlanta Street next to the city hall, moved to West Spring Street to the Masonic Lodge building in the mid-1950s.

❖

*The population of Smyrna was
approximately 5,000 and had more
than doubled the official 2008 census
of 1950 when the photograph was
taken of "downtown" Smyrna on a
Saturday morning in 1955. That was
just a few months after Belmont Hills
opened in November 1954. The
intersection is Atlanta Road and East
and West Spring Streets looking north.
The entrance to the present-day
Market Village is on the left. With the
exception of the two-story Whitfield
building (with the Coca Cola sign) all
of the structures on the right side of
the road were demolished in the late
1980's street-widening project. The
traffic light at this intersection was the
only one in the city from about 1953
until 1962 when one was installed at
Atlanta Road and Cherokee (now
Windy Hill). Stoplights at Church &
King Streets, Atlanta Road and Sunset
Avnue and at Atlanta and Love Street
had been removed around 1952-53.
The need for additional parking space
that was acquired when Jonquil Plaza
opened in 1959 is certainly reflected
in this photograph.*

CHAPTER V

SMYRNA IN THE TWENTIETH CENTURY

When the 1900 United States census was completed, the Town of Smyrna, Georgia, was found to have 238 residents. This number was down from the 416 that had been enumerated in the census of 1890. The reason for the town having 172 fewer residents was that on December 8, 1897, the Georgia Legislature amended Smyrna's corporate charter to change the town limits and for other purposes. One of the other purposes was to elect a town marshal and a city clerk. The maximum tax that could be collected was 25 cents on each $100 of property evaluation. The mayor and council also were given authority to compel every able-bodied male to work on the city streets a specified number of days each year, or to pay $3.00 per day if they refused to work.

But the reduction in the number of residents had little effect on the character of the area or the community. The economy of Smyrna, for the most part, was still based on agriculture. Ninety percent of the workforce was farmers or farm laborers. The social and civic life was still built around the churches, schools, and clubs.

The Smyrna post office that was authorized to sell its first money order in 1898 had been in operation since May 2 1870. From then until January 14, 1902, five males had served in the postmaster position. On that date Alma Reed, later to be Konigsmark, became the postmistress of the Smyrna post office and remained in that position until 1915. There wasn't another female postmistress until 2006. John J. Baldwin, became the first rural route mail carrier for Smyrna on October 22, 1902, but it was almost fifty years before in town Smyrna residents got home mail delivery. It had been rumored in 1948 that it would be available soon, but "soon" didn't arrive until 1952.

Another first in Smyrna came in July 1898 when the Southern Telegraph & Telephone Co. announced the installation of a pay phone inside Gilbert's Grocery store. You could call around the county for a nickel or dime. It wasn't until 1905 that Smyrna got its own telephone office and that year, 24 residents hooked up. By the end of 1910 the system had expanded to 62, and in October 1973 Smyrna reached the 50,000 mark. With a zillion cell phones, who knows what it is in 2010?

Perhaps Smyrna's best known business in the early 1900s was a name that is still familiar today—Belmont. Back then, it was Belmont Farms, owned and operated by a new man in town, Ed Wight and his son, who had moved here from Albany in 1899 along with Loring Brown, a well known Georgia poultry fancier, who was the general superintendent.

The Belmont operation was described as the largest plant of its kind in the state by the Georgia Historical and Industrial Directory. It was two hundred acres and raised chickens, ducks, turkeys, geese, pheasants, Jersey cattle and Berkshire hogs. The farm boasted a large two-story six hundred foot long incubator which could turn out 7,000 little chicks every three weeks that within sixty days, could be sent to market. From the twelve Berkshire hogs on the farm, several thousand dollars' worth of pigs were produced. Milk was another of the marketable products from the farm and was shipped to Atlanta, Marietta and other places.

Smyrna resident Henry Konigsmark, Sr., who lived on the farm from 1901 to 1908 and served as the corporation's secretary, related that the farm shipped fifty gallons of milk and butter each day to the Kimball House Hotel in Atlanta by rail, both train and trolley.

Belmont Farms won many prizes and awards at exhibitions throughout the country, but like many other enterprises, changing times brought an end to the large operation, and by the 1920s the farm was being divided and sold for real estate development.

As early as 1908 when Atlanta Road was still a muddy mess during rainy weather, some people, through the *Marietta Journal,* were clamoring for the installation of curbs on the town's major thoroughfare. One of the businesses that would benefit from the curbs in January 1910 was the first Bank of Smyrna, headed by President Parker M. Rice. A December 1, 1911 bank statement filed with the State of Georgia showed assets of $60,920.33. Cash on hand at the time was $1,257.31.

John Corn, who later became mayor of Smyrna, was cashier and manager of the original bank until 1922, when he joined the Citizens Bank in Marietta. A year later bank officials named J. W. Ridley to vice president and general manager. Another of Smyrna's mayors, J. Gid

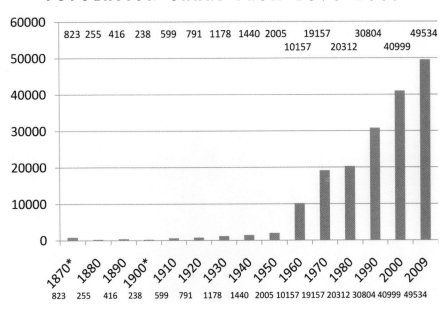

POPULATION CHART FROM 1870-2009

1870*	1880	1890	1900*	1910	1920	1930	1940	1950	1960	1970	1980	1990	2000	2009
823	255	416	238	599	791	1178	1440	2005	10157	19157	20312	30804	40999	49534

Morris, also was associated with the bank. But it, like so many other businesses, failed in the 1920s and Smyrna didn't have another bank until August 1946 when a completely different Bank of Smyrna opened.

The Rice family had actually become associated with Smyrna in 1872 when Daniell and Ruff sold to Rice, Love, and Porter but by 1906 John W. Rice had purchased the remaining interests of Love and Porter and he immediately sold the woolen mill plant to Annie E. Johnson of Rome, Georgia. Mrs. Johnson was the literary editor of the *Rome Tribune & Herald* and a social activist. She had plans to reactivate the factory by providing employment for displaced Russian Jews through an association with the Galveston Movement. The plan failed and the firm went into receivership in 1916. Mrs. Johnson was able to repurchase the property but defaulted again in 1928 to the Decatur Bank and Trust.

John W. Ruff sold the Daniell-Ruff gristmill to Parker M. Rice in 1897 and he sold it to M. A. and T. B. Martin in 1914. Dr. Clinton Reed, an Atlanta physician, purchased the entire 313-acre property from the bank. Dr. Reed initially planned to use it as a weekend retreat but subsequently moved into the miller's house to live until his death. His survivor, Carolyn Reed Bush, sold various parts of the acreage in the 1950s and '60s to individuals and developers. William Freeman and his wife Janice purchased the miller's house and a portion of the land around it from Mrs. Bush in 1967 and they sold

*Above: *Smyrna was enumerated in the Lemon's District in 1870. Smyrna was not incorporated until 1872.*
POPULATION CHART COURTESY OF BILL LYONS.

Below: Smyrna Postmistress Alma Reed Konigsmark, c. 1920s.

❖

*Right: This photograph courtesy of
Parker Lowry, grandson of the bank
president, was taken on the day the
Smyrna Bank was dedicated March
10, 1911. Left to right, front row:
Brant Eidson (boy), Dr. W. T. Pace,
Georgia Knott, Newt Dodgen, W. F.
Walker, Smyrna Bank President
Parker M. Rice, unknown, Loring
Brown, unknown, unknown, Ireland
and Hubert Ireland (sons of S. J.
Ireland) who owned a grocery store
on a lot on the right of the bank, and
W. Norris Pace, who owned a grocery
store at the corner of Spring and
Atlanta Street across from Dr. Pace's
Drug Store. The city of Smyrna
purchased the building in the mid-
1930s and it served as the Smyrna
City Hall, police station and jail
before it was demolished in 1971 by
the city. Today, this site is the
approximate location of Shane's BBQ
in Market Village.*

PHOTOGRAPH COURTESY OF PARKER LOWRY.

*Below: The Belmont House was
located east of Atlanta Road and
Windy Hill railroad underpass,
c. 1940s.*

to Gordon and Alice Ruckart in 1976. They in turn sold to Dr. Bob and Pat Burns Roche, the present owners, in 1988.

In 1980 Marietta attorney Gary Eubanks and his family purchased approximately 138 acres of the property between Concord Road on the north and Fontaine Road on the south that included all of the land containing the woolen mill ruins, but not the covered bridge or the gristmill.

In the meantime the area had been designated Cobb County's first historic district and the "Second Battle of Ruff's Mill" began. Cobb County commissioners proposed that the long-planned East-West Connector from Smyrna to Austell Road and points beyond be constructed through the Historic District on the right-of-way then-owned by the State of Georgia. The multi-lane highway would have been just a few hundred feet east of the gristmill and the woolen mill ruins. Cobb County purchased part of the acreage owned by the Eubanks family that contained the woolen mill ruins and other land needed for the right-of-way.

Historic district residents protested the location and preservationists from around the county and state of Georgia joined the protest. Gordon and Alice Ruckart, who owned the Ruff's Mill property at the time, organized "The Friends of the Concord Covered Bridge" and Pat Seay and her husband organized "Protect Endangered Areas of Cobb's History"

❖

Above: Ruins of the Concord Woolen Mill stand today as part of Cobb County's incomplete Heritage Park that was developed as mitigation for routing the East-West Connector highway through the Concord Covered Bridge Historic District. The ruins have been stabilized with the skelton supports to outline the original roof line of the building.
PHOTOGRAPH COURTESY OF TOM DOWNING AND THE SMYRNA MUSEUM.

Below; Nelms Masonic Lodge Number 323 of Free and Accepted Masons dedicated October 7, 2001. Located on Concord Road west of Hurt Road.

(PEACH). They enlisted the help of hundreds of other citizens, gathered petitions, and eventually won the battle to move the proposed East-West Connector approximately a quarter-mile to the east of the original route.

After numerous public hearings with Cobb County and city of Smyrna officials, Georgia and Cobb DOT departments and the Army Corps of Engineers, an agreement was reached. The East-West Connector would be constructed farther east and the roadbed lowered to leave and protect the natural terrain and other features of the landscape of the historic district. It was also agreed that no curb-cuts would be made from the East-West Connector on the portion from Hicks Road to Fontaine Road inside the historic district.

As part of the mitigation Cobb County agreed to participate in constructing the Silver Comet Trail and Heritage Park. Some of the promised features of Heritage Park have been completed but funds have not been appropriated in recent years for its completion.

Very little is known about the City of Smyrna government operations between 1872 and 1924 because a fire destroyed the official records and council minutes at that time. Newspaper accounts of some activity have

provided information on some of their activities. Scrapbooks and minutes of some of the churches and social and service clubs have given an insight into some of the social life.

Other than the First Baptist, First Methodist and the Presbyterian churches, the Nelms Lodge Number 323 of Free and Accepted Masons is the longest continuous organization in Smyrna. Its charter was granted on November 2, 1886, and named in honor on John W. Nelms for his untiring efforts in getting the charter granted in hard economic times for the area which was still recovering from the War Between the States. The Grand Lodge was hesitant to issue a new charter at the time and Captain Nelms traveled to the state headquarters in Macon and paid two years' advance dues for each charter member from his own funds and the charter was granted.

The charter members of the lodge were John Stone, W. H. Baldwin, John Henry Cantrell, J. N. Dodgen, Rufus A. Eaton, T. P. Whitfield, J. R. Kendley, Stephen Blair, John W. Irelan, A. T. Hill, John L. Reed, John H. Turner, Thomas M. Hooper, James R. Love, Benjamin F. Mackey, and John W. Nelms.

They have occupied four different buildings in Smyrna. The original one was on Atlanta Road near the present day Second Baptist Church. It burned in 1924. The second one was on East Spring Street. It was originally the Smyrna Boy's Academy. They demolished it in 1954 and replaced it with a similar looking

building on the same site. It was demolished in 1999 to make way for the construction of the Market Village. The newest lodge hall is located near the intersection of Concord and Hurt Roads. It was dedicated on October 7, 2001.

Some Smyrna elected officials have served as Worshipful Master of the Lodge over the years including Mayors H. H. Arrington, C. Mayes Hamby, George Kreeger, P. F. Brinkley and W. T. Pace. Smyrna councilmen who served in that position are T. P. Whitfield, Martin Ruff, F. D. Cargal and R. H. Bacon. Sam Whitfield, a long-time member of the lodge, has served as Worshipful Master and in a variety of offices. He was an elected member of the Cobb County Board of Education for several years.

Another Smyrna organization of considerable longevity and uniqueness is the Smyrna Social Club. It was founded on November 8, 1908. Present for the first meeting were Leila Gilbert, president; Nettie Fuller, vice president; Olive Hamby, treasurer; Hallie Moore, corresponding secretary; Ada Gann, secretary; Mable Timothy, Nina Ruff, Ida Gilbert, Alma Gilbert, Leetha Durham, Emma Durham, Kathleen Fowler, Donna Lee Pace, Mary Fleming, Grace Timothy, Myrtle Morris, Olive Daniell, Lena Mae Gann, Lucy Stovall, Alma Konigsmark and Coral Reed. It was organized in the home of Ida and Leila Gilbert. To be eligible for membership a young lady had to be single and at least seventeen years old. Another requirement was that the member had to be a resident or former resident of Smyrna. Membership was originally limited to 20 and later changed to 24. A vacancy in the club could be filled when someone died or moved away. Often the replacement was filled by a daughter or descendant of the original member. Mary B. Carson, in a history of the club that she prepared in 1976, said "the object of the club" as stated in the constitution, "shall be bringing together the ladies in a social way and for self-improvement."

The Smyrna Woman's Club was chartered in 1925 and federated in 1926. They engaged in a variety of activities to raise funds for various projects, both for civic improvements and for social purposes. There were hay rides, chicken dinners, fish frys, outings to Concord and Cooper Lake, little theater productions, dances, concerts and a variety of other things.

Smyrna Social Club members observing their 90th year, November 14, 1998. Left to right, front row: Rachel Dabney, Lillie Wood, Virginia Carmichael, LeoDelle Lassiter Jolley, Reese Stovall Landers, Kathy Hardage Hatcher and Jacque Hyde Lander. Second row: Claudia Mitchell Owens, Claudia Hamrick Adams, Ruth Mackay, Lois Matthews, Gayle Colquitt Ruddell, Judy Howard Hawkins, Evelyn Edwards Pressley, Linda Ruff Smith, Rosemary Nally Hardage, Martha Rambo Wyatt and Mary Brawner Rambo. Back row: Ellen Hamrich Cambron, Malinda Jolley Mortin, Becky Nash Paden, Marian Dabney and Nancy Konigsmark.

In 1929 the club bought a residence on Atlanta Road to use as their meeting place and club house. They were becoming somewhat of a major force in helping to influence what was going on in the city, and that might have been partially responsible for the organization of the Smyrna Men's Club that came along in 1933. It was a pre-chamber of commerce-type operation. For the most part it was made up of local businessmen and others interested in promoting the development of the town and local businesses. Smyrna's population was still less than 1,200 in the 1930s.

In 1936 the Woman's Club and the Men's Club joined forces to help the town start a library and all the financing was provided by the two clubs. When the independent Smyrna City Library had its grand opening ceremony Tuesday, September 15, 1936, its only other source of books and financing was from donations of the people of the town and their friends. Boy Scouts and others went door-to-door collecting books in wheelbarrows and small wagons to provide the city with its "first" library that consisted of one shelf, containing about fifty books. One of those books was a recently published copy of Margaret Mitchell's *Gone with the Wind*, donated by Miss Billie Shelton, a representative of the Smyrna Deluxe Tennis Club.

By 1938 there were approximately 1,400 books on the shelves. The next year the Woman's Club added a room to their club house and that served as the Smyrna library for the next twenty-two years.

The City of Smyrna and the Woman's and Men's Clubs were able to work out a contract with the depression-era Federal W. P. A. (Works Progress Administration) that agreed to provide $20 per month for a librarian if the two clubs would donate $5 each for a total of $30. The club members signed pledges that they would pay the money. The contract was renewed each year until the 1940s when the Federal Agency was abolished.

The governing board at the beginning consisted of three representatives from each club. Representatives from the Men's Club were Dr. W. C.Mitchell, W. P. Gresham and C. L. Groce. The Woman's Club representatives were Mrs. F. W. Dowda, Mrs. R. R. Manning and Mrs. G. C. Green.

The library remained in that building until December 17, 1961, when a modern brick building was dedicated at 2873 King Street during the first administration of Mayor George Kreeger.

Officers of the Smyrna Area Ministerial Association participating in the dedication ceremonies were Reverends Ridley Smith, John W. Rogers, Eugene Davis, Roland Walker and Arvie Thornton. The librarian at the time was Mazie Whitfield Nelson.The Library Board members were Mrs. G. C. Green, chairman, J. B. Ables, Mrs. Neva Cano, Mrs. Ruby Carmichael, Hubert Colquitt, Mrs. R. P. Hosch and Mayor Kreeger. The library board was abolished shortly after the new library opened and those duties were assigned to a committee of the city council.

On December 6, 1970, the "Jonquil Room" was dedicated to Mrs. G. C. Green, the long-time chairman of the library board during the administration of Mayor Harold Smith.

Mrs. Callie Jay, September 10, 1936 to 1944, Mrs. Clarence (Pearl) Power, dates unknown, Mrs. Floy Williams, 1944 to 1957, and Mrs. Mazie Nelson, 1957 to December 31, 1963, each served as director when the library was in the Woman's Club house on Atlanta Road. Mrs. Nelson's tenure carried over into the new building on King Street shown above. The following directors served only at the King Street facility: Mrs. J. W. Estes, December 6, 1962 to 1966, Mrs. Evelyn Ashton, October 11, 1966 to August 15, 1967, and Mrs. Kathryn Jones, 1967-March 26, 1982. Mrs. Doris Morris, 1982-1987, (Interim Director May-July, 1997) and Mrs. Laurel Best, November 9, 1987, to May 12, 1995, served in both the King Street

Several members of the Smyrna Historical and Genealogical Society are members of the Smyrna Social Club now: Kathy Hardage Hatcher, Lillie Fulghum Wood, Jacque Hyde Landers, Evelyn Edwards Pressley, Linda Ruff Smith, Mary Brawner Rambo, Malinda Jolley Morton, Ann Konigsmark Johnson and Becky Nash Paden. The club observed its 100th anniversary on November 15, 2008, at the rehabilitated and restored Taylor/Brawner House.

❖

Clockwise, starting from top left:

This is the library dedicated in 1961 at 2873 King Street.

Long-time Smyrna Library Director Doris Morris. Mrs. Morris' library career covered a period of fifteen years with five years as director. She was honored on December 31, 2007 when the large public meeting room in the new library was named in her honor. Mrs. Morris died April 7, 2009.

Dedication ceremonies for the new 28,000 square foot Smyrna Library and the 55,000 square foot Community Center and Village Green were held Saturday, August 3, 1991, 119 years after its first incorporation on August 23, 1872. The celebration started a tradition that continues today and draws crowds of 15,000 to 20,000 residents and visitors.

and the newest facility at 100 Village Green Circle. Michael Seigler has been director since July 24, 1995, and has served only in the newest facility which was dedicated on August 3, 1991.

The whole idea of redevelopment came in 1988 when Mayor Max Bacon and members of the city council decided the city needed an extreme makeover. They submitted a proposal to the Georgia Legislature to create a downtown development authority as a vehicle to accomplish the financing of the plan. The legislation passed the general assembly in

February 1989 and the authority members were sworn in on April 17. The original members of the authority were Hubert Black, Alton Curtis, C. J. Flouts, Dr. Jim Pitts, Willouise Spivey, Jimmy Wilson and Charles "Pete" Wood, Mayor Max Bacon was chairman.

As plans were made, the thirty-year-old library was included in the first phase for replacement along with the construction of a large community center that included two gyms and meeting rooms for public activities. Plans also called for a Village Green for outdoor activities.

In a complete departure from the traditional Smyrna structures, the city fathers turned to Colonial Williamsburg for inspiration and the City of Smyrna launched a program to change the face of the town that *National Geographic Magazine* had called "Redneck". The result was an award-winning city that has been recognized by the National League of Cities as a "City of Excellence".

The residences and commercial buildings that were demolished to make a place for these facilities were located on portions of Atlanta Road, Hamby Street, Sunset Avenue, Bank Street, Fuller Street, King Street, Powder Springs Street, East Spring Street and West Spring Street.

One of the most familiar structures in the downtown area was that of Dr. W. C. Mitchell. He moved to Smyrna in 1933 and constructed, the "Mitchell Building", on the northwest corner of Atlanta Road and Sunset Avenue in 1948.

In addition to treating Smyrna's citizens for various and sundry ailments, he was a community leader who was a co-founder, charter member and first president of the Smyrna Men's Club. He was also a charter member of the Smyrna Lion's Club in 1948 and co-founder of several of the city's most active civic organizations. He was an eleven-year member of the Cobb County Board of Education representing the Smyrna area.

After Dr. Mitchell retired, a new non-profit organization, Cobb Services for the Blind, purchased the building in April 1984. The agency was founded in 1983 by Sarah Sentell Scott and her husband Leon. It served as their headquarters and treatment facility for vision-impaired persons until 1990 when the city purchased it in the downtown redevelopment program. The agency changed its name to Blind and Low Vision Services of North Georgia and moved to new facilities at 3830 South Cobb Drive.

Dr. Mitchell's new concrete building had replaced the frame grocery store building that was first owned by J. M. Stone. After Judge Stone moved to Marietta, W. L. Southern bought the store building and the house on the property that faced Powder Springs Street. His daughter, Bonnie, and son-in-law R. H. Stephens lived in the house.

Mr. Southern started selling "motor oil" in his grocery store for the quickly-expanding

automobile tourist traffic traveling U. S. 41, known as the "Dixie Highway" (Atlanta Road) through Smyrna. During the tenure of a certain city councilman who operated a large service station on Atlanta Street just a few blocks from the Southern Grocery Store, the city passed an ordinance in 1932 that required grocery stores to buy a business license to sell motor oil in the store in addition to the regular business license. The fee was set at $7.50 per year.

The Jonquil Theater was located on the southwest corner of Sunset Avenue and Atlanta Road, across the street from the Mitchell Building. It was constructed in 1948 by Leonard Branscomb, a local entrepreneur who published a weekly newspaper named *The South Cobb Advertiser*. It was a forerunner of *The Smyrna Herald*.

The two-reel movie house was a favorite place for the young people to go to see the "cowboy"

Above: Office of Dr. W. C. Mitchell at the intersection of Atlanta Road and Sunset Avenue, former location of John Stone Grocery.

Below: Jonquil Theater opened in 1948 and closed in the 1950s. The intersection of Atlanta Road and Sunset Avenue across from the Mitchell Building.
PHOTOGRAPH COURTESY OF JOAN AND JEAN BENNETT.

❖

The Smyrna Community Center opened in August 1991.

movies and "chapter pictures" like the *Lone Ranger*, *Flash Gordon* and a variety of other movie heroes who were always left hanging on a cliff or about to be run over by a speeding train, or being attacked by a bunch of Indians or a wild animal. Miraculously the next Saturday, the hero would escape from certain death without a hitch.

You could get into the movie for five or ten cents, or use a quarter-sized token that your family had received in a bag of Capitola Flour. Anyone skilled at using a sewing machine could use the "print" flour bags for making clothing, curtains or other needed items.

The Jonquil Theater closed in the mid-1950s after the Belmont Hills Theater and Drive-In opened. Later the Cobb Center Theater and the Miracle Theater opened in the mid-1960s and '70s when merchants started moving out of the downtown area to nearby shopping centers like Belmont Hills, Dickson's Shopping Center and later Cobb Center and Cumberland Mall.

Following the Jonquil Theater's closing it was used for a variety of businesses including an auto repair garage and a plastic firm and then demolished in 1990 to make way for the redevelopment. The present-day entrance to the Village Green Circle, the fountain, the Community Center and the Library was the approximate location of Sunset Avenue

The original name of Sunset Avenue was Nickajack Street. It was only one "long" block from Atlanta Road to a dead end at Hamby Street. Harry H. Arrington's family lived on the street and when he was elected mayor of Smyrna in 1933, the story goes, his mother was fascinated with the beautiful sunset over the trees at the west end of the street and asked him to change the name to Sunset Avenue. He was able to grant her request with agreement of the other council members.

The buildings shown at the top of page 61 were south of Sunset Avenue and were the "heart and soul" of "downtown" in the 1950s, '60s and early '70s. The Western Auto building, which had also served as the Smyrna post office, was next door to the Smyrna city hall/police station and was owned by V. G. "Bud" Blakeney. He rented the building from former Mayor John Corn. Druggist Bill Atkins and former Mayor Harold Smith later purchased the building from Mr. Corn.

Atherton's Drug Store (1948) and Bill Atkins' Drug Store (1970s) were gathering places for politicians and would-be politicians, rumor-makers and town folks who just came in to eat at the lunch counter or soda fountain and pass the time of day.

The drug store was also frequented by two owner/editors of *The Smyrna Herald*, Bill Miles and the person he sold to, Bill Kinney, who later became Associate Editor of the *Marietta Daily Journal*. The printing plant and office of the *Herald* were located behind this row of buildings. Miles and Kinney would go to the drug store to "pick up" on the gossip for the day.

❖

Clockwise, starting from top:

The event depicted—was a "grand remodeling sale" where shoppers were waiting for the store to open for a chance to win a new black and white TV and a variety of other door prizes. The town had a population of a little over 2000 at the time.

A service station was located on the small triangular shaped piece of land between Atlanta Road and Memorial Drive from 1920 to the mid-1950s. The lot is now a small city beautification spot. This Anchor Oil Station was owned by the Joe Wine family.

Bank of Smyrna at Atlanta Road and Church Street. It opened in 1946 and has changed ownership several times. It is now the Wacovia Bank across the street from the Smyrna Museum.

One of Kinney's favorite stories about the drug store went like this: "One day Mayor Smith parked his Triumph TR6 convertible out front, came in and sat on "his" stool at the drugstore. He wore a red cap, blue pinstripe sports coat, a black shirt, white tie, red pants and white shoes. 'Who's that' asked a visiting drug salesman. 'That's our mayor' replied Druggist Atkins. Then in walked a lady known for her "generosity" around town. She had on a black leather mini-skirt, black fishnet hose, an off-the-shoulder blouse, a black beret and high-heeled shoes. She sat down on a stool, then slowly crossed her legs. The salesman eyeballed Mayor Smith, ogled the lady, then cracked, "Who's that! the city clerk?" Wrong again.

The Bank of Smyrna was the second one with that name. Smyrna had been without a bank since the 1920s when the first Bank of Smyrna went broke. It opened on Atlanta Street, August 5, 1946. W. P. Gresham was president, B. F. Reed, Jr., vice president, W. C. Patterson, cashier. Directors were W. P. Gresham, B. F. Reed, Jr., W. T. Crowe, Jr., D. C. Landers, J. W. Nash, and G. C. Green. The capital and surplus at the time was $70,000 and the telephone number for the bank was 228.

The bank remained at that location until December 19, 1956, when a more impressive structure was constructed a few hundred feet south in the triangle that is formed by the convergence of Atlanta Road and Memorial Drive. The space had previously been occupied by the D. C. Osborn service station for many years, the Smyrna Boarding House, or hotel, and some residences, but at the time of the construction of the bank it was occupied by the Anchor Oil service station owned by Joe Wine.

The red brick building on the right side of the original bank was a barber shop. The gabled structure north of the barber shop was the telephone exchange building where live operators manned the "switchboards" and said "number please" when a telephone customer lifted the ear piece from its holder on the side of

❖

Above: Sunnyside Inn was located on Atlanta Road directly across the deadend of Campbell Road near present-day Campbell Middle School, apartments, condos, and commercial buildings.

Below: North side of Bank Street, 1970s, looking northwest. The Smyrna City Hall was located directly across the street from this row of buildings.

the phone. In the early days Dr. Pace, and later his daughter Lorena, had telephone number 1, The next nine in the top ten numbers were N. T. Durham 2, Smyrna Drug 3, Mrs. Parker Rice 4, D. J. Ray 5, J. C. W. Turner 6, Mrs. Carl Prichard 7, L. A. Tedder 8, T. Q. Richardson 9, W. and H. O. Williamson 10. In 1938 there were 200 homes and businesses that had telephones in Smyrna.

Those were the days of long-distance calls from Smyrna to Atlanta where you had to pay an extra 10 cents per call for a station-to-station or 25 cents for a person-to-person call. The initial price was for 3 minutes and if you talked longer there was an additional charge.

It was also a time of "party lines" where you might have to share a line with one or more customers. Each customer had a distinct number of rings and you were supposed to answer only your own ring. But you had to be careful of your conversation and language because someone on the line might be listening without your knowledge. For the most part

operators were eliminated in Smyrna and some other metro communities in 1951 when "dial" phones were put in operation. With the exception of "person-to-person" and station-to-station long-distance calls, the live operator was eliminated. Most homes had only one phone in it. Some folks had "extensions" but there was no call waiting, forwarding, caller ID, answering machines, cell phones, etc. All that came eighty years later.

The building on Bank Street directly behind the 1930s to 1958 Smyrna City Hall was constructed as the Howard Hardware store. Later it was converted to house a large flatbed press to print the *Smyrna Herald* newspaper. In addition, the owner/publisher, Bill Miles, did job printing for local businesses and the city of Smyrna. Bill Kinney purchased the *Smyrna Herald* and moved the office to Atlanta Road near the Belmont Hills Shopping Center and then to Cherokee Road (now Windy Hill). Eventually, Kinney sold the *Herald* to the *Marietta Daily Journal* (*MDJ*) and the *Smyrna Neighbor* became the prototype for the "Neighbor" newspapers and Kinney became Associate Editor of the *MDJ*.

The flat-top building between the two residences was constructed as a Colonial Store Supermarket in the 1950s, later purchased by the Southern Acceptance Corporation and in 1981 by the city of Smyrna. The Parks and Recreation Department had offices in it for a while and later it was converted to the Smyrna Judicial Building where part of the court operation took place.

Eventually all the property on Bank and West Spring Streets, between Atlanta Road and King Street was acquired by the city.

Smyrna's population grew by only about 1,800 during the fifty years from 1900 to 1950. Even World War II and the construction of the Bell Bomber Plant in Marietta and the Access Highway (now South Cobb Drive) on the west side of town had little effect on Smyrna's growth.

Women and men, living in Smyrna, who didn't go into the military were hired to fill some of the 95 cents per hour assembly-line jobs and other positions in the large plant. But for the most part, people from Atlanta and other surrounding towns filled those jobs. In the decade of the 1940s, Smyrna's population grew only by about 600.

The old Dixie Highway, U. S. 41, when it was first laid out, came through the middle of Smyrna. It didn't get paved until the mid-1920s through Smyrna and it was called the Marietta Highway. It was the most direct route from the mid-west to Florida and the automobile traffic spawned some tourist courts where travelers could rent a room for a night. The Sunnyside Inn was one of the well-known tourist courts in the area. It was located on the west side of Atlanta Road where Campbell Road deadends. It was operated by the Parks family and consisted of a series of one-room structures in a circular drive-way behind the main building that was a service station and convenience store.

A more widely known tourist court, approximately one mile south of Sunnyside, at the intersection of then unpaved "Vinings Road" (now Paces Ferry Road) was Stonewall Court, named for famous Southern Confederate General "Stonewall" Jackson. The site was said to be a part of a 202 acre land lot awarded to the Lemon Family; however, the Cherokee Land Lottery records do not bear this out. It's possible the Lemon family did purchase the land from the original lottery winners but the land lots in this area were all forty acres. Stonewall Court was owned by Edgar Anderson and over the years had a number of different managers. It, too, had one-room structures with enclosed parking but they were constructed of stone. There was a restaurant on the property that had an extensive display of War Between the States memorabilia that would rival a fairly good size museum. It attracted many tourists. However, the dining room and museum burned in 1946 and only a few of the War Relics were salvaged. The 2000 Paces subdivision of upscale housing occupies that site at the present.

When U. S. 41 was moved about three miles to the east in 1939, to its present location, it became known as "The Four-lane Highway" and completely by-passed Smyrna. There were no more tourists coming through town and some of the "tourist courts" started catering to a local trade and clientele.

One story that was reported in the local newspapers concerned a Cobb County Sheriff's raid one weekend at Stonewall Court. There was a large number of well-known local men who were said to be occupying some of the rooms with someone other than their own wives and there was known to be some illegal whiskey in large quantities there. When the sheriff entered one of the rooms, he immediately recognized the man in the room as a long-time acquaintance. The man

Left: Copy of a postcard from Stonewall Court, south of downtown Smyrna at the intersection of Paces Ferry Road. Now site of 2000 Paces subdivision.

Right: Cover for the menu at Stonewall Court Restaurant. The cover art recreates a condensed history of the Battle of Kennesaw Mountain and Atlanta.

❖

Above: J. M. "Hoot" Gibson.

Below: Belmont Hills Shopping Center as it appeared in the fall of 2009. It opened as the south's largest shopping center on November 18, 1954, and attracted shoppers from metropolitan Atlanta, Alabama, and Tennessee. Currently in demolition mode, the original 48-acre retail strip center opened with eighteen businesses. It will be replaced with a mixed-use development of 127,000 square feet of retail space and 900 residences including single-family units, condos, apartments and luxury rentals, and facilities for senior citizens. Halpern Enterprises, the city of Smyrna, and Cobb County agreed to finance the $250 million project through a tax-increment financing plan. Atlanta Road parallels the CSX Railroad at the bottom of the photograph. The street on the right is Windy Hill Road.

begged the sheriff not to tell his wife that he had been caught with another woman in the motel. The story goes that the sheriff responded, "you can tell her yourself, she's down in cabin # ???"

The major change and growth in Smyrna didn't come until the 1950s. Bill Miles, the editor-owner/publisher of the *Smyrna Herald,* in his *People of Smyrna* book published for the City of Smyrna during its Centennial celebration in 1972, recorded it this way: "In a meeting in 1949 with Stuart Murray, the owner of the beautiful Belmont Farm at that time, and Smyrna Mayor J. M. "Hoot" Gibson developer Bill Ward is quoted as saying, "This town isn't even a decent throw-off for a mail bag, let's make a city out of this place". He was referring to Smyrna, of course, and that meeting led to the construction of the Belmont Hills Shopping Center and a number of sub-divisions. From the very beginning it was promoted as the South's largest shopping center, and editor Miles said that it was exactly three feet longer than any shopping center existing in the south at the time.

When they first started planning the shopping center for Smyrna, Murray and Ward were not aware that the Lockheed Aircraft Corporation, based in California, had already made a deal with the U. S. Government to lease the former Bell Bomber Plant in Marietta. They learned of it when Ward tried to lease the plant for another of his endeavors. That's when he found out that Lockheed would employ thousands of people. Lockheed already had a contract for a number of planes for the military. Smyrna's Mayor, J. M. "Hoot" Gibson, thought it was a great idea and the city would be willing to be a part of it if they would annex the property into the city limits.

This is some of the property that had been de-annexed in 1897. It would become the first addition to the city limits in fifty-four years.

Originally the subdivision nearest the shopping center was to be named Lockheed Heights and all the streets were named for cities around the company headquarters in California: Ventura, Glendale, Burbank, San Fernando, Inglewood, Wooddale and Pasadena and those names stayed with the development. But the Belmont Hills name is the one that was eventually chosen at the urging of Smyrna area native, Jimmy Carmichael, who was the first general manager of the Bell Bomber Plant.

In the meantime, primarily through the efforts of A. C. Shepherd, a retired attorney, a Smyrna Chamber of Commerce was organized with eighteen members on July 9, 1951, and by 1953 there were ninety active members. With new people moving into the area, many of the civic and service organizations became interested in helping promote the Jonquil City. Some of the organizations that joined in this effort were: The Smyrna Lion's Club, Smyrna Citizens Council (made up of churches and civic group representatives), American Legion Post 160, Smyrna Woman's and Jr. Woman's Clubs, Nelms Masonic Lodge, Eastern Star, P.T.A.s for the Smyrna Elementary and High School, Jonquil Garden Club, and Boy's and Girl's Scout Troops.

Mayor Gibson and Councilmen C. W. Jones, Howard Hames, Stanley McCalla, H. L. McEntyre and P. P. Shaw, secured the help of Georgia Tech in conducting an extensive study of Smyrna. The study was entitled *Survey of the City of Smyrna, Georgia Tech Planning Study No. 13.* The finished report was delivered to the

city in the spring of 1953 with this partial explanation: "The present study is our first to concern itself with a small Georgia town which we hope is just one of a series to come. Smyrna is by no means a typical small Georgia town; its close proximity to Atlanta and the reactivated Lockheed Aircraft Plant, and its exceptional rate of expansion due to this reactivation made this study and, we believe, further analysis and more detailed studies imperative." The study pointed out that it was particularly difficult to overcome "great obstacles" in conducting the study because of the lack of recent planning data and the nonexistence of a base map of the community. Georgia Tech secured the help of the Georgia State Highway Department that provided an aerial survey of Smyrna that enabled Tech to provide a map showing every building in the Smyrna area. For all this work conducted and for the almost 90-page report, the City of Smyrna generously voted a payment of $350 to Tech to help "defray the expenses incurred by Tech."

With the enthusiasm generated by the growth, the re-energized social, civic, service community and city government of Smyrna was ready for the South's Largest Shopping Center.

Belmont Hills had its grand opening on November 18, 1954. Movie actress Anita Eckberg, from the John Wayne Studios, participated in a motorcade and parade that included a tour of the recently opened Lockheed Aircraft Plant and the shopping center. Neva Jane Langley, the 1953 Miss America, visited every store in the center and had photographs made with the customers. There was a drawing for a 1955 Dodge 4-door sedan. Other prizes included washers and dryers, TVs, steam irons, silverware sets, cameras and other door prizes. The fanfare and celebrities helped the merchants attract shoppers in the upcoming Christmas season. The 107 new houses that had been constructed on Smyrna's north side were selling and Smyrna was on a boom. The new center drew customers from Tennessee and Alabama as well as from all the surrounding metropolitan cities and suburbs. One of the big draws to the center was 2,500 free parking spaces in this new "regional shopping center" for the metro Atlanta area.

There were eighteen businesses, both local and national, including the A & P, Kroger, W. T. Grant, F. W. Woolworth, Singer Sewing Machine, Dunaway Rexall Drug Store, Economy Auto Store, Shell Oil, Butler Shoes, Belmont Sinclair, Florence Fashions, 12 Oaks Restaurant, Walter R. Thomas Jewelry, Home & Hobby Shop and Belmont Barber Shop

This was, perhaps, a prelude to the exodus of businesses from the downtown Smyrna area. Over the years family-owned enterprises like the grocery and general merchandise stores belonging to Whitfields, Gilberts, Black and Webb, W. N. Pace, J. F. Petty, T. E. Legg, S. J. Ireland, J. F. Dunton, J. F. Cates, Hubert Colquitt, J. D. Daniell, M. L. Collins, Harold Davis, Bud Blakeney, George Howard, along with a couple of the chain grocery stores like Rogers and Colonial and family-owned drug chains like Dunaway and Atherton, had been the mainstays of downtown Smyrna.

But the downtown area was unable to handle the increased traffic. There were few places to park other than on the street where there were meters. The population during the decade of the '50s had increased from 2,005 in 1950 to 10,157 in 1960. The increase in population in ten years was four times more than it had been in the last fifty years. Lockheed had attracted many of the newcomers but changing demographics in Atlanta had encouraged what became known as "white flight" to the suburbs that brought even more people looking for new homes.

Smyrna's first official map prepared in 1953. The map shows Smyrna's city limits from 1897 to 1950 with 1951 additions.
MAP COURTESY OF GEORGIA TECH'S SCHOOL OF ARCHITECTURE.

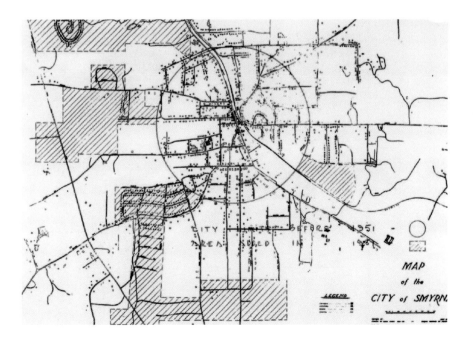

Top, left: Smyrna City Hall at 128 Atlanta Street during the 1920s and 1930s.

Top, right: Smyrna City Hall at 210 Atlanta Street, from 1933 to 1959.

Right: Smyrna City Hall at 1306 Bank Street 1959 to 1996.

In an effort to save downtown Smyrna in 1958-59 J. D. Daniel and some other merchants, including property owners M. H. Tatum, D. J. Ray and the Koningsmark family, developed Jonquil Plaza Shopping Center. It was located on the east side of Atlanta Street halfway between East Spring Street and the deadend of Love Station. (now Spring Road)

Mr. Daniel had operated his Red Dot Grocery Store on the southeast corner of Atlanta and East Spring Streets for a number of years and another one in Oakdale. The area had previously been a mixture of older residences, and houses that had been converted for business use. The new strip shopping center brought 400 much needed parking spaces to downtown. Today, that property is vacant, the center having been demolished, and awaiting financing for another mixed use facility named Jonquil Village that will include retail space and multi-family dwellings.

The year before Jonquil Plaza opened December 9, 1959, the mayor and council decided to construct a new city hall on Bank Street. They purchased a house that had been converted to commercial use as a real estate office and demolished it to make way for a new city hall. One of the two known previous ones had been constructed as a bank. There are no known existing records that identified the location of Smyrna's first city hall, but in interviews with Mrs. Agnes Feeley, the widow of S. E. Faucett, April 20, 1982, and Hoyt Langston, a former police chief, and his wife January 28, 1982, they said the first city hall and jail was a little frame building on Roswell Street "where the plastic factory is located now and where the ice house used to be." Records do indicate the city sold a lot on Roswell Street to the Southland Ice Company on May 3, 1943, for $750.

The second known location was 2893 (formerly 128) Atlanta Street on the east side. The building backed up to the railroad. An interior snapshot of the city hall during the John Corn administration showed City Clerk S. E. Faucett, who served from 1933 to 1938, sitting at a large wooden table with a typewriter on it. There was one window behind the table and a blackboard and a chart holder on the wall behind Mr. Faucett.

The next city hall was originally the Smyrna Bank building that was located at 2810 (formerly 117) Atlanta Street located diagonally across from the previous one on the northwest corner of Bank and Atlanta Street. It served as the city hall from the late 1930s until October 18, 1959. The building also served as the police station and jail until May 1970 when a new

police station was started during George Kreeger's first administration and finished during the Harold Smith administration.

The first "modern" building constructed as a city hall was during the administration of Mayor "Hoot" Gibson. Dedication ceremonies were held 11:00 a.m. to 1:00 p.m. what with Mayor Gibson in charge. The Smyrna American Legion provided a color guard and Reverend John Knight of the Smyrna Presbyterian Church dedicated a rare version of the Bible to the citizens of Smyrna that had been donated by Bill Ward, the owner of the Belmont Hills Shopping Center. City employees greeted the visitors and escorted them on tours of the building. Located at 1306 Bank Street, with a couple of additions, a fire and a renovation, it served as the city hall during the administrations of Mayors J. M. "Hoot" Gibson, George Kreeger, Harold Smith, John Porterfield, Arthur Bacon, Frank Johnson, and a return administration of Arthur Bacon until he died in October 1985 and his son Max, the present mayor was elected to fill the vacancy.

It was thirty-eight years before a new city hall was constructed in 1996 and it came during the extreme-makeover period.

Dedication ceremonies for the current city hall at 2800 King Street took place on Sunday, September 8, 1996. It is a $3.8 million facility that houses the council room that doubles as the courtroom, offices for the mayor and council members and a number of administrative departments like taxes, utilities, etc.

Some of the activities for the day included the ribbon-cutting ceremonies, guided tours of the new building, music by the Atlanta String Quartet and refreshments for the more than 300

❖

Top, left and right: Jonquil Festival activities on Bank Street across from the city hall April 1970.

Below: The Jonquil Plaza Shopping Center, from 1959-2007. This location presently is awaiting financing and construction as J. D.'s Jonquil Village.

Above: Smyrna Administrative Services building, 2800 King Street, dedicated on September 8, 1996.

Bottom, left: Smyrna Soap Box Derby starting ramp near the intersection of Concord Road and South Cobb near Dickson's Shopping Center.

Bottom, right: July 4, 1960, South Cobb Drive looking from Cherokee Road (Windy Hill) toward Concord Road.

who attended. Television Channel 11 news personality Jill Becker was Mistress of Ceremonies for the day. Participating in the program were: Mayor Max Bacon, Councilman Pete Wood, Reverend Steve Kimmel of the Smyrna First Baptist Church, County Commissioner Joe Thompson, Dwight Morgan of the Beers Construction Company, Architect Mike Sizemore and keynote speaker 7th District Congressman Bob Barr.

From 1958 until 1991 the area that was Bank Street and West Spring Street and their intersections with Atlanta Road were, or became, the heart of the city. The city hall, fire

station, police station, judicial department, health clinic, library, justice of the peace courthouse, bank, grocery and drug stores, a passenger and freight railroad station and almost anything a citizen could want or need was concentrated in those few blocks.

But it was much more. In 1963 several of the clubs and business organizations joined together to sponsor what was termed "Smyrna Days". That was the forerunner of the first "Jonquil Festival" held in 1964. It lasted a whole week with special events almost every night. One event was the Jonquil Queen beauty contest sponsored by the Civitan Club with

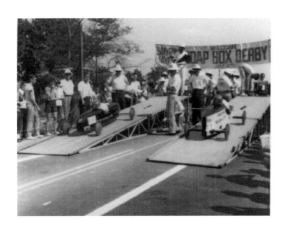

assistance from the Jaycees, Jaycettes, the Opti-Mrs. and the Business and Professional Women. Another event was a flower show with 150 entries. It was sponsored by several garden clubs including the Greenridge, Azalea, Jonquil and Dogwood Clubs. There were games and prizes, TV appearances, etc.

The climax of the festival was a big parade the following Saturday. It boasted more than forty-five floats and other units including bands from Campbell High School, The United States Third Army, and the 116th Air National Guard at Dobbins Air Force Base. Hundreds of people filled the streets from Nash Junior High School on Ward Street to Cherokee and Atlanta Roads past Belmont Hills Shopping Center and ending at Jonquil Plaza. The Rainbow Girls, Smyrna Jaycees, Lockheed Aircraft, Chamber of Commerce and others entered floats.

Some years later the Smyrna Parks and Recreation Department adopted the Jonquil Festival as one of the activities that gives Smyrna a "small town feeling" that attracts newcomers to the area and makes it a great place to live, work, and play.

The 1950s and early '60s brought some new civic and service organizations to Smyrna. The Smyrna Junior Chamber of Commerce (the official name was later changed to Jaycees), was one of them. The first organizational meeting was July 21, 1959, with 45 young men in attendance. One week later 75 charter members voted to establish a club with the following officers and directors: President Tommy Oglesby, Internal Vice President Barry Goodson, External Vice President Cecil Haralson, Secretary Bill Atkins, Treasurer Pete Wood, Directors Harold Nix, Frank Boykin and Sam Whitfield. When charter night ceremonies were held at the Marietta Country Club on August 27, 1959, there were 163 in attendance for one of the largest charter night ceremonies ever held in the state of Georgia The membership was limited to males ages 18 to 36 and on the 36th birthday the member was ceremoniously dismissed from active participation in the club.

After the charter night the Smyrna Club got down to business with the motto *Young Men Can Change the World, also the title of* a recently published book by Booten Herndon about the founding of the Jaycees. In the next twenty years

or so they went about their task with energy and enthusiasm to make major contributions to Smyrna and the surrounding area. They sponsored projects like the area Junior Miss America Pageant, safety checks for automobiles, voter register drives, turkey shoots, Christmas tree sales, United Way collections, poll managing for city elections, sponsoring free shots for polio for more than 4,000 when vaccines first became available, blood drives, Young Man of the Year Banquets and others.

Perhaps one of the most memorable projects of all was the Smyrna soap box derby races held on July 4. The first one was in 1960 and it drew several more than 5,000 visitors. Two-lane South Cobb Drive was closed to regular traffic from Concord Road to Cherokee Road (now Windy Hill) from 6:00 a.m. until noon. The road was lined with hay bales and the race was run in heats of two until the winner was determined. Present-day Ward 7 City Councilman Pete Wood was chairman of the Jaycee committee for that first race and also served as the club

Above: Western and Atlantic Railroad Depot located on the south side of East Spring Street near the intersection of Atlanta Road. The state of Georgia owned the railroad leased to the NC & St. L., L & N and currently to CXS. The station was demolished in 1959. The City of Smyrna constructed a replica of it on Atlanta Road close to the original location and it serves now as the Smyrna History Museum.
PHOTOGRAPH COURTESY OF OATES STUDIO.

Below: Atlanta Northern Interurban Railway Depot and Substation located on the east side of Atlanta Road across the street from the entrance to the present day Village Green Circle. It was demolished in the 1990s in the downtown redevelopment program.

Above: The trolley in the photograph was at the intersection of East Spring Street and Atlanta Road. In addition to the Black and Webb Grocery, the site had served as Dr. W. T. Pace's Drug Store, J. D. Daniell's Red Dot Grocery and Harold Davis' Department Store. When the building was finally demolished it made way for the Drive-In Sur-Way Dry Cleaners and Laundry owned by A. B. Ware.

Below: G. B.'s Place, in about 1970.

PHOTOGRAPH COURTESY OF KEITH DUNN.

president and later a National Director for the Georgia and U. S. Jaycees.

Another project that had a long-lasting impact for the city was constructing a new health clinic building for the city and the Cobb County health department. It was during the presidency of Sam Turriglio in the mid 1960s that the Jaycees completed a new brick structure at 2875 King Street to replace the one room frame building on West Spring Street that had served as the Justice of the Peace Court House and the health clinic. The club won the first place award for "Service to Humanity" at the Jaycee International convention in Paris, France, for the project.

When the Smyrna Health Clinic moved to South Cobb Drive, the city allowed the Smyrna Historical Society to use the facility for Smyrna's first History Museum from 1991 until April 1999 when the museum moved to Atlanta Road in a newly constructed replica of the old Smyrna railroad depot. It was the second depot constructed in Smyrna on the Western and Atlantic tracks by the State of Georgia during the years of 1836 to 1845. The first depot was destroyed during the War Between the States. The construction of the railroad was one of the factors that determined the permanent location of the city of Smyrna and made it a desirable "bedroom" community between Marietta and Atlanta. The railroad was used by both Union and Confederate forces during the war and became world famous with the help of *The Great Locomotive Chase* movie.

Over the years a number of railroad companies leased the tracks from the state of Georgia, including the Nashville, Chattanooga and St. Louis, and the Louisville & Nashville railroads and the current lessee CSX Railroad. The telegraph office was also located in the building. Passenger and freight service was discontinued in 1959 after hearings conducted by the Georgia Public Service Commission. The railroad offered the building to the city of Smyrna, but Mayor J. M. "Hoot" Gibson called it an eyesore and wouldn't accept the building. It was demolished.

Forty years later Mayor Max Bacon and members of the city council, as part of the downtown redevelopment, constructed a replica of the building, added a basement to it and faced it on Atlanta Road for use as the Smyrna History Museum. At the same time the city moved and restored the world famous Aunt Fanny's Cabin Restaurant building next door to the museum and made it into a welcome center and an activity facility for Smyrna citizens. Both buildings were dedicated in ceremonies in April 1999.

Located directly north across East Spring Street from the railroad station was G. B.'s Place, a favorite hangout for Smyrna's young people of the day. You could get enough food for two people for less than a dollar, including a couple of dogs, hamburger, chips and soft drinks. He sold bread, a small number of canned goods, coffee, candy and other goodies that are now considered "fast foods."

There was a counter and a few stools where you could sit and eat your food He also sold cigarettes, cigars, snuff, and chewing tobacco. G. B.'s was a small, early version of today's convenience store.

Another thing that made the operation unique was that being located next to the railroad track where the trains stopped from time to time to let passengers on or off, it became an early facility with a "drive-up" window—for train passengers, not automobiles. Note the small structure attached to the right side of the building.

The owner of the business was G. B. Williams, who was known as a frugal and wise investor and over the years acquired a large tract of land where he developed G. B.'s Lake and Stables. He was one of the original stockholders in the second Bank of Smyrna that opened in 1946.

From 1937 until 1973 dozens of Smyrna teenagers had the opportunity to work part-time in the facility and earn some money and learn about the small business world. G. B.'s Place closed when he retired in 1973 and the building was rented for a variety of businesses until it, too, became a victim of the city's wrecking ball in the extreme makeover of the city in the 1990s and early 2000s.

G. B. Williams died in July 2002. On April 4, 2004, a small park, just north of his old place of business, was dedicated to his memory. Smyrna mayor Max Bacon and city councilmen Pete Wood and Bill Scoggings provided personal comments about their association with the Williams family. at "the place." 11th District U. S. Congressman Phil Gingrey also spoke.

Approximately a quarter-mile north of the W & A Station and G. B.'s Place was the depot for the Atlanta Northern Railway—the interurban trolley line that ran from the Marietta square to downtown Atlanta right through downtown Smyrna. It's maiden trip was July 17, 1905, and the last trip was January 31, 1947.

This building was often confused with the W & A Railroad Station by some of the newcomers moving to Smyrna in the 1950s. This "rapid transit" of the day was another factor that contributed to Smyrna's popularity as a "bedroom" community. The trolleys were powered by electricity with an overhead wire For the most part, the rails were located on their own private right-of-way between the W & A Railroad tracks and the old Dixie Highway (U.S. 41). In downtown Smyrna the rails came onto the public road from just below Love Street to north of this station that was located across the street from Sunset Avenue. The entire trip from Marietta to the turnaround in Atlanta was a little over eighteen miles. Smyrna was a "transformer" station. There was a total of six transformer stations along the line. The others were located in Marietta, Fair Oaks, Gilmore, Bolton and Ashby Street. Fares were based on the distance between "transformer zones". The fare for riding the trolley was five cents between each of the six fare zones with the exception of the one between Hills Park and the turnaround at Walton and Fairley Streets in downtown Atlanta, which was 10 cents. For 35 cents you could make the 30 to 40 minute trip from Marietta to Atlanta.

Six trolley cars and two trailers were assigned to this line. Several of the trolleys had their own distinctive names honoring someone who had made major contributions to the state of Georgia: *John B. Gordon* (No. 484) *Joseph E.*

Ladies of the Smyrna Woman's Club enjoy a rest at the Belmont stop after picking up trash on Atlanta Road.
PHOTOGRAPH COURTESY OF ELIZABETH ANDERSON.

Whitfield's Grocery store, c. 1910.
It remained an important part of
"downtown" from the late 1800s until
1970 when the City of Smyrna
purchased it for demolition. It might
have been the first acquisition of the
city for the eventual widening of
Atlanta Street. Left to right: Tom
Moss, Albert Ireland, Robert Baldwin
(he identified the people in this
photograph), Voss Baldwin, T. W.
Whitfield (holding a cabbage),
Tom Barnes, Jack Thrash, Ann D.
Manning, Clara Dunn and Louise
Tollerson. Over the years this building
was occupied as Whitfield Grocery,
Black and Webb Grocery, Hendrix
Radio and Television Repair, and
Bernstein TV Repairs. For several
months in the early 1960s it served as
a campaign headquarters for Eaton
Chalkley, a 7th district congressional
candidate from Georgia who was the
husband of movie actress
Susan Hayward.

Brown (No. 485) *Joel Chandler Harris, A. Stephens Clay* (No. 488) *Evan P. Howell* (No. 491) and *Lemuel P. Grant* (No. 492).

Prior to World War 11, the high point in ridership was in 1920 when 1,402,503 passengers made the trips to their particular destinations. But by the mid-1920s the trolley line was starting to have competition from automobiles running along a recently paved Dixie Highway (U.S. 41) that was a direct route from the mid-west to Florida.

Tragedy struck the line on January 2, 1928, when a head-on collision occurred, just north of the Jonesville station, between a northbound and a southbound trolley. Six people died from the injuries they received. Two of them were on the southbound car. An investigation revealed no malfunction of the equipment and eventually the blame was laid on the northbound trolley operator.

The ridership was also affected when U.S. 41 was moved from the old Dixie Highway to its present location about 1939.

After World War 11 started following the Japanese attack on Pearl Harbor December 7, 1941, Marietta was chosen as the site for constructing the Bell Bomber Plant to build the B-29 Superfortress. The Atlanta Northern Railway became the major means of getting the construction work crews and other personnel to

Top: This building was constructed as the Smyrna Boy's Academy in 1849, purchased by the Nelms Masonic Lodge in the 1920s and demolished in 1954. It was replaced by a similar looking building that remained on the site until it was demolished in 1998 to make way for the Market Village complex. The Masons were the last owners.

Middle: Brooks Brothers' taxi stand, c. 1950s.

Bottom, left: Memorial to founders of the Masonic Lodge.

Bottom, right: Number 1 fire station looking south from Centennial Park 1966-1999.

Top: The restored and relocated Aunt Fanny's Cabin at 2875 Atlanta Road in the heart of Smyrna serves as the City's Welcome Center. It is available to the public for parties, receptions, meetings, etc. The Smyrna Museum is left of the cabin.

Middle: Interior reception area for Aunt Fanny's Cabin Restaurant when it was in operation 1941 to 1992. The wall is covered with the photographs of movie stars, sports figures, politicians and other celebrities who visited the cabin. Some of the photographs and furniture are on display in the Smyrna Welcome Center.

Bottom, left: These unidentified employees of the Aunt Fanny's Cabin Restaurant gave everyone a cheery greeting and the young man sang the menu to the customers.

Bottom, right: The Old Cabin Trace residential complex replaced the Aunt Fanny's Cabin Restaurant on Campbell Road.

work at the Marietta Plant. Many of them lived in Atlanta and the other metropolitan areas south of the Chattahoochee. Because of gas rationing during the war, many of the "bomber plant" workers left their cars at home and rode the trolley. In 1943 the trolley line gained another million passengers.

Something that almost everyone remembers about the trolley line are the unique "stops" they had for the passengers. Each station had a name and the name was printed on both ends of little station to enable the passengers to see them from both directions.

One of the more unusual ones was the Springhill station. It was located on Atlanta Road just south of Vinings Road (now Paces Ferry). The typical one was like the Belmont stop on Atlanta Road near the Belmont Farms, pictured on page 71. Although the trolley had stopped running on January 31, 1947, the "Belmont" stop was still in place until the major road widening in the 1980s. The ladies of the Smyrna Woman's Club went on a clean-up project along Atlanta Road after their November 1967 meeting and stopped for a rest. The picnic tables were added to the area long after the trolley had stopped running.

In addition to providing an inexpensive way to make a fast trip to Atlanta or Marietta, the trolley cars became somewhat of a social function also. Most of the passengers knew the motormen personally and their families. Many of them lived in Cobb County. The passengers who rode to their work places daily got to know their fellow passengers.

William C. Janssen, in his history of the Atlanta Northern Railway, where most of the information for this story was obtained, said it like this: "During its lifetime the Atlanta Northern Railway enjoyed a large measure of popularity. In its early days in Marietta, according to one account, the society columns rarely failed to mention that visitors to the town had arrived and departed by the electric trolley".

Most of the names of the stops that were used for the electric railway are still in use today to identify locations: Starting at the Marietta Square and coming south, some of the stops were Waterman Street, Fraser Street, Clay Street, Dixie Avenue—in 1943 the bomber plant line was added—Jonesville Station, Fair Oaks, Mozley, Belmont, Smyrna Depot, Spring Road,

Church Street, Love Street, Campbell Road, Jane Lyle Road, Vinings Road (Paces Ferry), Lee Road, Gilmore, Oakdale, Conway, Carmichael and Crestlawn.

The Smyrna Station was used for a variety of businesses after the trolley was discontinued, and it was one of the last buildings to be demolished in the redevelopment program. A sample of the unusual bricks used in its construction are on display in the Smyrna Museum along with a section of the rail that was on Atlanta Road in front of the museum.

Another event that had and continues to have a long-time impact on the City of Smyrna was the establishment of the world-famous Aunt Fanny's Cabin Restaurant just one week before the start of World War 11 in December 1941. The Campbell family's involvement in Smyrna was covered in Chapter IV, but it was the creation of Isolene Campbell McKenna, the daughter of Richard Orme Campbell and his wife, the former Hariett Bunn Wimberly, that brought Hollywood movie stars, sports figures, politicians, and celebrities of all kind to the little town of Smyrna that had a population of less than 1,500.

She took an 1890s tenant house on the property of the Argyle Estate on Campbell Road in Smyrna and created Aunt Fanny's Cabin. Mrs. McKenna named the cabin for her childhood mammy, Fanny Williams, who had been with the Campbell family for more than fifty years. When the cabin opened for business on November 27, 1941, it was filled with antiques that Mrs. McKenna had collected during her years of traveling the world as an Atlanta debutante. The first foods served in the restaurant were Aunt Fanny's recipes of vegetable soup, goulash, ginger bread, squash and other fresh vegetable dishes. They also sold farm products that were raised on the property as well as chickens, ducks, turkeys, hams, country-made sausage, molasses and corn meal. There was also a collection of jellies, preserves and canned fruits for sale. In 1946 a circular room was added to the rear of the original cabin to accommodate the increased business. The *New York Herald Tribune* printed a glowing review on May 7, 1949, by Clementine Paddleford, of a trip to the cabin. She described it this way, "the building is on the plantation owned by the family

Springhill "trolley line" stop.
PHOTOGRAPH COURTESY OF ANNETTE CARSON JONES AND TOM CAMP.

❖

The old Teen Canteen building was demolished and transformed to a state-of-the-art building for senior citizens. The new facility is The Aline Wolfe Adult Recreation Center.

of Mrs. Max Don Howell (Isolene Campbell McKenna). Its decoration is a bit of everything, old copper pots and pans, school desks, hanging lamps, hornet's nests, antique Colonial china and three open fire places. Two young lads come to your table to sing out the menu and carry a blackboard around their necks and say 'Aunt Fanny says Howdy Folks-wot'll it be?"

By this time Harvey Hester, the former owner of the Miami Seahawks and fight promoter for Jack Dempsey, and his partner Mrs. Marjorie Bowman, were managing the restaurant. Hester is the person credited with having created the myth of a slave cabin occupied by Aunt Fanny Williams who was around during the War Between the States. When Harvey Hester and Mrs. Bowman had the cabin it became widely known and was visited by celebrities who would have their pictures made with Harvey or other friends. The autographed photographs by the celebrities were exhibited on the walls in the restaurant as an added attraction for the regular customers. His Hollywood connections brought people from all over the world to the cabin and made Smyrna one of the best known small towns in the south. Harvey Hester died in March 1967 and Mrs. Bowman died December 14, 1968.

George "Pongo" Poole, another widely-known promoter, and his wife Gretna, bought the restaurant and during their ownership several additions were made to the cabin. In the 1970s and '80s the restaurant could seat over 500 in all of the facilities. Approximately forty people, mostly black, were employed there. Pongo died in October 1988 and Mrs. Poole continued the operation until 1992. She sold it at auction below the assessed value to realtor Frank Johnson (not the former Mayor of Smyrna with the same name). Tom Posey, an operator of

a number of restaurants in the Atlanta area tried to keep it open for a while but Aunt Fanny's days were over. Frank Johnson donated the cabin to the city of Smyrna and much of the memorabilia to the Smyrna Museum. He sold the property for a subdivision that became Old Cabin Trace. The cabin was put in storage on the property of the Smyrna Public Works department until it was restored at its present location on Atlanta Road and opened as the Welcome Center in April 1999.

Ground-breaking ceremonies for Smyrna's Market Village took place on August 4, 2001, the day the city celebrated its 129th anniversary. That kicked off the last phase of the downtown redevelopment program that had started in the late 1980s. The structures were formerly located on West Spring Street which is now the heart of Market Village. One building was originally constructed as the Smyrna's Boy's Academy in 1849. It was the site from which the original Smyrna city limits were measured—one mile in every direction from that building and again in 1897 when the city limits were reduced to one-half mile in every direction. The building also served as a worship center for the Smyrna Presbyterian Church, the Smyrna First Baptist Church, the Smyrna Elementary and High Schools and ultimately the Nelms Masonic Lodge, the last owners. They purchased the building in 1924. In 1954 they demolished it and constructed a similar looking one in which parts of it, and subsequent additions, were rented out to the U. S. post office, Colquitt's Five and Dime Store, Diahn's Answering Service and others. The taxi stand was located on the northwest corner of Atlanta and West Spring. The No. 1 fire station was constructed in the early 1960s and was replaced with a new one on

Atlanta Street that was dedicated on August 7, 1999. The memorial was located next to the Nelms Masonic Hall near the sidewalk and was dedicated to its charter members and leaders who had contributed so much, not only to the lodge, but to the city itself in the early years of Smyrna's development. It was fitting that it was one of the very last structures to be demolished in the makeover.

Although most of the old, historic commercial buildings and residences are gone from the "heart" of Smyrna, the memories of the people and activities that made them important will last as long as they live. Their experiences and stories will be passed on to their children and grandchildren and will not be lost.

Rather than considering it a loss it might be thought of as a "heart transplant" that brought new life and vigor to a worn out town. Fifty years from now today's citizens will have warm memories of today's activities, events and people.

The grand opening for the Market Village on October 26, 2002, brought Smyrna into the twenty-first century with a bang. It included six restaurants, sixteen condos/townhomes over the retail space with prices starting at $300,000. A variety of other businesses filled the spaces, including a beauty shop, florist, and arts and crafts retailers. The Smyrna City Hall is located at the west end of the Market Village complex on King Street.

The highlight of the grand opening was the ribbon-cutting and serving slices of a 7-foot-diameter key lime pie provided by Kenny Burts, the owner of Smyrna-based Kenny's Key Lime Pie Company. It was designed to feed a thousand people and was said to be the largest key lime pie ever made in Georgia.

After thanking the citizens of Smyrna, members of the city council, the developers, city employees, Smyrna business people and the many organizations that had a part in the completion of this massive effort, Mayor Max Bacon was quoted by the *Marietta Daily Journal* as modestly saying "We are glad we were able to complete the project like we predicted in 1988."

But it didn't end there. The city continued to make improvements, not only in downtown but in other areas as well. When the building, located at 884 Church Street, opened July 9, 1957, as the Smyrna Teen Canteen, 372 showed up for the activities It was one of the first facilities in the metropolitan area to cater to teenagers.

The city constructed the building. The Smyrna Junior Woman's Club, Smyrna Lion's Club, Teen Canteen board and the city furnished it with a juke box, eighteen booths, pool, ping pong tables, board games of all kinds, and other recreation items.

The Lolli Pop Lounge and live radio broadcasts from the canteen over radio station WFOM brought in large crowds to enjoy dancing, swimming, and other activities.

One of the earliest adult boards was made up of President Bill Blount, First Vice President Aline Wolfe, Second Vice President Frances Reed, Secretary Gladys Causey, and Treasurer Dereld Abner.

The early teen officers were: President Steve Harris, Vice President Tommy Allen, Secretary Peggy Watkins, and Treasurer Betty Matthews. Lester Weathers, a faculty member at Campbell High School, was the full time director of the canteen in the early days.

Mrs. Aline Wolfe, a founding member who continued to serve and work with the teenagers

The Teen Canteen when it opened in 1957. It was later changed to a senior daycare center and a distribution station for Meals on Wheels.

Entrance to Smyrna's Market Village.

for many years, died September 5, 1968. The Smyrna City Council named the facility The Aline Wolfe Teen Recreation Center for her years of service to the teens and the community. The ceremony was on a rainy Sunday afternoon, November 24, 1968, with Judge Conley Ingram, a former Smyrna city attorney, as master of ceremonies and Reverend Nelson Price Pastor of the Roswell Street Baptist Church delivering the invocation.

Eventually the building was converted for use as a recreation center for all ages. The upstairs and downstairs meeting rooms were used by a variety of organizations including the Smyrna Historical and Genealogical Society that met there in the late 1980s. A number of dance clubs and musical groups also used the facility.

Cobb County and the City of Smyrna cooperated in establishing it as a senior day care center and a distribution point for delivering Meals on Wheels until 2007. The original building was demolished. to make way for the new facility that is now catering to some of the previous teenagers—the baby-boomers who have now reached the status of senior citizen.

The new building, on the old site, is approximately 8,000 square feet. It features a large meeting room, arts and crafts room, exercise and dance room, classroom/computer lab and a fitness and exercise room equipped with state-of-the-art equipment designed especially for senior adults.

The $2.8 million cost was funded by general obligation bonds for parks and recreation that was passed by the citizens in 2005 and a community development block grant. The center is adjacent to the Senior Aquatic Center that opened in 1996.

Ribbon-cutting and dedication ceremonies were held March 28, 2009. Patty Bacon, the Senior Recreation Coordinator for the City of Smyrna, welcomed everyone and did the introductions. Reverend Al Turnell, retired pastor of the Smyrna First United Methodist Church gave the invocation. Mayor Max Bacon, Mark Reed, a member of the Campbell High School class of 1964, and Ward 5 Councilman Jimmy Smith, chairman of the Parks and Recreation Committee provided the closing remarks.

The ribbon-cutting and refreshments followed.

CHAPTER VI

SMYRNA CITY GOVERNMENT

To the best of my knowledge a list of the names of all the Smyrna mayors, city councilmen, police chiefs, fire chiefs, city attorneys, judges and various other appointed or elected city officials has never been published in a single document. Unless a miracle happens and the records and minutes of the city council meetings that burned in a fire in the early 1920s suddenly appear out of the ashes, or the missing newspapers and other publications that might have reported the elections reappear, a complete list will never be published.

The town of Smyrna was incorporated and created by the Georgia State Legislature on August 23, 1872, when it passed House Bill number 169. That legislation named the first officials who were to serve until the first election could be held in July of 1873. The terms were specified to be for one year. In the ensuing years the term of office was changed from one to two years, and after more than 100 years they were changed to four year-terms.

The original city limits for the Town of Smyrna was set at one mile in every direction from the Smyrna Boy's Academy that, at the time, was located just north of the Smyrna Memorial Cemetery currently near the south side of Smyrna's Market Village and more specifically near where Café Michel was located when it opened in 2001.

The first change to the city charter came in 1897, when, for some unknown reason, the city fathers decided their town was too large so they reduced the limits to a half-mile in every direction from the same building, although it had a different owner—the Smyrna Presbyterian Church.

Entrance to the 1838 Smyrna Memorial Cemetery. The structures in the background are condominiums, mixed-use retail stores and restaurants in the Market Village.

❖

*Installation of mayor and council at
the Smyrna City Hall, January 5,
1970. Left to right: Clarence Canada,
Ward 5; Arthur Bacon, Ward 3;
Hubert Black, Ward 7; J. P. White,
Ward 2; Ken Chalker, city judge;
George Carreker, city attorney; Les
Charles, city clerk; Homer Kuhl,
Ward 4; John Porterfield, Ward 6;
Marston Tuck, Ward 1; seated, Mayor
Harold Smith.*

The second charter change was in 1931 and again in 1951 when it annexed property on the north city limits to take in the area that was to become the South's largest shopping center, Belmont Hills, and some acreage on the southwest edge of town for constructing new housing in the area of Concord and King Spring Road, McLinden Avenue, Dale Avenue, Hollis Street, etc. Since then thousands of acres of property have been annexed into the city.

For the years from July 1873 to January 1900, we have been unable to find any information about the Smyrna city elections. As previously mentioned, the official records of the city were lost in a fire in the early 1920s. Harold Smith and his late wife Betty, who died in 1993, began looking for the names of those early office holders and other officials in the 1950s. Smyrna police Lieutenant Curtis Cook, who died August 30, 2006, joined the research after Betty Smith became ill in 1993. More recently Norma McHann, the associate editor for the Smyrna

Historical Society newsletter, *Lives and Times* continued the search in 2005 when Curtis became ill.

Every available edition of the *Marietta Journal*, *Cobb County Times*, *The Atlanta Journal* and *Atlanta Constitution* and other publications prior to 1900 were searched for reports of the early Smyrna elections. None were found. Hopefully, one of these days somewhere in someone's attic or basement or a long forgotten secret hiding place, the missing records will be found.

The information and name listings for the period from 1900 to 1924 were found in the previously mentioned publications and some papers donated by Rex Pruitt, the son of Mayor Lorena Pace Pruitt. The listings from 1925 to the present, except as noted, were compiled from the official minutes of the mayor and council meetings, various publications in the state of Georgia Archives with additional information from other publications and the personal knowledge of the author.

1872-1873
Mayor John C. Moore
Council: W. R. Bell, G. P. Daniel, W. L. Davenport, E. D. L. Mobley

1900
Mayor Matthew Varner Ruff
Council: P. Y. Daniel, B. B. Hamby, Bob Love, J. T. Pace, J. L. Reed

1901
Mayor J. T. Pace
Council: A. J. Morgan, J. F. Petty, J. L. Reed, M. V. Ruff, T. W. Whitfield

1902
Mayor J. T. Pace

1903
Mayor J. T. Pace
Council: L. W. Fowler, M. S. Gilbert, Laban Magbee, J. L. Reed, T. W. Whitfield

1904
Mayor J. T. Pace
Council: L. W. Fowler, M. S. Gilbert, J. L. Reed, P. M. Rice, T. W. Whitfield

1905
Mayor J. T. Pace
Council: J. W. Fuller, P. Y. Gann, J. L. Reed, P. M. Rice, T. W. Whitfield

1906
Mayor J. T. Pace

1907
Mayor J. F. Petty
Council: B. F. Walker, T. W. Whitfield, P. Y. Gann, J. R. Deavors, J T. Segars

1908
Mayor J. T. Pace
Council: G. L. Fambrough, M. V. Ruff, J. T. Rutledge, J. T. Segars, C. D. Timothy

1909
Mayor Joe L. Stopplebein
Council: M. V. Ruff, J. W. Segars, D. A. Sewell, C. D. Timothy, B. F. Walker

1910
Mayor Jake Moore
Council: J. W. Fuller, P. M. Rice, M. V. Ruff, Captain Thompson, ? Youmans

1911
Mayor Jake Moore
Council: J. W. Fuller, P. M. Rice, M. V. Ruff, Captain Thompson, ? Youmans

1912
   Mayor W. T. Pace

1913
   Mayor J. W. Fuller
      Council: J. H. Dunn, G. L. Fambrough, G. C. Green, P. M. Rice

1914
   Mayor J. W. Fuller
      Council: Isaac Eidson, G. C. Green, J. L. Pollock, P. M. Rice

1915
   Mayor J. W. Fuller
      Council: Isaac V. Eidson, John L. Pollock, P. M. Rice, P. Y. Westbrook

1916
   Mayor J. W. Fuller

1917
   Mayor J. W. Fuller
      Council: Isaac V. Eidson, G. C. Green, John L. Pollock, P. M. Rice, P. Y. Westbrook

1918
   Mayor B. F. Whitney
      Council: J. L. Fuller, ? McKelvey, John L. Pollock, J. W. Ridley

1919
   Mayor B. F. Whitney

1920
   Mayor B. F. Whitney
      Council: N. T. Durham, W. T. Earwood, C. L. Groce, P. M. Rice, M. V. Ruff

1921
   Mayor M. V. Ruff
      Council: C. L. Fambrough, T. F. Hamby, C. C. Jones, W. A. "Lon" McBrayer, B. F. Whitney

1922
   Mayor John L. Pollock
      Council: J. R. Brewer, T. M. Martin, R. G. Ray, J. C. Stephens, B. F. Whitney

1923
   Mayor John L. Pollock

1924
   Mayor John L. Pollock
      Council: W. H. Besherers, P. M. Rice, R. G. Ray, W. A. Wright, Joe Pruitt

1925
   Mayor J. Gid Morris
      Council: L. H. Baldwin, P. M. Edwards, J. W. McCollum, Joe R. Pruitt, W. A. Wright

Matthew Varner Ruff

John L. Reed

A. J. Morgan

P. M. Rice

Jake C. Moore

Dr. W. T. Pace

Dr. G. C. Green

W. A. "Lon" McBrayer

John L. Pollock

J. Gid Morris

Pat M. Edwards

Paul Gresham

Hugh L. Marston

P. F. Brinkley

Hiram Cicero McLarty

Harry H. Arrington

D. C. Osborn

Milton L.Collins

T. W. Huffstutler

Chester Benefield Austin

John Corn

Henry Konigsmark

D. C. Landers

John Tatum

C. M. Hamby

A. B. S. Lowry

J. O. Hargis

Roy Howard McLarty

William Alfred Quarles

J. Y. Wootten

Lorena Pruitt

William A. Pressley

1926

 Mayor J. Gid Morris

 Council: L. H. Baldwin, P. F. Brinkley, P. M. Edwards, H. H. Tollison, W. H. Williamson died and replaced by F. T. Wills

1927

 Mayor P. M. Edwards

 Council: P. F. Brinkley, T. W. Huffstuttler, J. C. Stephens, E. H. Tollison, F. T. Wills

1928

 Mayor P. M. Edwards

 Council: P. F. Brinkley, W. P. Gresham, H. H. Harden, T. W. Huffstutler, Hugh L. Marston

1929

 Mayor P. M. Edwards

 Council: H. H. Arrington, P. F. Brinkley, W. H. Gresham, C. L. Groce, H. L. Marston

1930

 Mayor P. M. Edwards

 Council: H. H. Arrington, J. T. Blount, P. F. Brinkley, C. L. Groce, C. C. McKelvey

1931

 Mayor P. F. Brinkley

 Council: J. M. Bramblett[1] replaced by C. W. Flowers, J. T. Blount, E. M. Hamby, H. G. McLarty, P. J. Voss

1932

 Mayor P. F. Brinkley

 Council: J. T. Blount, E. M. Hamby, J. W. McCollum, H. C. McLarty, P. J. Voss

1933

 Mayor H. H. Arrington

 Council: J. T. Blount, E. M. Hamby, T. W. Huffstutler, J. T. McCollum, H. G. McLarty

1934

 Mayor H. H. Arrington

 Council: T. W. Huffstutler, T. R. McCollum, H. G. McLarty, D. C. Osborn, Ralph Stephens

1935

 Mayor H. H. Arrington

 Council: Milton L. Collins, T. W. Huffstutler, T. R. McCollum, D. C. Osborne, Ralph Stephens

1936

 Mayor H. H. Arrington

 Council: Milton L. Collins, T. W. Huffstutler, T. R. McCollum, D. C. Osborne, Ralph Stephens

1937

 Mayor H. H. Arrington[2] resigned and in a special election was replaced by Mayor T. W. Huffstutler

 Council: Milton L. Collins, T. W. Huffstutler, T. R. McCollum, D. C. Osborne, Ralph Stephens

 The unexpired term of Huffstutler was filled by Chester Benefield Austin

1938

Mayor T. W. Huffstutler[3] resigned due to ill health and replaced by Mayor John Corn
Council: C. B. Austin, J. T. Blount, M. L. Collins, J. C. Johnson, Henry Konigsmark, D. C. Landers

1939

Mayor John Corn
Council: J. T. Blount, J. C. Johnson, Henry Konigsmark, D. C. Landers, John Tatum

1940

Mayor John Corn
Council: W. P. Cochran, C. M. Hamby, J. J. Hill, D. C. Landers, John Tatum

1941

Mayor P. M. Brinkley[4] died in office and replaced by Mayor John Tatum
Council: J. R. Arrington, W. P. Cochran, C. M. Hamby, J. J. Hill

1942

Mayor John Tatum[5] resigned and replaced by Mayor C. M. Hamby
Council: J. R. Arrington[6] resigned and replaced by A.B.S. Lowry, F. D. Cargal was appointed to fill the vacant seat of C. M. Hamby who had been elected mayor, C. O. Garvin[7], J. J. Hill

1943

Mayor C. M. Hamby
Council: F. D. Cargal, C. O. Garvin[9] resigned and replaced by J.O. Hargis, J. J. Hill, A. B. S. Lowry, Roy. H. McLarty

1944

Mayor C. M. Hamby
Council: F. D. Cargal, C. W. Flowers, J. O. Hargis, Roy H. McLarty, W. A. Quarles

1945

Mayor J. Y. Wootten[10] resigned and in a special election, replaced by Mayor Lorena Pruitt
Council: C. W. Flowers, E. E. Jackson, William Pressley, W. A. Quarles

1946

Mayor Lorena Pruitt
Council: R. H. Bacon[12], Emmett F. Cox, C. L. Groce died and replaced by E. E. Jackson[11], B. H. Hanson[12], William Pressley

1947

Mayor Lorena Pruitt
Council: Homer Durham, B. H. Hanson, E. E. Jackson, Herbert P. McCollum, W. A. Quarles

1948

Mayor Lorena Pruitt
Council: M. L. Collins, Homer D. Durham, Henry Konigsmark[13] resigned and the unexpired term was filled by H. L. McEntyre, Herbert P. McCollum, P. P. Shaw

1949

Mayor J. M. "Hoot" Gibson
Council: R. S. Brinson, M. L. Collins, R. B. Logan, H. L. McEntyre, P. T. Shaw

C. L. Groce

B. H. Hanson

Homer Durham

Herbert P. McCollum

H. L. McEntyre

J. M. "Hoot" Gibson

Howard Hames

Guy Duncan

James E. Quarles

A. M. "Red" Poston

Roy H. Wood

J. B. "Dusty" Rhodes

William Tyrannus Rutledge

George Kreeger

Bob Austin

R. J. McCurry

John K. Chastain

Bill Sanders

Bill Keck

Harry E. Ingram

J. B. "Jake" Ables

James W. Webb

Blake Thomas

Cyrus Chapman

Homer Kuhl

C. W. "Chuck" Armour

Dan Mixon

Bill Stewart

Clarence O. Canada

Harold Smith

Marston Tuck

J. P. White

1950

Mayor J. M. "Hoot"Gibson

Council: R. S. Brinson[14] resigned and replaced by Howard Hames, R. B. Logan[15] resigned and C. W. Jones was elected to fill the unexpired term, Stanley McCalla, H. L. McEntyre, P. P. Shaw

1951

Mayor J. M. "Hoot" Gibson

Council: C. W. Jones, Howard Hames, Stanley McCalla, H. L. McEntyre, P. P. Shaw

1952

Mayor. J. M. "Hoot" Gibson

Council: C. M. Hamby, Harry Mitchell, Eugene Rice, C. C. Terrell, Glenn Yarbrough

1953

Mayor Guy Duncan

Council: John Collier, C. M. Hamby, H. L. McEntyre, Harry Mitchell, Glenn Yarbrough

1954

Mayor Guy Duncan[16] died in office and replaced by James E. Quarles who had already been elected in the November election.
Council: Norman E. Brenner, John Collier, H. L. McEntyre, Virgil R. Sidall, Glenn Yarbrough

1955

Mayor James E. Quarles

Council: John Collier, H. L. McEntyre, A. M. "Red" Poston, Virgil R. Sidall, Glenn Yarbrough

1956-1957[17]

Mayor James E. Quarles

Council: Councilman-at-large Norman Brenner; J. S. Collier replaced by James White, Ward 1; Max Sonenberg, Ward 2; Roy H. Wood, Ward 3; Max Scarbrough, Ward 4; A.V. Bolton replaced by A. S. Dodd, Ward 5; J. E. Johnson, Ward 6; J. B. "Dusty" Rhodes[18] replaced Councilman-at-large Norman Brenner

1958-1959

Mayor J. M. "Hoot" Gibson

Council: Councilman-at-large George Kreeger; J. B. "Dusty" Rhodes, Ward 1; J. B. Ables, Ward 2; Roy Wood, Ward 3; Bill Sanders, Ward 4; L. G. Dodd, Ward 5; Jack Brooks resigned January 6, 1959, and replaced by William Ty Rutledge, Ward 6

1960-1961

Mayor George Kreeger

Council: Councilman-at-large Bob Austin; R. J. McCurry, Ward 1; J. B. Ables, Ward 2; John K. Chastain, Ward 3; Bill Sanders, Ward 4; Bill Keck, Ward 5; Harry E. Ingram, Ward 6

1962-1963

Mayor J. B. "Jake" Ables

Council: Councilman-at-large, J. B. "Dusty" Rhodes[19]; R. J. McCurry, Ward 1; Jim Webb, Ward 2; Roy Wood, Ward 3; Harold Smith, Ward 4; W. L. "Bill" Keck resigned and replaced by Blake Thomas, Ward 5; Harry Ingram[20] resigned and replaced by John Porterfield in a special election, Ward 6

1964-1965

Mayor George Kreeger

Council: Councilman-at-large Cyrus Chapman; R. J. McCurry, Ward 1; James Webb[21], Ward 2; Roy Wood, Ward 3; Homer Kuhl, Ward 4; Blake Thomas, Ward 5; John Porterfield, Ward 6

1966-1967

Mayor George Kreeger

Council: C. W. Armour, Ward 1; J. B. "Jake" Ables, Ward 2; Roy Wood, Ward 3; Homer Kuhl, Ward 4; Dan L. Mixon, Ward 5; John Porterfield, Ward 6; Bill Stewart, Ward 7

1968-1969

Mayor George Kreeger

Council: C. W. Armour, Ward 1; J. B. "Jake" Ables, Ward 2; Roy Wood, Ward 3; Homer Kuhl, Ward 4; Clarence O. Canada, Ward 5; John Porterfield, Ward 6; Bill F. Stewart, Ward 7

1970-1971

Mayor Harold Smith

Council: Marston Tuck, Ward 1; J. P. White, Ward 2; Arthur Bacon, Ward 3; Homer Kuhl, Ward 4; Clarence O. Canada, Ward 5; John Porterfield, Ward 6; Hubert Black, Ward 7

1972-1973

Mayor John Porterfield

Council: Marston Tuck, Ward 1; Forster Puffe, Ward 2; Arthur Bacon, Ward 3; Homer Kuhl, Ward 4; Clarence O. Canada, Ward 5; Elbert Coalson, Ward 6; Jack Miles, Ward 7

1974-1975

Mayor John Porterfield

Council: Marston Tuck, Ward 1; Forster Puffe, Ward 2; Jerry Mills, Ward 3; Homer Kuhl, Ward 4; Clarence O. Canada, Ward 5; Elbert Coalson, Ward 6; Earle Cochran, Ward 7

1976-1977

Mayor Arthur Bacon

Council: Jim Tolleson, Ward 1; Bill Darby, Ward 2; Jerry Mills, Ward 3; Homer Kuhl[23] resigned and replaced by Jim Hawkins, Ward 4; Clarence O. Canada, Ward 5; Elbert Coalson, Ward 6; Rem Bennett, Jr., Ward 7

1978-1979

Mayor Frank Johnson

Council: Jim Tolleson, Ward 1; Bill Darby, Ward 2; Jerry Mills, Ward 3; Jim Hawkins, Ward 4; Jack Shinall, Ward 5; Elbert Coalson, Ward 6; Rem Bennett, Jr., resigned and replaced by John Steeley, Ward 7

1980-1981

Mayor Frank Johnson

Council: Jim Tolleson, Ward 1; Max Bacon, Ward 2, Jerry Mills, Ward 3, Jim Hawkins, Ward 4; Jack Shinall, Ward 5; Elbert Coalson, Ward 6; John Steeley, Ward 7

1982-1983

Mayor Arthur Bacon

Council: Jim Tolleson, Ward 1; Max Bacon, Ward 2; James Williams, Ward 3; Jim Hawkins, Ward 4; Jack Shinall, Ward 5; Elbert Coalson, Ward 6; Sarah Jones, Ward 7

1984-1985

Mayor Arthur Bacon died and replaced by his son, Mayor Max Bacon

Council: Jim Tolleson resigned and replaced by Bob Davis, Ward 1; Max Bacon resigned to become mayor and replaced by Joel Harrell, Ward 2; James Williams, Ward 3; Jim Hawkins, Ward 4; Jack Shinall, Ward 5; Kathy Brooks, Ward 6; Hugh Ragan, Ward 7

Hubert Black

John Porterfield

Forster Puffe

Elbert Coalson

Jack Miles

Earle Cochran

Arthur Bacon

Jim Tolleson

Bill Darby

Jerry Mills

Jim Hawkins

Rem Bennett

Frank Johnson

John Steeley

Jack Shinall

James Williams

Sarah Jones Monsour

Max Bacon

Bob Davis

Joel Harrell

Kathy Brooks

Hugh Ragan

Bob Beatenbaugh

Wade Lnenicka

Bill Scoggins

Charlie "Pete" Wood

John Patrick

Ron Newcomb

Jack Cramer

Charlene Capilouto

Melleny Pritchett

Paula Weeks

Mike McNabb   Jimmy Smith   Teri Anulewicz

1986-1987

Mayor Max Bacon

Council: Bob Davis, Ward 1; Joel Harrell, Ward 2; Jerry Mills, Ward 3; Jim Hawkins, Ward 4; Jack Shinall, Ward 5; Kathy Brooks, Ward 6; Hugh Ragan resigned to run for State Senate and replaced by Bob Beatenbaugh, Ward 7

1988-1991 (4-year terms)

Mayor Max Bacon

Council: Bob Davis, Ward 1; Wade Lnenicka, Ward 2; Jerry Mills died May 16, 1988, and replaced by Bill Scoggins, Ward 3; Jim Hawkins, Ward 4; Jack Shinall, Ward 5; Kathy Brooks, Ward 6; Bob Beatenbaugh died May 30, 1989, and replaced by Charles "Pete" Wood, Ward 7

1992-1995

Mayor Max Bacon

Council: John Patrick, Ward 1; Ron Newcomb, Ward 2; Bill Scoggins, Ward 3; Jim Hawkins, Ward 4; Jack Cramer, Ward 5; Wade Lnenicka, Ward 6; Charles "Pete" Wood, Ward 7

1996-1999

Mayor Max Bacon

Council: Charlene Capilouto, Ward 1; Ron Newcomb, Ward 2; Bill Scoggins, Ward 3; Jim Hawkins, Ward 4; Jack Cramer, Ward 5; Wade Lnenicka, Ward 6; Charles "Pete" Wood, Ward 7

2000-2003

Mayor Max Bacon

Council: Charlene Capilouto resigned and replaced by Melleny Pritchett in a special election June, 19, 2001, Ward 1; Ron Newcomb, Ward 2; Bill Scoggins, Ward 3; Jim Hawkins resigned and replaced through appointment by Paula Weeks, Ward 4; Jack Cramer, Ward 5; Wade Lnenicka, Ward 6; Charles "Pete" Wood, Ward 7

2004-2007

Mayor Max Bacon

Council: Melleny Pritchett, Ward 1; Ron Newcomb, Ward 2; Bill Scoggins, Ward 3; Mike McNabb, Ward 4; Jimmy Smith, Ward 5; Wade Lnenicka, Ward 6; Charles "Pete" Wood, Ward 7

2008-2011

Mayor Max Bacon

Council: Melleny Pritchett, Ward 1; Ron Newcomb, Ward 2; Teri Anulewicz, Ward 3; Mike McNabb, Ward 4; Jimmy Smith, Ward 5; Wade Lnenicka, Ward 6; Charles "Pete" Wood, Ward 7

MAYOR
LORENA PACE PRUITT

Long before female politicians were in vogue, Lorena Pace Pruitt was elected to the Smyrna City Council in 1944. When Mayor J. Y. Wootten resigned on May 4, 1945, a special election was held and Mrs. Pruitt won over C. Mayes Hamby, who had been on the council since 1940. She was reelected for the next term and served until the end of 1948.

Mrs. Pruitt was said to have been the first female elected mayor in Georgia and became somewhat of a celebrity throughout the state and she made the national spotlight when she was invited to New York as a guest of then Mayor William O'Dwyer.

Mayor Pruitt had three major projects during her term. She wanted to upgrade the city water system which, at the time, was fed from a series of wells and springs. When she couldn't work out a satisfactory agreement and cooperation from Cobb County Commissioner George McMillan she went to Mayor William B. Hartsfield in Atlanta. Negotiations with that city administration brought an Atlanta water line into Smyrna to solve the water problem. As a part of this effort, Smyrna became known nationally and internationally as the first city to win a Georgia Supreme Court test case on combining water and sewage anticipation revenue certificates as a method of financing major capital improvements. With this arrangement a new sewage treatment plant and other improvements were made including the installation of fire hydrants and some street lights.

The details of the bonds and revenue certificates were worked out in conjunction with Smyrna City Attorney Scott Edwards and Smyrna resident Lex Jolley whose firm handled general and special obligation bond issues for cities and counties throughout the state of Georgia.

Her second major project was paving Smyrna's dirt streets. During her three years as mayor fourteen streets were paved for the first time.

The third project of her administration concerned a dispute over a request to the Georgia Public Service Commission by the Greyhound Bus Company to the Georgia Public Service Commission to permit their busses to compete with the Atlanta Northern Railway that had a station in Smyrna and had provided trolley service through the city since 1905. The city council passed a resolution to deny the permit. Eventually Marietta joined Smyrna in a suit to keep Greyhound out but it was to no avail. The Atlanta Northern Railway discontinued service from Marietta to Atlanta on January 31, 1947, and the matter was resolved.

During the years Mrs. Pruitt was mayor the annual city operating budget was about $25,000 and her salary was $25 per month. The population was less than 2,000.

Mrs. Pruitt distinguished herself in a variety of other ways including her employment with the state of Georgia as Director of the State Training School for Girls, superintendent of the Confederate Soldiers Home in Atlanta, and as the manager of one of the large cafeterias in the huge Bell Bomber Plant in Marietta during World War II.

Her parents, Dr. W. T. and Janie Bentley Pace, were long-time Smyrna residents. He represented Cobb County in the Georgia Legislature, and he, like his father J. T. Pace, served Smyrna as a mayor in the early 1900s. Mrs. Pruitt was born in Smyrna June 30, 1896. She married Joe R. Pruitt, April 28, 1914. He was an employee of the Georgia Railway and Power Company. They had two boys, Joe, Jr., who was born January 1, 1919, and Rex, born January 20, 1920. Both are deceased.

Mrs. Pruitt moved to Augusta to live with son Rex in 1981. She died there December 22, 1982, at age 86. In a visit to Smyrna in 1991 Rex donated a number of his mother's documents, family photographs, newspaper clippings, etc. to the Smyrna Museum. Several are in this book.

MAYOR A. MAX BACON

The longest serving mayor in the city's history is the current one—A. Max Bacon.

❖

Above: Mayor Lorena Pace Pruitt.

The children of Dr. W. T. and Janie Bentley Pace. Left to right, standing: Donnie Lee (Mrs. Harvey Williamson), Sidney, Lorena (Mrs. Joe Pruitt). Seated, Helen Irena (Mrs. John Schley Thompson).

Below: A Greyhound bus at the intersection of Atlanta and Spring Streets, c. 1948. The man in the street is standing near the covered tracks of the Atlanta Northern Railway (street car line). This is the current entrance to the Market Village.

A native of Smyrna, he was elected councilman to represent the city's Ward 2 in November 1979. Two years later his father, Arthur Bacon, was elected mayor for the second time. Arthur had previously served as mayor during the 1976-1977 term but chose not to run for re-election at the end of that term. Both Arthur and Max were re-elected in the November 1983 election. After Arthur was diagnosed with lung cancer in 1984 he wrote a note stating, "Obviously I will not be able to attend or hold any meetings. My intention is resigning on November 1 and hope that I will be able to swear in the new mayor and council member for Ward 2."

In September 1985, after three days of qualifying had ended, Max Bacon was the only person to qualify for the mayor's race. In the meantime, his father Arthur died October 26, 1985, just a little over a week before election day. As a result Max was elected mayor by the council on November 18, 1985, to fill out his father's unexpired term. When his current term ends on December 31, 2011, he will have served as Smyrna's mayor for twenty-six years and two months.

The Smyrna mayor's office, as well as the members of the City Council, are part-time positions. Mayor Bacon's full-time employment during most of the time he has served as councilman and mayor was with the U. S. Postal Service. He began his postal career in 1965 as a clerk/carrier at the Smyrna post office when it was located on West Spring Street. In 1969, after a new post office had been constructed and dedicated on July 5, 1970, on Cherokee Road (now Windy Hill), he was promoted to supervisor of delivery and collections at the Smyrna post office. He served in a variety of other management positions until August 15, 1987, when he was named postmaster in Mableton, Georgia. The swearing in ceremony took place August 20, 1987.

Mayor Bacon continued as Mableton postmaster until November 2002 when he was appointed postmaster for the city of Smyrna and served there until his retirement on January 3, 2006.

For a short time he was employed by the Northwest Exterminating and Pest Control Company as public relations director from January, 2006 to January 2008 but since his resignation he spends more time with his grandchildren and horses and more time in the office at the Smyrna city hall.

None of the present members of the Smyrna city council were on the council when Max was first elected in 1979. Some of the original members died, some resigned on moving out of the city, some were defeated for re-election and some chose not to run for re-election.

Other than Mayor Bacon, Councilman Wade Lnenicka of Ward 6 is the most senior on council and serves as mayor pro tem. He was first elected in November 1987. Charlie "Pete" Wood of Ward 7 is next in longevity. He was elected in 1989 in a special election to fill the unexpired term of Bob Beatenbaugh after his death. Ron Newcomb of Ward 2 was first elected in November 1991 and took office in January 1992.

All the members of the Smyrna city council elected since November 1987, had a part in Smyrna's "extreme makeover" that continues to this day.

The mayor/council form of government for Smyrna was established in the original charter in 1872 but the number of council members and the ward lines have changed a number of times over the years. In the beginning all were elected in a city wide vote and all voting was done at the city hall or another designated place. As the town grew more council members were added but still remained on a city-wide vote. Later when the city limits were extended and the city was divided into wards, the council members were required to live in the ward and be elected only by the registered voters in that ward.

For many years the Smyrna City Elections were held on the first Saturday in January and later changed to November. When the elections were on Saturday the turn-out of registered voters sometimes ran as high as 80 to 85 per cent. State law now requires that polls be open from 7:00 a.m. to 7:00 p.m. Previously the city would set it at varying time. Sometimes from 8:00 a.m. to one or two o'clock and at other times from 10:00 a.m. to 4:00 p.m. The city hall was the only polling place and there was only one ballot box. It is currently on display in the Smyrna Museum.

The city had its own three-member board of registrars and a three member board of election managers. Both boards were appointed by the mayor and members of the city council. Smyrna was one of the very early cities to register

Above: City Councilman Pete Wood and wife Lillie enjoy a stroll at the Jonquil Festival with their granddaughter Lillie Rose.

Below: Mayor A. Max Bacon.

❖

Above: This ballot box was retired in 1969. It had been used in city elections at the one polling place in city hall for more than sixty years. It now serves as a donation box in the Smyrna Museum.

Below: Willouise Spivey.

Bottom: Melinda Dameron.

eighteen year olds. Requirements for registering to vote were simple:

1. Be eighteen years old or older.
2. Be a citizen of the state of Georgia for two years.
3. Be a resident and registered to vote in Cobb County for one year.
4. Be a resident of Smyrna for six months.
5. Be able to read one sentence from the Georgia State Constitution or another designated document.

A few years after the Smyrna Jaycees were chartered in 1959 they volunteered their services to the city in helping with the registrations and assisted with managing the elections at the city hall without any cost to the city.

When the state voting laws changed in the late 1960s the city of Smyrna was required to have a polling place in each of the wards. The city election of 1969 was the first year to have an election where all the votes were not cast and counted at the city hall. A few years later, because of the expense of manning seven polling places (number of wards) Smyrna changed its election date to the first Tuesday in November and found it more economical to contract with the Cobb County elections department to conduct the Smyrna municipal elections. Some twenty years later, expenses of conducting the elections were cut in half by going to four year terms for the mayor and council positions

The mayor/council form of government has worked well for the city even with those elected officials serving on a part time basis. They are responsible for providing the city with the most effective government services possible consistent with the needs of the community. They are responsible for the city's financial matters, taxes, etc. They appoint the city administrator, city clerk, municipal court judges and the various commission members.

The mayor usually appoints each council member to chair one major committee that over-sees the operations of a particular department and to serve on two or more committees as a member. The regular public City Council meetings are held at 7:30 p.m. on the first and third Mondays in each month. Agenda meetings are held on the Thursday prior to the regular twice monthly meetings. All meetings are open to the public.

During his first term Mayor Kreeger attempted to change Smyrna to a city manager form of government, but in the public referendum in May of 1960 the measure was soundly defeated and it has never been attempted again although it was discussed.

Many of the early major changes and growth in Smyrna's city government came in the decade of the 1950s when the population grew from 2,005 to 10,157 in 1960. Even in the mid 1960s Smyrna still only had 15 full-time police officers and 8 full-time fire fighters. Both departments were supplemented by volunteers. The city almost doubled in population again from 1960 to 1970 when it reached 19,157.

A great deal of that growth was attributed to the "white flight" from Atlanta to the suburbs and to the new contract that Lockheed-Georgia had obtained to build the C-5A. Almost 35,000 people were employed at Lockheed at that time.

Smyrna's growth slowed somewhat from 1970 to 1980 but the population has increased approximately 10,000 per decade since that time. A new state law that went into effect in 1970 allowed municipalities to annex property into the city limits without approval of the Georgia Legislature. Prior to that law, a majority of the legislative delegation from Cobb County had to be in favor of the annexations and then the entire general assembly would approve it and the governor would have to sign the bill. Under the new law certain requirements had to be met before the annexations could be complete including a request from a majority of the property owners within the district to be annexed. The property could be annexed without approval of the property owners where the city had completely surrounded the property. There were other stipulations that had been met also.

Besides the elected officials many of the activities and responsibilities of the city are carried out by appointed people. Two of the early appointed people were the city clerk and the police chief.

When the town of Smyrna was first chartered in 1872, no provisions were made for a city clerk. Two major changes were made in a new charter approved by the Georgia Legislature in 1897. The first one was that it reduced the city limits fifty per cent from one mile to one-half mile. The second one was that it provided for a city clerk and police chief. For the most part, at the beginning the role of the city clerk was to record the minutes of the meetings of the mayor and council and to handle whatever correspondence, and other clerical work was associated with the job. Homer Durham, a city councilman in the 1940s recalled in his memoirs to the *Lives and Times* that as late as the early '40s the city only had three employees: the city clerk, the police chief and the superintendent of the sanitation and water department. All fire personnel were volunteers.

City Clerk C. C. Terrell made his annual financial report to the city on December 31, 1940, showing total receipts for the year from all city functions. They had $158.78 in the bank on January 1, 1940. During the year income totaled $14,659.40. Expenses for the year were $13,960.81, finishing the year on December 31, 1940, with $857.59 in the bank. Accounts receivable were $1,844.55 and accounts payable were $1,545.44.

As the city grew, the responsibilities of the city clerk grew along with it. From the early 1950s to the 1970s Smyrna was transformed from a town to a city and additional personnel were needed for handling the clerical and administrative details, budgets, payrolls and other paperwork for all departments. These workers all came under the supervision of the city clerk until 1986 when the city hired its first city administrator

The city clerk was the contact person for citizens who came into the city hall looking for services or help. With few exceptions, the part time mayor and members of the city council had full time jobs and were only available during the twice a month council meetings or when a citizen might see them at a church or social function or call them at home after hours. For many years, the city clerk was the single public face and public relations person for the entire city government.

Les Charles was hired as city clerk in 1958 during the last administration of Mayor J. M. "Hoot" Gibson. It was during the tremendous growth period of the 1950s and '60s and he played a major part in getting the city ready for expansions in every direction. He was the "front" man for the city. He took part in ribbon cuttings, ground breaking ceremonies, grand opening, and social activities with the civic and service clubs.

He served in that "appointed" position longer than any other person in the city's history through the administrations of "Hoot" Gibson, George Kreeger, J. B. "Jake" Ables, Harold Smith and John Porterfield. He retired at the beginning of Arthur Bacon's first term. The *Marietta Daily Journal* quoted Arthur as saying that if he had known Les Charles was going to retire, he would not have run for mayor.

Prior to taking the city clerk job with Smyrna Mr. Charles was employed by the Lockheed-Georgia Company as an efficiency expert. The story goes that when he was evaluating his own department, he concluded the company could save some money by eliminating his job. That's when he became available for the city clerk's job in Smyrna.

As a tribute to Les Charles the city dedicated the Municipal Complex at King Springs Park (now Tolleson Park) to him at ceremonies on April 22, 1979. The complex included a heated Olympic size swimming pool, lighted tennis courts, a bath house, office and handicap facilities. The complex was Phase II of an $800,000

Above: Les Charles, city clerk from 1958-1975.

Below: City Clerk Susan Hiott.

CITY CLERKS OF SMRYNA

1900	John Baldwin	1929	R. G. Lewis	1950-1952	Martha Theodocian
1901	P. Y. Daniell	1930-1939	S. E. Faucett	1953	Mrs. A. J. Hackney (19 days)
1905	Bob Love	1940-1942	C. C. Terrell	1953-1957	Helen Baldwin
1908	J. R. Deavers	1942	C. W. Hawkins	1958-1975	Les Charles
1909	S. J. Ireland	1943-1944	C. C. Terrell	1976-1985	Willouise Spivey
1910	L. Q. Yancey	1944	L. R. Briggs (died)	1987-1999	Melinda Dameron
1919	C. L. Fambrough	1944	Louise Pavlovsky (resigned)	1999-2001	Candis Joiner
1924	S. W. Dodgen	1944-1945	Maude Paris	2001	Kelley Barber
1925-1926	M. D. Lewis	1946-1947	Ober Hensley (resigned)	2002-present	Susan Hiott
1927	S. W. Dodgen	1947-1948	Thelma Myers (resigned)		
1928	J. W. McCollum	1949	James L. Pierce		

Top: City Administrator
Robert Thomson.

Above: City Administrator
John Patterson.

Below: City Administrator
Howard Smith.

expansion program at the park. Mr. Charles had moved to Melbourne, Florida, and was unable to attend the dedication ceremonies.

Following Mr. Charles was Willouise Spivey. She was employed by the city for twenty-two years—first as an accountant, assistant city clerk and the last eleven years as city clerk. She supervised all office personnel in addition to her regular duties as city clerk until July 1985 when the city hired its first city administrator. She had the distinction of being the first certified city clerk in Cobb County with 100 course hours at the University of Georgia. Mrs. Spivey celebrated her retirement at a reception at Aunt Fanny's Cabin, November 23, 1986, with fellow workers, friends and well wishers.

Melinda Dameron had been employed by the city for twelve years as assistant to the mayor and city council and was elevated to the position of city clerk January 5, 1987, following Mrs. Spivey's retirement. She served until December, 1999 and was replaced by two short term clerks: December 1999 to April 2001 Candis Joiner and May 2001 to June 2001 Kelley Barber (interim).

The current city clerk is Susan Hiott. She was appointed to the position by the mayor and council on May 20, 2002, although she actually took over the duties May 13 after the resignation of Kelley Barber.

Ms. Hiott started her career in government in 1996 when she was hired as assistant to the city clerk for Smyrna but she left to accept city clerk positions in Acworth and Roswell before returning to Smyrna.

The city clerk is the official record keeper for the city. Responsibilities include recording and maintaining the council's official actions in minutes, maintaining contracts, ordinances, resolutions, agreements and coordinating the records management and retention program for the city. The city clerk is also the administrator and clerk of the municipal and environmental courts and oversees the court services.

It had become obvious with the growth of the city and the additional departments and personnel that someone was needed to handle the day-to-day business, activities and operations. Smyrna's first city administrator was hired in May 1985 during the last administration of Mayor Arthur Bacon. However, he

was not able to come to work until July 1, 1985.

Immediately prior to coming to Smyrna, at age 32, John Patterson had been employed by the city of Conway, South Carolina, for two years as city administrator. Previously he was the finance director for the city of Myrtle Beach, South Carolina, for four and a half years.

His arrival at that time put him in the position to play a major role in the planning and development of Smyrna's complete makeover in the late 1980s and early 1990s.

He worked with the mayor and council, the downtown development authority and other city commissions, committees, department heads and eventually the architectural firm of Sizemore and Floyd to lay out the plans for the downtown redevelopment program that brought national recognition to the city.

The first phase of the program included the new Smyrna library, the Village Green, the community center, office and retail space and new upscale housing.

Four months after the grand opening of the first phase and six years after coming to Smyrna, to the surprise of city officials and the community, Mr. Patterson gave the city a 30-day notice of his resignation. He had accepted the position of city manager of West Valley City, Utah, a city with more than twice the population of Smyrna. He and the family moved from Smyrna in mid-December to start his new job in January 1992.

Robert Thomson came to Smyrna from the position of city manager of Powder Springs where he had been employed since December 1987. He had ten years of experience in public administration and was chosen from a field of five selected from 300 applicants for the job.

He started to work on April 1, 1992, after having been hired on March 6, as the planning for a new city hall, fire and police stations and the Market Village were underway.

Thompson resigned and his last city council meeting was July 8, 1996. He left to enter private business. He was replaced by Howard Smith.

Smith was head of the Rome, Georgia,. chamber of commerce when he was approached by the city of Smyrna to become its city administrator on September 3, 1996. Smyrna had just completed its new city hall and another phase of the downtown revitalization was underway. The public safety buildings for the police and fire departments and the Market Village complex were yet to be completed.

The mayor and council members were familiar with Mr. Smith. They had known him for some thirteen years as the host for their annual planning retreat and through their association with him when he worked for the Carl Vinson Institute of Government at the University of Georgia.

Through the five years or so that he was with Smyrna his relationship with the mayor and council became somewhat "strained" because of "communication" problems and a variety of other reasons. In a special called meeting on November 1, 2001, on a split 4 to 3 vote the council terminated his employment immediately with the city and voted to give him six months severance pay.

The following week Chris Corey, the human resources director for the city, was named interim city administrator. He served in that position until June 10, 2002, when Wayne Wright officially assumed the duties of city administrator.

At the regular council meeting on June 3, 2002, after a presentation of his educational background and his experience in government work he was appointed city administrator with an effective date of June 10, 2002. Ward 7 Councilman Pete Wood's motion, with a second by Ward 6 Councilman Wade Lnenicka, to appoint Mr. Wright was unanimous.

Mr. Wright's immediate past employment was as city manager of Powder Springs. He had been there since July 1993, and was previously the city administrator for Garden City, Georgia, from October 1987 to July 1993.

Mr. Wright resigned in July 2009 to accept a position with a private company that provides personnel for the recently chartered city of Sandy Springs as their operations director.

The current city administrator, Eric Taylor, was appointed by the mayor and council effective August 17, 2009, following less than a month as Interim. He has been with the city since March 2006 and served as the assistant city administrator, a position that brought him in direct contact with the city department heads. He also served as the human resources director for several months.

During the redevelopment program the duties of the city administrator changed due to the particular program underway. The current administrator is charged with updating the mayor and the council on city business and makes policy recommendations. He is charged with presenting a balanced annual budget to the mayor and the council for approval. He also manages department heads for the following departments: community development, community relations, finance, fire, human resources, information systems, Keep Smyrna Beautiful, library, parks and recreation, police and public works/engineering.

Appointed officials that have not been full-time employees of the city are the city attorneys. In the past they were usually hired on a retainer basis to handle specific assignments that might arise in the business of the city.

Today the city attorney is appointed by the mayor and city council and is responsible for advising the mayor and council, administrator, city clerk, department heads and advisory boards on legal matters. He reviews ordinances, resolutions, contracts, and other official documents for their legality and impact. He serves as the parliamentarian for city council meetings and represents the city in civil litigation.

The current city attorney is Scott Cochran. He has been in that position since the death of Charles "Chuck" Camp on December 16, 1999, at the age of sixty. Camp had been the city attorney since 1976. Both men were associated with the law firm of Cochran, Camp and Snipes. The Cochran in the firm's title is J. Al Cochran, the father of the present city attorney, who died April 1, 2008, after a long bout with cancer. He attended council meetings on many occasions when his partner "Chuck" or his son Scott could not be present.

The firm was associated closely with the city beginning with the first administration of Mayor Arthur Bacon in 1976.

Records are "sketchy" but we have located the following names in the city council minutes who have served as city attorney for Smyrna.

In the early years of Smyrna when someone was arrested and charged with an infraction of a city ordinance they were cited to the "mayor's court." The mayor would hear the case and decide the appropriate punishment. The original charter limited the town to a fine of

❖

Above: City Administrator Wayne Wright.

Below: City Administrator Eric Taylor.

CITY OF SMYRNA JUDGES

1956-1957	Judge John B. Kelley	1968-1969	Judge C. V. Reeves	1994-1999	Judge Michael Whaley
1958-1959	Judge J. M. Sitton	1970-1970	Judge Ken Chalker	2000-present	Judge E. Alton Curtis
1960-1965	Judge C. V. Reeves	1970-1971	Judge Ken Nix		
1966-1967	Judge George Bridwell	1972-1994	Judge C. V. Reeves		

no more than $5 and no one could be put in jail for more than 24 hours.

Somewhere along the way the city was given the power to fine as much as $50 and 10 days in the calaboose, depending on the infraction. Currently the law is very specific as to the limits of the city court and the fines they may impose.

Possibly it didn't take long for the mayor to find out that holding court wasn't the way to make friends and influence the town's voters nor the most popular thing to do especially around election time. The mayor's court was later changed to the recorder's court.

Today the Smyrna municipal court is the judicial branch of the city government of Smyrna. The court services division includes five full-time employees, two part-time employees, a solicitor and a judge. The court services division is responsible for processing all traffic citations and misdemeanor state law violations issued by the police department. The court services division holds separate sessions for traffic and environmental court citations. The environmental court addresses property maintenance, animal control, and other environmental degradation cases before the court judge.

Judge E. Alton Curtis was appointed to the judgeship January 3, 2000, and has made many innovations in the municipal court operation. The sessions are held in the council chambers at the city hall. It is equipped with cameras and projection equipment that is used often for a ten minute power point presentation on the rights of the defendants. On some days as many as 200 cases are heard. Everyone entering the court room passes through a metal detector with Smyrna Police officers on duty

Other than the judges mentioned above, we have found in the official minutes of the Smyrna city council the following who have served in the recorders/municipal court as judge.

During the first few months of the administration of Mayor Gibson there was no recorder and the council authorized the mayor to fill that position. He resigned as recorder court judge June 2, 1958.

The city charter had been changed on January 25, 1958, to allow a non-resident of Smyrna to serve as judge of the recorder's court.

After C. V. Reeves had served from 1960 until 1965 it was discovered that his appointment was probably in violation of a state law that required a person in this position to pass the state bar examination. Mr. Reeves had a law degree but was not a member of the Georgia Bar.

To remedy the situation, during the 1966-1967 term of Mayor Kreeger, Smyrna Attorney George Bridwell was appointed to fill the post while the legalities could be worked out regarding Judge Reeves. He was appointed again at the beginning of the 1968-1969 term of Mayor Kreeger

Attorney Ken Chalker was appointed judge in January 1970 by Mayor Harold Smith and the council. He had just started his law practice in

CITY OF SMYRNA ATTORNEYS

1925	Gordon Gann	1941-1945	Glenn Giles	1966-1969	Berl Tate
1925	Fred Morris	1946-1948	Scott Edwards	1970-1971	George Carreker
1926	F. T. Wills	1951	Harold Willingham	1972-1975	Berl Tate
1927	Harold Hawkins	1952	Raymond Reed	1976-1999	Charles "Chuck" Camp
1932-1933	F. T. Wills	1953-1957	Harold Willingham	2000-present	Scott Cochran
1934-1938	James Carmichael	1958-1965	Conley Ingram		

Judge C. V. Reeves   Judge Ken Chalker   Judge Ken Nix

Judge Michael Whaley   Judge E. Alton Curtis

James Carmichael   Harold Willingham   Raymond Reed   Conley Ingram

George Carreker   Charles "Chuck" Camp   J. Al Cochran   Scott Cochran

A small portion of the 15,000 that gathered on the Village Green to celebrate the city's 131st Anniversary in 2003.

underway, Smyrna was recognized as the City of Excellence in 1997 by the Urban Land Institute. The award was presented in New York City on September 7, 1997. Mayor Max Bacon and Mike Sizemore of the architectural firm of Sizemore and Floyd that provided the design concept, accepted the award on behalf of the citizens of Smyrna.

Smyrna was selected from 102 entries. Citing Smyrna's redevelopment program the Urban Land Institute's Awards Jury stated: "Smyrna's success represents a powerful example for many decimated suburban communities across America. Their success occurs at a time when many living in the suburban areas of the U. S. are unhappy with the congestion and are yearning for a sense of community and a small town feeling."

Smyrna and, in November, stating that the part-time job was taking more time than he thought it would he resigned. The monthly salary at that time was $150 for holding court twice a month.

Smyrna Attorney Ken Nix served the remainder of the 1970-1971 term. He was elected to the Georgia House of Representatives, the Cobb County State Court and presently serves as Cobb County Superior Court Judge.

Judge C. V. Reeves was returned as city judge in the administrations of John Porterfield, Frank Johnson, Arthur Bacon and Max Bacon. He retired in 1994 by continued to work part-time until 1996 with Judge Mike Whaley.

Shortly after the second phase of the downtown redevelopment program, or as called by some, "the extreme makeover", was well

Smyrna was recognized again on January 26, 2004, when the Georgia Municipal Association cited Smyrna as one of ten "Cities of Excellence" in the state. Smyrna received this award for excellence in fiscal management, public safety, infrastructure, citizen participation, cultural activities, community partnerships and downtown viability. Smyrna has become widely known as a model for redevelopment and serves as an example to other communities.

Smyrna has maintained the small town feeling in the midst of tremendous growth even as 10,000 to 15,000 people gather on the Village Green in August every year to celebrate the city's birthday and at the twice a year Jonquil Festivals.

Other administrative personnel and department heads currently employed by the city:

Rosemary Rivera, executive assistant to city administrator
Lizette Bryan, executive assistant to mayor and council
Assistant City Administrator Tammi Saddler
Deputy City Clerk Lee Miller
City Engineer Keith Williams
Community Development Director/City Planner Ken Sudderth
Information Systems Manager Chris Addicks

Library Director Michael Seigler
Community Relations Jennifer Bennett
Finance Department Director David Boyd
Human Resources & Risk Management Director Kay Bruner
Parks & Recreation Steve Ciaccio
Keep Smyrna Beautiful Ann Kirk
Public Works Director Scott Stokes

In addition to the full and part-time personnel employed by the city through the years listed within this *Historic Smyrna* book there have been literally thousands of volunteers from the community who have helped make Smyrna what it is today. These include the individuals from the businesses, civic, social and service clubs, schools, church organizations and families.

The mayor and council recognizes the individuals and groups through a variety of special awards programs and activities annually for their contributions. Some of those people work through official commissions and boards appointed by the mayor and council but the major portion comes through the membership organizations. Some of the organizations mentioned in this list that provided the leadership, encouragement, financial assistance, manual labor and the people for the city, county, state and national elected positions have long since been gone but many of them are still functioning today as a vital part of the religious, social and civic life of Smyrna.

Unfortunately time and space prevents sharing the names of all those who have made Smyrna one of the most desirable places in the whole state to live, work and play, but we will share the names of the organizations that many of them belonged to: + indicates the organization no longer exists.

American Legion Auxiliary, 1946
American Legion Post 160, 1941
Bennett Woods Garden Club, 1974
Bethel Baptist, 1882+
Boy Scouts
Calvary Baptist, 1952
Carmichael Funeral Home, 1976
Castellaw Funeral Home, 1960
Church of the Nazarene, 1962
Collins Spring Primitive Baptist, 1856
Concord Baptist, 1832
Eastern Star, 1951
Faith Methodist, 1963
Fellowship Christian Center, 1964
Friends of the Smyrna Library, 1990
Greater Zion Hill Baptist, 1950
Green Acres Baptist Church, 1948
Hurt Road Baptist, 1968
Jonquil Garden Club, 1937
Keep Smyrna Beautiful, 1989
King Springs Baptist, 1958
Legend Heights Baptist, 1965+
Leonidas Polk Camp 1445, SCV
Vinings First Baptist, 1948 Smyrna
Locust Grove Baptist, 1909
Maloney's Spring Primitive Baptist, 1852
Mount Zion Baptist Church, 1877
Nelms Masonic Lodge, 1886
Parent Teacher Associations
Phillips Legion U.D.C., 1961
Retail Merchants Association, 1952+
Saint Thomas Catholic, 1966
Sharon Baptist Church, 1942
Smyrna Assembly of God, 1953
Smyrna Business Association

Smyrna Cemetery Association, 1994
Smyrna Chamber of Commerce, 1951,
    merged with Cobb Chamber in the 1960s
Smyrna Christian Church, 1954
Smyrna Citizens Council, 1951+
Smyrna Civitan Club+
Smyrna Clean & Beautiful changed to
    Keep Smyrna Beautiful, 1989
Smyrna Community Chorus, 1975
Smyrna First Baptist Church, 1882
Smyrna First United Methodist Church, 1838
Smyrna Golden K Kiwanis, 1988
Smyrna Historical & Genealogical Society, 1985
Smyrna Jaycees, 1959+
Smyrna Junior Woman's Club+
Smyrna Kiwanis Club
Smyrna Lion's Club, 1948+
Smyrna Men's Club, 1935+
Smyrna Oakdale Moose, 1962
Smyrna Women of the Moose, 1962
Smyrna Optimist, 1962
Smyrna Presbyterian Church, 1874
Smyrna Rotary, 1963
Smyrna Second Baptist Church, 1942
Smyrna Social Club, 1908
Smyrna Veterans Memorial Association, 1999
Smyrna Woman's Club, 1925+
Smyrna's Little League and other sports
Spring Street Baptist, 1933
Taylor/Brawner House Foundation, 2004
The Entertainers, Windy Hill Senior
    Center, 1988
Tillman Memorial Methodist, 1954
Trinity Baptist, 1973+
Vinings First Baptist, 1948

1   Resigned on August 6, 1931, because he was moving out of the city. He was replaced by C. W. Flowers who was elected by the council on a vote of 3 to 1.

2   Arrington resigned on June 7, 1937, and was replaced by T. W. Huffstutler in a special election on June 26, 1937. C. B. Austin was appointed to fill the council post vacated by Huffstutler.

3   Huffstutler resigned May 2,1938. He was replaced by John Corn.

4   Mayor Brinkley died on April 3, 1941, shortly after taking office. John Tatum was elected to replace him in a special election on April 5, 1941. He won over J. O. Hargis 141 to 43. F. D. Cargal was appointed by the mayor and council to replace John Tatum on the council.

5   Mayor Tatum resigned August 2, 1942, giving as a reason his work load with the railroad as a result of the beginning World War II. Mayor pro tem C. Mayes Hamby assumed mayoral duties until the election in November.

6   W. F. Stewart was elected to a council post on November 1, 1941, for a two-year term beginning on January 1, 1942. On November 11, 1941, before taking office he resigned because he worked for the federal government and was concerned about the "Hatch" Act. C. O. Garvin was appointed by mayor and council to fill that term.

7   J. R. Arrington resigned April 6, 1942. He was replaced by A.B.S. Lowry by vote of the city council on July 15, 1942.

9   J. O. Hargis was elected councilman to fill the unexpired term of C. O. Garvin on August 2, 1943.

10   J. Y. Wootten resigned May 4, 1945. A special election was held December 29, 1945, and Lorena Pruitt was elected.

11   E. E. Jackson, June 3, 1946, was sworn in to fill the unexpired term of C. L. Groce, who died.

12   June 17, 1946, Robert Bacon resigned from the council. On July 24, 1946, Emmett F. Cox was elected to fill the unexpired term.

13   Konigsmark resigned May 4, 1948. H. L. McEntyre was elected on a tie vote broken by the vote of Mrs. Pruitt. J. L. Collins had nominated J. F. Bradfield, second by P. P. Shaw. Homer Durham nominated H. L. McEntyre, second by H. P. McCollum.

14   April 17, 1950, R. S. Brinson resigned because he was moving out of the city. He was replaced by Howard Hames.

15   C. W. Jones was elected to fill the unexpired term of R. B. Logan on November 7, 1950.

16   Mayor Duncan died in office December 6, 1954. His successor, James E. Quarles had been elected in November.

17   The city charter was changed in 1953, effective on the first Saturday in November 1955, to elect a mayor and seven councilmen, one from each of the six wards and one at large, for a term of two years with elections being held biannually (every other year).It required the candidate to live in the ward in which elected. The charter was changed again in 1964, effective January 1, 1966, to provide for seven council members representing 7 wards and eliminating the council-at-large post. A seventh ward was added to the city at that time and all wards were redrawn.

18   J. B. "Dusty" Rhodes was appointed to fill the unexpired term of Norman Brenner. In November of 1957 he was elected to a full term. The at large position was eliminated and a seventh ward was added to the council.

19   Rhodes resigned in July 1963 in a dispute with Mayor Ables. Since an election was scheduled for November no one was appointed to fill his unexpired term.

20   Ingram resigned May 18, 1963, when he moved out of the city. John Porterfield won a special election against Amby Hughes to serve out the unexpired term.

21   Jim Webb resigned because of moving out of the city and the ill health of his wife. J. B. Ables, a former councilman and mayor, won over Hugh Lee McDaniel to fill the unexpired term.

22   Keck resigned because he was moving out of the city. Blake Thomas, who had won that post in the city election in November, was appointed to fill out the unexpired term of Keck.

23   Kuhl resigned and moved to Columbus, Georgia. Jim Hawkins was appointed to fill the unexpired term on August 1, 1977.

24   Melleny Pritchett was elected in a special election held on June 19, 2001.

CHAPTER VII

SMYRNA'S
PUBLIC SAFETY DEPARTMENTS

Smyrna Police Chiefs were almost as numerous as the mayors and members of the city council. The reason was, for the most part, until the 1960s the chiefs served at the pleasure of the mayor and/or the members of the City Council. The mayor would make a recommendation and the council would approve it.

Traditionally, even before a new mayor was sworn in, he would have someone in mind to fill the top law enforcement position for the city and, for many years, there was only one person in the police department, and he was chief. Also in the early days that position was only a part-time job.

In the last term of Mayor J. M. "Hoot" Gibson, 1958-1959, the Smyrna city council asked the Georgia Legislature, through the Cobb County delegation, to amend Smyrna's charter to allow the city to establish a civil service board and to authorize the city to hire a "recorder" (city judge) that did not live in the city.

However, it was in the first term of Mayor George Kreeger in 1960, that the legislation was put into law and the police and fire department personnel, including the two chiefs, were placed under a three person civil service board. The board was charged with the responsibility of making recommendations for all personnel in those two departments. After the adoption of the ordinance, when there was a vacancy in the departments, the civil service board would screen the candidates and recommend the top three candidates to the mayor and council, and the new chief would be chosen through this process. That process lasted until August 1994 when the city administration removed the two chiefs from civil service and made the board an appeals body and transferred the responsibility of screening and testing job applicants to human resources. Department heads make the final hiring decisions. The civil service board serves as an appeals board for police and firefighters. Other city employees take their appeals directly to the city council.

❖

The Smyrna police department and jail located at 2646 Atlanta Road was dedicated on Saturday, August 2, 1997. It replaced the 1970s Bank Street building that had originally contained the department headquarters, the jail, the courtroom and the civil defense department. The police department had outgrown that facility years ago and the city had obtained several other buildings in the vicinity to house the judicial operation, the traffic division and the detective division.

1878	W. N. Pace		1939	Hoyt Langston
1898	W. K. Bickers			C. T. White
	Charlie Fleming		1940	Hoyt Langston, E. G. Peek
1899	E. J.Morri			J. F. Marshall
	Joe Grizzard		1941	Hoyt Langston
1901-1902	Joe Grizzard			B. F. Black, C. C. Mohon, E. G. Peek,
	George Morris			J. E. Wright
1905	Joe Grizzard		1942	Sam Morris, R. M. Argo
	W. K. Bickers			W. H. Gann, Fred Addison
1906	Jack Norris		1943	R. M. Argo
1907-1910	Paul Chaney			W. H. Gann
1911-1912	R. H. Wall		1944	R. M. Argo
1915	G. K. Parnell			B. A. Walker
1920	W. F. Earwood		1945	E. G. Peek
	M. V. Ruff			W. D. Anderson
	N. G. Durham		1946	S. G. Sexton
1923	S. W. Dodgen			W. W. Day, W. H. McCollum
1926	J. Z. Foster, I. W. Foster		1947	S. G. Sexton, W. C. Lowe
	J. P. Pair, (3 days)			W. A. Wright
1927	E. N. Brooke		1948	S. G. Sexton
1928	I. W. Foster, F. Lex Jolley			R. N. Neese
1929-1930	I. W. Foster		1949	J. H. Stephens
1931	R. L. Barfield, G. C. Griggsby			R. N. Neese
	Sam Morris, Night		1951-1953	J. C. Hardy
1932	R. L. Barfield, Sam Morris		1954	Broughton May, A. B. Hodnett
	J. W. Akins		1955-1956	Paul Epps
1933	Sam Morris, Charles Turner		1956-1958	Marshall Tanner
1934	J. R. Folsome, Claude Turner		1958-1960	M. L. Robinson, Paul Epps
1935	A. R. Collins, Claude Turner		1960	Paul Epps died, Bill Burgess
	W. H. Mapp		1960-1962	Elmer Dyke
1936-1937	A. R. Collins, Claude Turner		1962-1976	Robert L. Drake
1938	A. R. Collins		1976-1989	R. Everett Little
	W. A. Wright		1989	Kent Sims
			1989-2010	Stanley E. Hook

Editor's Note: If no year is listed it means we could not find any information regarding who served in the year.

1926 Paul Hensley, according to the minutes of the Smyrna city council, served one day as chief of police in 1926. There was no explanation as to why such a short time, but later on his wife Ober served as city clerk during the administration of Lorena Pace Pruitt, Smyrna's only female mayor.

After moving to Smyrna from Ball Ground, Georgia, Paul became a self-educated surveyor and engineer and was elected Cobb County surveyor. He was also involved with the annexation of the property that eventually became Belmont Hills.

Chief Stanley E. Hook, the current chief, has served longer than any other police chief in Smyrna's history. He celebrated his twentieth anniversary with the department in December, 2009. He came to the city after the retirement of R. Everett Little who was the second longest serving chief. He replaced Robert L. Drake who was the third longest serving Smyrna police chief. Major Kent Sims served as interim chief from the

Paul Hensley

I. W. Foster

Sam Morris

James C. Hardy, Sr.

Broughton May

Paul Epps

Marshall Tanner

M. L. "Robie" Robinson

Elmer Dyke

Robert L. Drake

R. Everett Little

Stanley E. Hook

Kent Sims

Jim Farley

Tilden C. Ledbetter

John Young

retirement of Chief Little in May 1989 until the arrival of Chief Hook in December 1989.

Chief Hook came on board just in time to take part in the "extreme makeover" planning of practically all of the city's facilities including

the police department. But it was eight years after he arrived before the beautiful, present day facility on Atlanta Road was completed.

Local, county, state and national elected officials attended dedication ceremonies for the new Public Safety Building on Saturday, August 2, 1997, during the city's 125th Anniversary Celebration. More than 200 Smyrna and Cobb County citizens enjoyed the outdoor ceremony, the tour of the building and the refreshments in spite of the sunshine with temperature nearing 90 degrees.

Cobb County Sheriff Bill Hutson was the keynote speaker and praised the city for its progress. Mayor Bacon spoke briefly.

Ward 2 Councilman Ron Newcomb, the chairman of the city's public safety committee provided information on the facility: He said the $7.6 million, 48,000 square foot structure

was financed through a general obligation bond issue approved by the citizens. The two story portion of the building houses the administrative offices and the 911 communications center. The jail is located at the rear of this building. At that time there were 88 officers and 33 administrative personnel. In 2010 the police department has 95 sworn officers, 17 detention and jail personnel and 27 administrative and communications personnel for a total of 139. The jail can house approximately 60 inmates. Judicial proceedings for the city court are held in the council room at city hall.

Councilman Newcomb compared the new building with the 1286 Bank Street building it replaced. and gave a brief history of past police facilities. The Bank Street building was constructed in 1969 and 1970 during the administrations of Mayor George Kreeger and Mayor Harold Smith. It was dedicated in April 1970 and housed the police administration personnel, the courtroom, the civil defense department and the jail which could house only sixteen inmates.

The 10,000 square-foot building cost approximately $175,000. The department had outgrown that facility years before and the city purchased several other buildings in the vicinity to house the judicial operation, the traffic division and the detective division.

When the new city hall was constructed on Bank Street in 1958 the police department took over the entire old city hall building located at the intersection of Atlanta and Bank Streets and converted the council room into a three cell jail. Several improvements were added to this facility, including a second floor in 1962 that provided space for lockers for the officers and the wrought iron rail for the steps. The old Smyrna Bank vault, with its three-foot thick reinforced brick walls served as the records and evidence storage room. The building was demolished in 1970 and a small beautification park was made on the 30 by 100 foot lot. Prior to that the city had remodeled the old Smyrna Cannery building at 101 West Spring Street that was constructed in August 1944 and converted it to a combination police and fire station in 1954.

There was a great deal of turmoil in the police department during the administrations of Mayor J. M. "Hoot" Gibson, Guy Duncan and

Jimmy Quarles. At least three of the police chiefs requested to go back to their positions before they became chief: A. B. Hodnett and C. Broughton May returned to patrolman and M. L. Robinson returned to his former sergeant position. Bill Burgess served as chief just a few months.

When the police department moved to the old city hall at the intersection of Atlanta and Bank Streets the fire department remained in the remodeled cannery building until it was demolished and replaced by a new number 1 fire department building on the same site in 1964.

During the same time frame, directly behind this police/fire dual purpose building, Smyrna's modest one room brick jail was located. There were no amenities like the ones in today's "adult detention facility" on Atlanta Road. A single door, two small windows with iron bars, a commode and wash basin were about as good as it got. The interior was as drab as the outside—not very inviting. It was demolished when the police department moved to the old city hall building on Atlanta Street

All the structures mentioned were located on the property that now make up the southern boundary of the Market Village mixed-use development with commercial enterprises on the ground floor and residential condominiums on the upper floors.

Volunteer or special policemen were mentioned in Smyrna's mayor and council minutes. On June 19, 1954, specific reference was made to "special" policemen Earl Cobb, W. H. Adams, A. V. Bolton, R. B. Swink, Jr., Earl Black, Carl Pearson, and R. D. Patterson. In the August 1955 minutes Bill Miles and Milton Bruce Chase were shown as volunteers and the September 10, 1955, minutes showed David Freeman and Marvin Landers (?) as volunteers. There was also a note in those minutes that said there were eleven members but they were not listed.

As mentioned earlier, over the years in addition to the regular police officers, dating back to the mid-1950s there were volunteers originally referred to as "special" or simply "volunteer" police who worked with the full time police in the department to supplement their efforts in a variety of situations in the department. However, the volunteers or reserve officers later became part of the civil

Opposite, starting from the top:

This 1953 photograph combination shows the portion of the old city hall (left) and the police station (right) that was added to the building for a council room where the public could attend the meetings. The police department's only patrol car is parked along the curb.

Police department facilities on 1286 Bank Street. This address was built and dedicated in 1970.

Smyrna Police Department 1995. First row, left to right: Ptl. Gene Crawford, Ptl. Mike Conti, Ptl. Clyde Cook, Ptl. Kerry McCoy, Ptl. Joe Tyson, Ptl. Norman Johnson, Ptl. Tim Strickland, Ptl. William Hegewood, Ptl. Ken Spencer, Capt. David Littlejohn, Ptl. Clark Pino. Second row: Det. Mike Moore, Ptl. Mitch Plumb, Capt. Fred Brack, Det. Chuck Wade, Sue Aiken, Francine Humpharies, Desiree' Caysey, Comm. Operator Haley Alexander, Det. George Folds, Det. Billy Hood, Sgt. Jerry Waldrop, Det. Officer Bill Hanke, Det. K. K. Wrozier. Third row: Ptl. Biller, Ptl., Jimmy Chastain, Major Kent Sims, Ptl. Cleveland McDuffie, Ptl. Larry Mazzoni, Park Ranger Ken Kelmer, Ptl. Randy Black, Lt. Douglas Carlson, Det. Larry Wood, Ptl. Clyde Cook. Fourth row: Det. Henry Cambron, Det. Bill Geter, Ptl. Keith Zgonc, Ptl. Layson Andrews, Ptl. Robert Harvey, Ptl. Sam Slover, Sgt. Joe Marks, Ptl. Ron Eaton, Ptl. Mike Ely, Ptl,. Barry McCurdy, Ptl. Frank Durrance, Chief Stanley Hook. Fifth row: Comm. Operator Randy Rogers, Lt. Joe Martin, Ptl. Scott White. It was two more years before police department personnel moved into the new department building at 2646 Atlanta Road.

Opposite, starting from the top:

The Smyrna police department on
April 26, 1956. Left to right:
Patrolman M. L. "Robie" Robinson
later served as sergeant and became
chief in 1958, Patrolman Herbert
Brown, Chief Paul Epps, Patrolman
J. L. Edge lost a leg when the driver of
a car he stopped put it in reverse and
pinned him between the two vehicles,
Patrolman Norman Castile later went
to the Cobb County police
department. Sgt. Marshall Tanner
later was promoted to chief and
Officer R. D. Patterson went to the
Cobb County police.

Smyrna police department, c. 1960.
Left to right: Thad Bates, Lee Poss,
Herbert Brown, Recorder Court Judge
C. V. Reeves, Don Atkinson, M. L.
"Robbie" Robinson, R. B. Brown,
? Neeley. Seated: James Adams,
Wayne Ellis.

Smyrna police department 1962-
1963. Front row, left to right: Horace
Holland, J. L. Edge, Buck Rudasill,
Chief Robert L "Bob" Drake, Sgt.
Clifford Brown, Barbara Nix, Police
Committee Chairman Ward 4
Councilman Harold Smith, Back row:
Thad Bates, Raymond Lowry, Bobby
Parker, Lee Chandler, James Free,
unknown, Bobby Stephens.

defense, first under the command of Director
Beverly Dubuc and later Director Jim Farley.
Unfortunately those records showing who
participated in the program at the time are not
available (if they still exist).

In 1972 Tilden C. Ledbetter, who had been a
volunteer for some fifteen years or so for the
police, fire, ambulance and emergency services,
approached Chief Robert Drake and some of the
other senior officers about reorganizing the
reserve police force (volunteers) that had dwin-
dled to only four members. Ledbetter had actually worked full-time for the department for
about six months in 1967 as a radio operator
and office clerk because of a shortage of man-
power. The chief was receptive to the idea and
asked him to present a plan. With the help of
Captain John Young and Communications
Officer G. R. Galloup, Ledbetter went about
gathering information for the organization. This
included application forms, record checks, fin-
gerprinting, uniforms, equipment, and training
etc. As soon as all this was done the program
was submitted to Chief Drake and the mayor
and council and was approved to move forward.

Rules of operations were adopted that the
reserve officers had to agree to follow pertaining
to dress, equipment, knowledge, courtesy,
deportment, demeanor, attitude and all the
other characteristics required that would give
the general public confidence and respect for
the reserve officers.

The number one rule, of the twelve, was
that each volunteer reserve officer had to ride
patrol with a full-time officer at least eight hours
per month.

In May 1972 applications for the auxiliary
force were accepted and the process was the same
as the regular officers including photographs,
fingerprints, record checks and the like.

The first training classes started with 12
applicants on June 10, 1972, to run for eight
weeks but only 8 officers completed the course
on July 22. The second training class started
August 26, 1972, and 14 officers completed the
course on October 14. With the completion of
that class the volunteer force was brought to 22
volunteers and enabled the Smyrna Police
Department to have available 50 officers for
duty in emergencies and special security work.

For many years, other than the full-time
chief of police and others he designated, Reserve
Major T. C. Ledbetter was in charge of the
reserve force. After reorganization the actual
chain of command changed from time to time
but basically was as follows: Robert L. Drake,
chief of Smyrna police department; Captain
John Young, a full-time employee of the Smyrna
police department was designated chief of the
reserve police; T. C. Ledbetter, assistant chief of
the reserve; full-time officer G. R. Galloup was
designated (for a period of time) captain of the
reserve police.

The basic training for the auxiliary or reserve
officers enabled eight of the reserves to go
to work in full-time law enforcement. David
Littlejohn, Danny Drake, Bart Jones, Mike
Brown, Jack Giesler, Jim Bone, Douglas Cole
and Dale Sims.

By 1975 the reserve force had grown to 26
members and with available records we have
been able to identify the following that served
the city as a volunteer. Charlie Adams, Michael
Babin, James Berry, Jerry Biggs, J. C. Blankenship,
Richard K. Britton, Michael Brown, Doyal A. Cain,
Donald F. Carney, Marvin Chapman, Douglas A.
Cole, Darrell R. Crowder, Carl Davis, Sr., Larry
Michael DeWitt, Robert M. Dunton, Garland
Estes, Larry Graves, George Hanson, Richard
Hartline, Robert January, Albert A. Kirt, Joseph W.
LaLonde, Michael W. Lanning, Carl C. Latini,
James G. Lipscomb, David Littlejohn, Paul W.
Meek, John Mike Porterfield, Harvey Lee Robert,
James E. Seay, Dale Sims, Francis L. Sims, George
Stevens III, A. B. Underhill, Carl Ussing, Fred A.
Wallace, William D. West, Donald Williams, Jr.,
Terrell Wilson, and Nathan D. Young, Jr.

There may have been others but this is all
we have been able to identify with available
records. Interviews with former Mayor John C.
Porterfield, former Mayor Frank Johnson and

former volunteer policeman Carl Ussing failed to reveal other names or when the volunteer force was actually discontinued.

In the meantime the tremendous growth in the metropolitan area and especially in Cobb County, from a population of 61,830 in 1960 to the current population of more than 900,000 and Smyrna's population inside the city limits is expected to exceed 50,000 when the 2010 census is complete, brought about the necessity of cooperating with other departments in certain law enforcement efforts.

At about the same time, September 1989, the Smyrna City Council approved the establishment of a S.W.A.T. team. (Special Weapons and Tactics) after Captain Bill Hayes made a report to the council. He had been working on the proposal for almost a year. The estimated time for the startup would be about eight months before the program could be carried out. Team members would be volunteers from the regular force and there would be no extra compensation for being a team member. Thirty-one officers volunteered for the duty. The list was narrowed to fourteen after physical training tests were administered. Captain Hayes said the annual operating budget would be about $20,000 for the unit. Councilman John Steeley said that $90,000 would be needed for start-up equipment like protective vests, shields, and some sharpshooter rifles.

A year before, in September 1988, the Smyrna police department had already received approval from mayor and council to convert to a semi-automatic, more powerful handgun for its officers. The weapon chosen to replace the old 357 Smith and Wesson 686 revolver that held six bullets was the Glock 17. It could hold twenty rounds and was much easier to reload than the Smith and Wesson. At the time the Glock could be purchased for $511 and it is manufactured in Smyrna by Glock, Inc.

Major Kent Sims was quoted by the *Marietta Daily Journal* as saying the transition to the Glock for the 73 officers would begin in November and be completed over a period of time.

Technology in communications also had changed. When the police station was on Atlanta Road there was a "radio operator" that manned the transmitter 24/7 with a large antenna on the station. On occasions the radio signal would hardly reach to Dickson's Shopping

Center on the west side of Smyrna. The few patrol cars the department had, for the most part, could not communicate with each other and most help calls had to be sent through the "radio operator." Cell phones were a God-send to public safety organizations like fire, police and medical rescue personnel.

❖

Mayor Guy Duncan, left is shown with Smyrna's entire paid fire and police personnel for the city in 1954. Left to right: Officers C. Broughton May, Grady Trailer, Albert B. Hodnett, Marshall Tanner, ? Stokes, Ray Schwarts, Fire Chief John Thomas, and firefighter and future Chief Joe Porterfield. This photo was made between April 1954 and December 6, 1954, when Mayor Duncan died. Official minutes show that Marshall Tanner was hired April 7, 1954, and the first full-time fire chief, John Thomas and the first full-time firefighter, Joe Porterfield were hired April 26, 1954. The building on the left was the Justice of the Peace Courthouse that eventually became the Smyrna health clinic.

By 1990 Smyrna's population had grown to almost 31,000 and a portion of the growth in population was attributed to the annexation of large and small tracts of land on South Cobb Drive near the recently opened East-West Connector and Interstate 285. Because of this expansion of the city limits planning started for the construction of Smyrna's second combination police and fire facility. (The first one had been demolished in the 1960s) and the mayor and council approved the purchase of a one-acre tract of land for almost $300,000 on the east side of South Cobb Drive just south of the East-West Connector near Lois and Main Streets.

The construction of the new facility that had its open house and dedication ceremonies on December 17, 1991, provided the police department with enough space to house the STEP unit and the motorcycle operation. Lt. Mike Brown was the commander of the STEP unit when the facility opened.

The new 6,500 square foot building had two 65-foot bays for fire equipment, sleeping and eating quarters, a locker room, showers, and exercise equipment for twelve fire personnel. This new location enabled the police and fire department to respond quicker to emergencies in this fast growing commercial, industrial and retail area. This is the city's only satellite police station and it is at least three miles south of the main police department headquarters on Atlanta Road in the heart of Smyrna.

The mission statement of the police department says it is a full-service municipal department, comprised of 93 sworn officers, 21 jail personnel, 22 full and part-time communications officers and 13 administrative support personnel.

The primary purpose of the Smyrna police department is to maintain social order within prescribed ethical and constitutional limits, while providing professional law enforcement services. To attain this, the department enforces the law in a fair and impartial manner, recognizing both the statutory and judicial limitations of police authority and the constitutional rights of all persons. Recognizing that no law enforcement agency can operate at its maximum potential without supportive input from the citizens it serves, the Smyrna police department actively solicits and encourages the cooperation of all citizens in decreasing opportunities for crime in facilitating the maximum use of resources.

FIRE DEPARTMENT

Unlike the Smyrna police department that, over the years, has had at least 46 different police chiefs that we are aware of, in the 138 years since the Village of Smyrna was first incorporated in 1872, and 113 years since its second incorporation as the town of Smyrna, in 1897, the Smyrna fire department has had only 7 full-time fire chiefs. John Thomas, P. A. Bond, Joe Porterfield, Don Atkinson, Hubert Cochran, Larry Williams and Jason Lanyon.

In spite of the fact that Smyrna had suffered numerous fire losses of residences and commercial structures in the 1800s there was no discussion in the available minutes of the city about fire protection until 1928. The city itself suffered a major loss of all its records from 1872 until 1923 when the city hall and fire shed on Roswell Street, near the present location of the G. B. Williams Memorial Park, burned to the ground. Probably one reason there was no urgency in having a fire department was because the city had no water system until the late 1920s and even then, the water was obtained from a series of wells and springs on the east side of town. The water was distributed through one-and-a-half-inch pipes and there would not have been sufficient volume to fight a fire.

Prior to the city hall burning, newspaper accounts from the *Marietta Journal* and the *Cobb County Times* on January 9, 1902, reported that one of the boarding houses at the Belmont farm was destroyed by fire due to a defective flue and the loss was $5,000. On March 3, 1924, the papers reported that Maggie Simpson's home was destroyed by fire.

On Monday, March 30, 1925, several buildings in downtown Smyrna burned including the original frame First Baptist Church building that had been constructed in 1886. The fire apparently originated in the church building, like the Belmont fire, through a faulty flue. The Baptists had sold their old building to the Nelms Masonic Lodge after they constructed their new rock building at the intersection of Church and King Streets. Both the church building and the Masonic Lodge were being used temporarily as schools because a school building constructed the year before burned shortly after it opened for classes in September 1924. A dwelling owned by Mrs. Harrison also burned. The townspeople set up a bucket brigade from the spring that was located near the present day Second Baptist Church on Atlanta Street but it was not enough to keep the buildings from burning. The Marietta fire department, six miles north of Smyrna, responded to the call for help but by the time they arrived the structures were gone. They did help keep the fire from spreading to more buildings in the area.

Dr. Nelms was instrumental in organizing the Nelms Masonic Lodge that was named in his honor. He operated a clinic in Smyrna for the treatment of clients with the opium habit. He guaranteed that his treatment would cure them or they didn't have to pay.

Another fire in the heart of Smyrna that consumed the two-story office and drug store building of Dr. W. T. Pace occurred in 1915. Only the bricks were salvaged from the building and a new building was being constructed shortly thereafter. The present Smyrna Museum adjoins the old site.

Perhaps members of the Smyrna city council had some of these fires in mind when they recorded the following in their March 1928 minutes: There was a mass meeting of citizens of the town held March 26, 1928, for the purpose of organizing a fire company. The following were elected officers: W. P. Coggeshall, chief; J. P. Anderson, day chief; W. R. Jackson, night captain; W. B. Carson, assistant. Said officers were to be under jurisdiction of the mayor and council and subject to discharge for cause by said mayor and council. Fire department

historian, retired assistant chief, Sam Wehunt said that Coggeshall's wife was interviewed in 1988 and confirmed that.

Ten years later on September 6, 1938, the mayor and council voted to "reorganize" the fire department and pay volunteer firefighters fifty cents for each call they answered and the chief would be paid $1 for each call he answered.

The names of some of the people who probably helped to "reorganize" the earliest fire department has been provided by Sam Wehunt. He is currently researching and writing a comprehensive history of the Smyrna fire department. The family names, prominent in the 1920s, are still familiar in Smyrna today and many of them take part in the civic, social and religious life of the community: J. P. Anderson, March 6, 1928; Robert Austin, January 15, 1938; Arthur Bacon, 1934; Lark Baldwin, June 15, 1924; Roy Barfield, June 15, 1924; Whit B. Carson, March 6, 1928; P. M. "Pat" Edwards; J. Mayes Hamby, June 15, 1928; W. R. Jackson, March 6, 1928; Max Parnell, June 15, 1939. There may have been others but we are unable to identify them at this time. However, Sam has been able to document the existence of a piece of fire fighting equipment identified as a hose cart with some type of chemical fire retardant.

At the next meeting on October 3, 1938, there was an extensive motion passed that established rules for operating the volunteer department fixing a specific night for one monthly meeting for discussions and for fire drills and training. Each person attending the meeting would receive $1. The fee paid for actually attending a fire would be $1.25 for all personnel. Names would be recorded of who

Several innovations in the department's approach to police work were carried out. One of these was the establishment of a county-wide DUI Task Force. It was made up of representatives of all of Cobb County's police and sheriff's departments as well as from the six Cobb municipalities: Left to right: Kent Brooks, Powder Springs police department; H. D. Floyd, Cobb County sheriff's department; Field Training Officer P. L. Wood, Cobb County police department; R. Higgins, Marietta police department; and Assistant Project Director J. W. Waldrop, Smyrna police department. M. L. Warren, Marietta police department; and R. E. Purdue, Cobb County police department. In the doorway is Project Director Sgt. Ken Ball, Marietta police department.

PHOTOGRAPH COURTESY OF MARK MILLER AND THE SMYRNA POLICE DEPARTMENT.

were present after the hose and equipment were returned to the truck. (apparently the truck that was used by the public works personnel). The motion also contained a provision for insurance to cover the firefighters while on duty and a requirement that a report would be made each month at the city council meeting. In the following years and months there was no mention of reports from the fire department in the minutes but on occasions the monthly financial report would indicate a few dollars had been paid to fire department personnel.

The next mention of the fire department was on January 1, 1940. A motion was made to reduce the department to six men. The fireman who attended a fire inside the city would be paid $1.35 If they answered a call outside the city limits the city did not pay. They were strictly on their own. Unfortunately no names of any of the firefighters appeared in the council minutes.

At the January 5, 1942, council meeting a motion was made to purchase a "modern" fire truck At their next meeting on January 27, 1942, they voted to place an order with the American-LaFrance Fire Equipment Company. However, the nation was now at war because of the Japanese attack on Pearl Harbor December 7, 1941, and the request had to be directed to the war production board for approval. The board refused Smyrna's request for the top priority fire truck and at the same meeting a Mr. George Pannell from Monroe, Georgia applied for the job of city marshall and fire chief. No action was taken on the application. On May 6 after council had been refused permission to buy a "modern" fire truck, the council voted to buy a pickup truck instead and use it temporarily for the vol-

unteer fire department. The pickup truck was bought from Carl Smith for $360 in May 1942. In March 1943 the city bought 500 feet of new hose to be carried on the truck and three months later on June 7, the council voted to build a fire house and work shop behind the city hall.

Because of World War II, the city also created a civil defense council made up of the following:

Mayor John Tatum	chairman
G. C. Green	information and publicity
C. Mayes Hamby	fire department
G. O. Garvin	police
J. J. Hill	warden
F. D. Cargal	emergency medical service
J. R. Arrington	public works
C. C. Terrell	utilities

On April 10, 1944, the city purchased 6 rain coats, 6 rain hats and 2 pairs of rubber boots for the fire department. An entry in the minute books on September 10, 1945, indicated that a Mr. W. H. Bennett was hired to take over fire and sanitation departments and be paid $200 per month for his services. The effective date for him to start the job was October 1, 1945.

During the month of October there was a disturbance at the local R & M Restaurant and it resulted in one of the policemen being discharged and a volunteer policeman no longer being able to "wear a badge and carry a gun" or assist the regular police officer. This brought about a great deal of turmoil in the council. At the regular monthly meeting on November 5, 1945, with all council members present and Mayor Wootten absent, Mayor pro tem Pressley presided at the meeting and handled a variety of items including a discussion about a disturbance in a restaurant in October.

In the same meeting, the recently hired Mr. W. H. Bennett, the new head of the fire and sanitation department, made his report of the work that had been accomplished in October. After the report Councilwoman Lorena Pace Pruitt made a motion that Mr. Bennett be made superintendant over the waterworks, sewerage, streets, sanitation and fire departments. His complete duties were outlined in the minutes and he was to have full charge of all work and men including the authority to hire and fire. He was to make a monthly report to the city council. Another stipulation was that he

Another feature of Smyrna's modern department is the use of motorcycles especially in traffic enforcement. This unit was introduced to Smyrna in 1989. Left to right: Officer Robert J. Martin, City Counilman John Steely, Officer Sam C. Glover, Smyrna Mayor Max Bacon and Officer Ricky A. Lee. They work in connection with the S. T. E. P. (Selective Traffic Enforcement Patrol) unit.

would be "elected Superintendant at a regular meeting of the council."

A special call meeting of the Mayor and Council was held on November 19, 1945, and again called to order by Mayor pro-tem Pressley. Mayor Wooten was present but he refused to preside because he did not call the meeting. Mr. Bennett's work and salary was brought up at the meeting and after a long discussion the council voted three to one to pay him his previously agreed on salary and he was also made responsible for all the city's tools and equipment and he was instructed to partition off an area in the city garage to store the tools and equipment and to keep it locked.

Another called meeting was held on November 23 and city clerk Maude Paris read Mayor Wooten's resignation dated November 20, 1945.

Dear Sirs: Due to confusion and disrespect to me by the councilmen, as Mayor, I hereby tender my resignation, effective immediately.

The council accepted the resignation The date set for the election of a new mayor was December 29.

Councilwoman Mrs. Lorena Pace Pruitt won the election 236 to 61 over former city councilman C. Mayes Hamby to become Smyrna's first and only female mayor.

At the same meeting on November 23, a policeman was fired and the much discussed Mr. Bennett was designated to take over that job also until the next meeting. At the first meeting of the new administration on January 9, 1946, Carl Mohon was elected to take the place of Mr. W. H. Bennett as superintendent of the sanitation, water and street departments at a salary of $160 per month.

The next mention of the fire department in the minutes came on June 17, 1946, when the city council members authorized Mayor Lorena Pace Pruitt to seek out a new fire truck for the city. At the same meeting Wilton Carson, Jr., was given permission to organize a fire department and help train twelve men.

In regards to the new truck, Councilman Homer Durham, who had been elected on November 2, to the 1947 term related a story in his memoirs that the city needed a fire truck because the city's only truck was used for other

work in the day time and not available for the volunteer fire department. "It was not long", Mr. Durham said, "that the City of Atlanta, through the influence of "Mr. Willie Medlin, an Atlanta fireman who lived in Smyrna, agreed to give Smyrna a pumper and install it if Smyrna would provide the chassis and of course we did and that was the first genuine fire truck we had. Mr. Earl Cobb who owned the Shell filling station north of Smyrna was our first volunteer fire chief."

Two years later on November 7, 1949, the city council authorized Volunteer Chief Earl Cobb to construct a building at 409 Atlanta Street to house the fire truck and equipment. In the March 4, 1950, council meeting the city made an agreement with Chief Cobb that the city would pay him $30 per month to house the fire truck and the equipment and $50 per month for his part-time job as fire chief. The city also signed a note with the Bank of Smyrna for $2,014 along with Chief Cobb to finance the construction of the building.

A comprehensive fifty-year planning study of Smyrna conducted by Georgia Tech in 1953 showed the Smyrna fire department made up of Chief Cobb and eight volunteers who were not named. The chief was paid $50 per month and each of the firemen were paid $10 per month. The assets of the fire department at that time were two fire trucks, 1800 feet of 2 1/2 inch-hose, 200 feet of 1-inch hose, 200 feet of 3/4 inch-hose, a 220-gallon booster tank on each truck and four ladders for a total of 100 feet.

Although the Georgia Tech study did not list the names of the individuals who made up the volunteer department, minutes of the volunteer fire department, various lists and published newspaper account show that in the late 1940s, '50s, '60s and early 1970s, the following were members for varying lengths of time. Bob

Left: Combination fire-police satellite facility on South Cobb Drive near the East-West Connector, opened in December 1991.

Right: Near the front entrance to the city of Smyrna police department on Atlanta Road stands this statue of a police officer with two small children. The statue is made in the likeness of retired Smyrna Police Captain David Farmer who served the city for thirty-eight years. He was known for his work with children in the schools. The inscription under the statues expresses the philosophy of the police personnel. The bronze marker on the left lists the names of Smyrna citizens, businesses, civic organizations and others who provided the funds for creating the memorial in honor of the Smyrna police department.

❖

Above: Another dwelling that burned in the heart of Smyrna was located on the southeast corner of Church and King Streets. It was a ten-room house that had been constructed by Dr. John Nelms in July 1895. The house is seen in the background of this photograph of Judith Rice Lowry, with her son, Parker, in the wagon. She lived across King Street from the Nelms residence. It burned shortly after this photograph was made on July 22, 1937. The site of Dr. Nelms' home is the approximate location of the original non-denominational brush-arbor religious campground worship center that started in 1838 and from which Smyrna got its name and eventually led to the establishment of the Smyrna Methodist Church. A couple of years after the fire, Dr. D. C. Landers, owner of the Smyrna Drug Store, and father of Bob Landers, one of the early volunteer firemen, constructed a brick house that still occupies the lot today.

PHOTOGRAPH COURTESY OF PARKER LOWRY.

Below: Ambulance and emergency rescue vehicle purchased with donations from the general public by the volunteer fire department and a contribution from the city of Smyrna. The volunteer fire department conducted a variety of fundraisers in the mid-1950s to finance the purchase of these rescue units for the citizens. Dances, concerts, BBQs, plays and selling hot dogs, hamburgers and other food in a booth at the North Georgia State Fair. They also signed notes to borrow money from the bank guaranteeing the loan.

Austin, Arthur Bacon, Harold Gann, T. H. Gann, Bobby Carson, Chris Dunn, Marcellus Hamby, Harold Davis, C. B. May, Harold Puckett, J. C. Strayhorne, Bobby Landers, Jerry Fouts, Don Kolda, Ralph Grady, Bob Logan, Tilden Ledbetter, Randall Barrentine, Jim Burson, Al Burris, Spurgeon Ware, Marston Tuck, Marshall Tanner, W. B. Stewart, Clyde Herren, James Lacey, Phil Page, Lee Poss, Harley Morris, John Mann, Wit Carson, Ted Barrett and others. Assistant Chief Sam Wehunt identified approximately 125 people that were part of the volunteer department at one time or the other.

The volunteers were a dedicated group of individuals who had a love for the work as volunteer fire fighters and were dedicated to the city. They paid dues to be members of the group, they conducted a variety of fund raisers to provide funds for equipment that the city was unable to afford at the time and above all they gave their time with little compensation.

When the West Spring facility was in operation both as a fire and police station, the volunteers raised money to purchase radio equipment for the station. They also helped by answering the telephone. When a call came in with a report of an emergency the siren, mounted on the railroad station or later on other downtown buildings, would be sounded and the volunteers who lived or worked in the downtown area would hurry to the station and board the fire trucks and equip themselves for handling the emergency. Sometimes the fire truck would be driven to the home of the volunteers to pick them up if they were in the vicinity of the fire.

In addition to answering the fire call, the volunteers had financed the purchase of two emergency rescue vehicles. Harold Davis was put in charge of this operation and received support from the whole volunteer group and the city of Smyrna, mayor and council.

With hundreds of people pouring into Smyrna every month in the early 1950s and the South's largest shopping center, Belmont Hills, scheduled to open in just seven months (November 1954) the mayor and city council members felt it was time to give the volunteers some full-time help. At the March 17, 1954, meeting of the council the city authorized the sale of the old fire truck and it was sold to the American Legion Post 160 on May 3, for $175. The council, at the April 5 meeting had approved an expenditure of $1,590 to renovate the combination fire and police station on West Spring Street. At the next meeting on April 15, the council authorized the hiring of two full-time employees for the fire department. On April 26, 1954, John Thomas was hired as the first full-time fire chief. Joe Porterfield was hired as the number two full-time man the same day.

Chief Thomas served until August 9, 1955, when his resignation was accepted "with regrets" by the mayor and council. Eight days later, P. A. Bond was named acting chief and then at the first city council meeting of the new city Mayor Jimmy Quarles' administration January 9, 1956, he was appointed (elected) by mayor and council to the position of fire chief. Chief Bond resigned in the spring of 1958 and Assistant Chief C. C. "Joe" Porterfield was promoted to chief, a position he held with the city until his retirement December 31, 1975.

Many changes took place in the department while Porterfield was chief. When he started with the department the Number 1 station was the old remodeled cannery.

By 1970 the city had gained almost another 10,000 people. The official census count for that year was 19,158. Much of the growth had been on the east side of town and the city limits had been extended almost to the Four Lane Highway (today's U. S. 41 and Cobb Parkway). In December 1972 the city received a check from the state of Georgia for $69,818. as part of a recently passed revenue sharing law by the Georgia Legislature. Part of the money was used for constructing Smyrna's first fire department substation.

Smyrna's first fire substation was on Spring Road across from the Argyle Elementary School during the administration of Mayor John Porterfield. The design departed from the traditional station architecture because the area was mostly residential except for the city's Jonquil Park that adjoined the fire department land. The park had been acquired through a general obligation streets and recreation bond referendum in 1961 in the administration of Mayor J. B. "Jake" Ables. It was designed to house two vehicles and a staff of three with expansion room for fifteen.

Chief Porterfield retired December 31, 1975, and long-time Assistant Chief Don Atkinson was appointed chief at the first city council meeting on March 22, 1976. He had been employed by the city since 1955—the first two years as a policeman—and the remainder as a fireman, which had been his childhood dream.

The very next month, in April, the second substation, originally named Station Number 3, was later changed to Station 2 to coincide with the police districts and the original No. 2 shown above was changed to 3. One of his first jobs as chief was to staff the new station.

Located at 640 Concord Road a quarter of a mile west of the South Cobb Drive intersection, it was in the perfect place to be able to respond much quicker to any emergency in the fast growing commercial area that is home to the Dicksons Shopping Center that had been annexed into the city in 1959. The Crossings Shopping Center, a variety of restaurants, Bennett Woods and Bennett Woods North subdivisions, Concord Woods, Lake Drive, Green Forest subdivision and three schools: Brown Elementary, Griffin Middle School and King Springs Elementary are located in the vicinity. Also, the recently opened Smyrna Hospital was nearby. The substation was located just a few feet from the site of a major fire at a cabinetmaking company that had burned just a few years before.

During the last year or so before his retirement in June 1981 the city had been discussing the possibility of merging the Smyrna fire department with the Cobb County fire department. Smyrna's starting pay for firefighters was a little more than the county, $931 per month to $915 but the county pay increased more rapidly than Smyrna's.

About the same time a special purpose local option sales tax referendum for the county was voted down by the citizens and the loss, in part, was attributed to fire department merger talk. Ward 2 councilman at the time (current Mayor Max Bacon) was chairman of the fire committee

❖

Above: Smyrna's first full-time paid Fire Chief John Thomas.

Below: Smyrna's first full-time paid firefighter Joe Porterfield.

Bottom: Fire Chief Don Atkinson pictured at his retirement June 1981.

Left: Smyrna public works truck used as the first fire truck by the volunteer fire department in the early 1940s.
PHOTOGRAPH COURTESY OF PATRICIA DURHAM BALDWIN.

Right: Smyrna's "modern" fire truck was delivered to the city hall in 1947. Mayor Lorena Pace Pruitt is in the drivers seat. The people identified with numbers are: City Councilman E. E. Jackson, Councilman Claude L Groce, Carl Mohon, superintendent of the sanitation and water departments, Volunteer Fire Chief Earl Cobb. Councilman Homer Durham noted in his memoirs for the Smryna Historical Society that Mrs. Pruitt could not drive a vehicle and someone had to drive her wherever she went.
PHOTOGRAPH COURTESY OF PATRICIA DURHAM BALDWIN.

at the time, after talks with the county officials in the spring of 1982 he concluded the proposal was dead. The county claimed it would cost it over a million dollars to merge and would only realize about $100,000 in returned taxes.

Shortly after Chief Atkinson's retirement, long-time Assistant Chief Hubert Cochran was named "acting" chief. He had been employed by the city since March 5, 1957.

Chief Cochran took over in another period of growth when the population went from 20,312 to 30,804—some of it due to annexations and some of it by new people moving into the city.

It was during his service as chief that the department acquired its first Aerial Platform fire truck. It was purchased from Emergency One Inc. of Ocala, Florida, and Chief Cochran went to Ocala and drove it to Smyrna on September 9, 1983. The cost of the 42-foot-long truck that had a ladder that could reach to the top of Smyrna's tallest building—10 story Smyrna Towers on South Cobb Drive—with its 125 foot reach. The $335,338 cost of the vehicle was more than the budget for the whole city administration department in the 1950s. Hubert Cochran served in the capacity of "acting" chief longer than any other person.

For his replacement the Smyrna civil service board tested, interviewed and investigated seven candidates for the chief's position and sent their recommendations to the mayor and council. They finally selected Larry Williams to become chief and his appointment was effective February 18, 1985. He is a native Georgian, having been born near Athens. His family moved to Gainesville when he was three years old. After finishing high school and

attending Gainesville Junior College he went to work for the Suburban fire department of Gainesville and later became the chief. Eventually Hall County formed it's own fire department and he was asked to be chief there. After the Hall County fire department was disbanded and fire service was privatized. he went to work for the Georgia Fire Academy. There he was a program specialist teaching and developing courses and supervising other instructors. He heard about the vacancy at Smyrna and since the Academy was moving to Forsyth and he didn't want to go there, he applied for the Smyrna position.

One of immediate results of Chief Williams efforts was a reduction in the fire rating for the city to a 3 which lowered fire insurance rates about forty percent for residences and commercial structures inside the city limits.

His arrival coincided with the city's beginning efforts to improve the image of Smyrna and redevelopment of the downtown area and the chief and his staff of dedicated men and women worked together to develop a plan that would make Smyrna fire and emergency agencies "second to none" to quote the chief. In 1987 Smyrna established its 911 center and one of the fire personnel, Lt. John Taylor, was selected to help set up the center and get it into operation. He eventually returned to his regular duties. At Chief William's urging and with skillful planning on his part and the help of the men and women of the department, a plan was submitted to the city for the purchase of three new pumpers. The plan was approved in June and the pumpers were secured from the Pierce Manufacturing Company for $418,876.

As mentioned earlier, over the years most of the emergency rescue squad had been made up of volunteers, first working with the volunteer fire department, then thru the volunteer civil defense department with Mrs. Beverly Dubuc as director during the time of the Cuban missle crisis. After Mrs. Dubuc resigned in 1970, Mayor Harold Smith asked Jim Farley, who was a longtime volunteer, if he would take over the department. He did and he continued to direct the emergency management program and organization for the next seventeen years ending in 1987. He submitted his resignation to Mayor Bacon and the council with the recommendation that the director's job be made full-time. The emergency rescue group was merged into the fire department. Under Chief William's leadership the transition was made smoothly and with the well trained EMTs and paramedics on the staff, the department assumed the duties without any problem.

At the request of the chief and his staff, the city allocated $27,000 in the 1987 budget for the purchase of a rescue truck. Fire department personnel spent the next four months equipping the new vehicle for service by using items removed from other vehicles owned by the department. An article in the *Marietta Daily Journal* quoted Chief Williams as saying if they had ordered the truck fully equipped it would have cost around $50,000.

However it was two more years before Chief Williams and other fire department personnel were able to realize their part of the "dream" in the downtown redevelopment project. with the same architectural design as Phase I and 2. The Smyrna Library, community center, and Village Green were completed in August 1991, the city hall in 1996, and the police and jail complex in 1997, the 125 anniversary of Smyrna's first incorporation in 1872.

The red letter day for the new Number 1 Fire Station and its move to 2620 Atlanta Road and possibly the highlight of Chief Williams' career with the Smyrna department was August 7, 1999.

The keynote speaker for the event was State Representative Randy Sauder who praised the

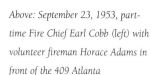

Above: September 23, 1953, part-time Fire Chief Earl Cobb (left) with volunteer fireman Horace Adams in front of the 409 Atlanta Street building.

Below: Smyrna Cannery building on West Spring Street. This 1958 photograph depicts all full-time fire department personnel standing in front of the West Spring Street Station that opened in 1954. Left to right: Assistant Chief Don Atkinson, Hubert Cochran, Sammy Sanford, E. D. Rampley, Church Harrison, James Swafford, Carl Carson and Chief Joe Porterfield. However, the volunteer firefighters continued working with the department until 1975 when it was disbanded. Enough full-time men had been hired to keep up with the growth of the city. That old building was replaced by a new one on the same site during the administration of Mayor George Kreeger and opened in June 1966.

❖

Top: The original No. 2 station on Spring Road adjacent to Jonquil Park, and across from Argyle Elementary School was demolished and replaced by a larger one and renamed No. 3.

Above: No. 1 fire station on West Spring Street, 1966-1999.

Below: Station No. 3 on Concord Road opened April 1976. It was later changed to No. 2.

Dedication ceremonies were held inside the garage portion of the new 2.5 million dollar facility that was "paid for in cash" according to Ron Newcomb, the chairman of the city's fire committee. The program was concluded with refreshments, a tour of the facilities by everyone, and a gathering around the three outside flag poles with a salute to the American flag as the Georgia and City of Smyrna flags waved nearby.

Chief Larry Williams retired April 16, 2005, and brought to a close his 41 years of fighting fires—the last 19 of them as chief of the Smyrna fire department. Retirement ceremonies were held in the training room in Station Number 1 with many of the city employees, firefighters, police officers and other well-wishers attending.

Four months later in August 2005 the city elevated assistant fire chief Jason Lanyon to the chief position. He was originally hired June 10, 1996, to work with the Smyrna fire rescue department after having served in Cherokee County for the Little River and the Hickory Flat fire departments.

Since Chief Lanyon assumed the duties many improvements and upgrades of equipment and facilities have occurred.

Dedication ceremonies for the station that replaced Smyrna's first fire department substation was held March 11, 2006. City Administrator Wayne Wright was the master of ceremonies for the dedication. Mayor Max Bacon, Fire Department Chaplin Brian Beaty, Council members Ron Newcomb, Ward 2; Melleny Pritchett, Ward 1; Wade Lnenicka,Ward 6; and Smyrna Fire Chief Jason Lanyon participated in the program.

Other members of the city council at the time were: Bill Scoggins, Ward 3; Mike McNabb, Ward 4; Jimmy Smith, Ward 5; and Pete Wood, Ward 7.

men and women of the fire department for their devotion to duty and putting their lives on line daily for the benefit of the citizens of Smyrna.

Mayor Bacon welcomed everyone and introduced the members of the city council and their spouses: Pete Wood, Ward 7; Wade Lnenicka, Ward 6; Jack Cramer, Ward 5; Jim Hawkins, Ward 4; Bill Scoggins, Ward 3; Ron Newcomb, Ward 2; and Charlene Capilouto, Ward 1. Other dignitaries present were State Representative Rich Golick, Cobb County District 2 Commissioner Joe Thompson, Cobb Superior Court Judge Ken Nix, school board member Curt Johnston, former Mayor Harold Smith, former City Councilmen John Patrick and Bob Davis, and retired Fire Chief Hubert Cochran.

That was the last major construction project of the Smyrna fire department. However, the equipment and services have continued to be updated and improved and the efficiency and expertise of the department personnel have been recognized by numerous organizations.

A notable event in the life of the department occurred when long-time Assistant Smyrna Fire Department Chief Samuel L. Wehunt, who had joined the department on January 2. 1975, retired after 34 years of service on January 31, 2009. He was honored in ceremonies in the training facility of the Number 1 station on Atlanta Road. There were many visitors and well-wishers from all departments of the city as well as fire and police departments and the general public He was recognized for his devotion to duty as a professional firefighter and his personal involvement in Smyrna civic, social and community programs and activities.

Retired assistant chief and fire department historian, Sam Wehunt, in his soon to be published history that has a very long name, "From Hose Carts To Hi-Rise, a Scrapbook History of Fire, Fire-fighting & Rescue Services in the City of Smyrna, Georgia, 1864-2010" relates many stories and events about the Smyrna fire department and chronicles dozens of articles and photographs from the *Marietta Journal*, *Cobb County Times*, and the archives of the Smyrna Museum.

The current city of Smyrna fire department has four areas of emphasis and expertise: emergency service training, bureau of fire prevention and emergency management. Each day, the Smyrna fire department excels at meeting needs and answering calls, never failing to treat each citizen with consideration. They work quickly, effectively, skillfully, and safely, regarding everyone as a customer. The city of Smyrna fire rescue department continues to maintain a fire insurance rating of "class 3," one of the best in Georgia. Fire stations are strategically located on the east, south, and west sides of the city and in the heart of town so they can respond quickly to any section of the city. Paramedics on the fire trucks provide advanced life support including drugs, airway intubation and electrical defibrillation to heart attack victims.

All city of Smyrna fire and rescue vehicles are equipped with hydraulic rescue systems, known as the "jaws of life," and flood lighting systems. The emergency management division of the fire department provides warning of imminent severe weather through a siren system and is responsible for all emergency planning, emergency management and subsequent paperwork. Education programs for children, the city's strong fire code, well-trained firefighters, and rapid response times help the fire rescue department meet and exceed the highest standards daily.

Above: Acting Smyrna Fire Chief Hubert Cochran.

Below: Smyrna Fire Chief Larry William.

Bottom, left: Retiring Assistant Fire Chief Sam Wehunt (middle) receives a commemorative mounted fire axe from Smyrna Fire Chief Jason Lanyon (left) and Assistant Chief Roy Acree as a gift from the department.

Bottom, right: Smyrna Fire Chief Jason Lanyon.

❖

Right: Located on Spring Road across from Argyle Elementary School, this building replaced one that had been constructed in the 1970s on the same site.

Below: New Fire Station No. 1 opened in 1999 at 2620 Atlanta Road.

SHARING THE HERITAGE

Historic profiles of businesses, organizations,

and families that have contributed to the

development and economic base of Smyrna

Leadership Sponsor

Castellaw Funeral Home

SPECIAL THANKS TO

GLOCK, Inc.

Motorcars International, Inc.

CASTELLAW FUNERAL HOME

Castellaw Funeral Home, Smyrna's first locally owned funeral home, was originally named Sanders Funeral Home when it was opened in 1960 in an old house on Concord Road by brothers Bill and Warren Sanders and B. C. Castellaw. It was back in the day when funeral homes provided ambulance service for five to twenty dollars.

four beautifully landscaped gardens, offering families a peaceful and tranquil setting to remember their loved ones.

"We are committed to providing superior service and being a vital part of the community," said Gale Castellaw Baker, who began working with her father in 1968 and became president when he retired in 1996. Today, she is the

❖

Above: The original Sanders-Castellaw sign.

Right, top: Founder and Smyrna civic leader B. C. Castellaw.

Right, bottom: The original Castellaw Funeral Home on Concord Road.

With Castellaw taking an increasingly prominent role and becoming a driving force in the business, in 1964 the name was changed to Sanders-Castellaw Funeral Home. And in 1966, with the idea in mind to expand and build a state-of-the-art mortuary facility to serve Smyrna, Castellaw bought out his partners and broke ground at 866 Church Street that year for an eighty-two-hundred-square-foot building, which was the first facility designed especially for a funeral home to serve the Smyrna area. He was joined in the new venture by local businessmen and friends, Attorney J. Al Cochran and CPA Jim Perry.

For the past four decades this modern, spacious facility, with four visitation rooms, a forty-five foot cathedral chapel with seating for more than 200 people and more than adequate parking space, has been an important part of the Smyrna community. It is located a few blocks from the new downtown Smyrna on eight beautifully landscaped acres. In 1996 the Castellaw facility was completely updated. The funeral home now sits amid

owner along with her brother, B. Coleman Castellaw, Jr., Mrs. J. Al (Leila) Cochran and Mrs. Jim (Loretta) Perry.

Manager Robert W. Dean has been a key member of the Castellaw staff since 1994 when he came to the Funeral Home as a Funeral Director/Embalmer. He was promoted to his present position in 1997. He also has an important role as Grief Facilitator for "Servicing the Teardrops" grief classes. Robert also is a licensed insurance agent and along with his other duties he cares for Castellaw's four beautifully landscaped gardens and a vegetable garden on the property. Active in civic affairs, he is a member of the Smyrna Kiwanis Club and a member of Central Church of Christ. "Robert's professionalism and versatility is a great asset to us and the community," Gale commented.

Lions Club and was later named Lion of the year. He also served on the advisory board of the Smyrna Emory-Adventist Hospital.

Gale has followed in her father's footsteps, being active in Smyrna's civic and community affairs. She has been on the board of the Smyrna Business Association for the past twelve years and was selected Business Person of the year in 2005. She has also served on the Emory Adventist Hospital Foundation for ten years.

B. C. Castellaw, a native of Macon and the son of a prominent builder there, came to Atlanta when he was sixteen to work in the warehouse of what was then one of the country's leading grocers, A&P. He had a career in the food service business for the next twenty years and used that experience to become commissary director for the Third Army at nearby Fort McPherson. He retired from the Civil Service in 1977. A long-time Smyrna civic leader, Castellaw was president of the local

Also active in community religious affairs, Gale was a member of Green Acres Baptist Church for forty-seven years and has been a member of Macland Baptist for the last two years.

Castellaw Funeral Home is a modern day Funeral Director Service and Caskets Retail specialist which also provides for crematories and cremation services. It is the first funeral home in the area to provide Worldwide Web Casting for funeral services. They offer Grief Seminars every quarter and has hosted a

B. C. and Hellan unveil architect's rending of Smyrna's first modern mortuary facility in 1967.

Candlelight Memorial Service in December for the past fourteen years with various clergy in the community participating.

Importantly, the firm has ties to thousands of quality funeral homes in the U.S., which enables it to extend services out of town.

and most complete selections of funeral and cremation services and products in the metro area. "Our staff is trained to provide ways for families and friends to participate in services which help in the healing process," Gale emphasized.

❖

Right: B. C. Castellaw, flanked by Smyrna Mayor George Kreeger (left) and State Representative Hugh Lee McDaniel (right) at Castellaw Funeral Home's ground-breaking ceremony.

Opposite, left: The modern, state-of-art Castellaw Funeral Home with beautiful landscaped gardens.

Opposite right: The current owners of Castellaw Funeral Home (from top to bottom): Gale Castellaw Baker, B. Coleman Castellaw, Leila Cochran, and Loretta Perry.

"Our professional staff regularly participates in continuing education with programs designed to keep on top of the industry," Gale pointed out.

Staff members assist families on a daily round-the-clock basis, offering one of the best

Gale enumerated an array of services the funeral home offers, giving assurance of its commitments to the families it serves: "Since the beginning of Castellaw Funeral Home, it has been the policy of our staff to make families aware of all alternative arrangements and the cost of those services. The disclosures are made in compliance with the requirements set forth by the Federal Trade Commission. Our prices have been computed according to the guidelines set forth by the F.T.C. Rule.

The goods and services listed are those we can provide to our customers. You may choose only those items you desire. However, any funeral arrangements you select will include a charge for our basic services and overhead. If legal or other requirements mean you must buy any items for which you did not specifically ask, we will explain the reason in writing on the statement we provide describing the funeral goods and services you selected."

our community with all of their financial and emotional needs, we have several different 'Funeral Packages.' These packages consist of specific services with a specific casket included at a reduced rate. We also include a worksheet to be used in comparing funeral related charges between funeral homes for those families who like to shop for better prices and better services. The worksheet lists the three areas of charges most funeral homes charge. Keep in mind some funeral homes place their mark-up on the services and charge less for the caskets and vaults. Other funeral homes have a lower service charge and their mark-up is on the merchandise. By using the worksheet, which shows a final total, a good and fair

She elaborated on the packages families may choose from: "We have found over the years serving families that many different financial situations occur during their lifetime. Some families don't see the need to spend a lot, some families only have a certain amount of insurance set aside for funeral expenses and some families can only spend a specific amount of 'out of pocket' funds for funeral expenses. In an effort to assist all families in

comparison is provided. "We firmly believe that 'everyone' deserves a dignified funeral service," she concluded.

On its fiftieth anniversary next year, Castellaw will celebrate its motto: "A Half Century of Caring; Three Generations of Trust."

For additional information or families with questions about Castellaw's services, please visit www.castellawfuneralhome.com. or call 770-435-9038.

EMORY-ADVENTIST HOSPITAL AT SMYRNA

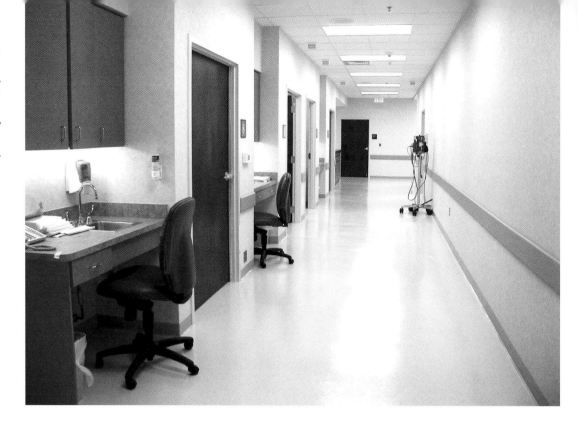

❖

Above: Equipped with a highly-qualified, responsive staff and state-of-the-art equipment, our Emergency Department treats approximately 24,000 patients per year.

Below: Ray Carney walking a camel, in the mid-1980s.

Emory-Adventist Hospital at Smyrna (EAH) was founded in 1974 when a group of physicians recognized the need for a hospital to serve their local community.

Still known today by many old time "Smyrnans" simply as Smyrna Hospital or the "old Smyrna Hospital" under the joint venture between Emory Healthcare and Adventist Health System, the hospital, by any name, continues to offer the community top quality comprehensive healthcare. "Extending the healing ministry of Christ" is its mission statement.

Adventist Health System purchased the hospital in 1976 and it became the first healthcare institution in the Atlanta area to be affiliated with the Seventh-day Adventist Church. Adventist Health System owns and manages hospitals, nursing homes, health agencies, healthcare systems and an array of other services. With hospitals located across the U.S., Adventist Health System is the largest not-for-profit Protestant hospital system in the country.

It was 1995 when Emory Healthcare joined with Adventist Health System to operate the hospital and the name was changed. Emory Healthcare has established a reputation as a leader in cutting-edge research and technology. As the largest, most comprehensive healthcare system in Georgia, Emory Healthcare has 1,184 licensed patient beds, 9,000 employees and more than 20 health centers located throughout Metro Atlanta.

Founding board members were Robert Fink, Walter Curry, Dr. Robert Kushner and then Smyrna Mayor John Porterfield. Fink later became a founder of the Ridgeview Institute in Smyrna. He recalls, "During the early seventies, the only hospitals available to Smyrna residents were the large hospitals in Cobb County. Often a patient would be required to delay surgery due to the waiting list for the small number of operating rooms available. Our founding group wished to develop a hospital for Smyrna residents in the city of Smyrna and provide the necessary facilities for the care needed by the residents. I am very proud to have been involved in the development of the hospital."

EAH is involved as a good citizen with many community and charitable affairs. An active community education program offers discounted or free screenings and health-related seminars presented by medical professionals. In addition, the hospital participates in the Cobb Chamber Partner in Education Program, and provides sponsorships for numerous community initiatives. Employees are also encouraged to get involved in the community and participate in various drives.

Visitors to the hospital may notice containers for collecting food for MUST Ministries, or clothes for the homeless, blankets and coats for the needy, school supplies, and used eyewear for Vision Rehabilitation Services.

Each year the hospital publishes a Community Benefits Report, which outlines the impact that the hospital has on the community. The report combines the charity care, unreimbursed costs for Medicare and Medicaid, and costs associated with community support and health education.

"The total direct benefit to the community was over nine million dollars in 2008," EAH President Dennis Kiley pointed out.

Commenting on his tenure at EAH, Kiley said, "I've been the president of Emory-Adventist Hospital for nine years and I can honestly say it has been a tremendous privilege. I have been especially impressed with the people of Smyrna and their support of our hospital. I continue to hear stories about how our hospital has impacted their lives throughout the years." Adding, "The residents are proud to have a hospital in their community and we are glad to be here to serve. We are

celebrating our thirty-fifth anniversary this year. With all the challenges that healthcare institutions continue to face, that, in itself, is remarkable!"

Ed Moyer's long and varied career with EAH began when he was seventeen years old and went to work as a nursing assistant. Today, he is the hospital's Chief Operating Officer. He recounts going from his nurse assistant job to ICU technician and then up the ladder to the Emergency Department as a paramedic. "In 1982, I became the Director of Emergency Center as we opened a new department," he recalls. "It is with this position that I had the opportunity to work with the community and fell in love with what Smyrna had to offer." He left briefly to work for another hospital but returned in 2008 to take his present position. "…It felt like I was coming home…Smyrna has really grown and there have been many changes but I still see that warm spirit of community."

Sharon Croyle, who has been affiliated with the hospital, first as a Trustee, and now as Foundation Director commented, "I like the idea that I'm part of a Christian-based facility. It's evident in the loving, family atmosphere. In my role, I work closely with community leaders and I always hear the same thing—'Your people are so nice and friendly' or 'I was a patient at your hospital and you have such a caring staff.' I hear this all the time."

Much of EAH's past history and activities offer fond memories for many in the community. For years the hospital's Foundation sponsored fundraising galas. One of its most memorable featured the popular vocalist Marie Osmond of the famous Osmond family. "We had 720 people at that Gala. It was very successful," states Croyle.

Vice-President of Business Development Peggy Seckler has been a hospital employee for thirty years. She remembers that one of the items that the hospital was well known for, ironically, had nothing to do with healthcare. "One of our most memorable past events, which people in the community still talk about, was the Live Nativity." She remembers, "It was complete with live camels, donkeys and many other animals. In fact, one year a camel got away and was running down South Cobb Drive! To this day, many Smyrnans remember that when they were children, Christmas wasn't Christmas until their family visited the Live Nativity."

EAH is at the forefront of disaster preparedness in Cobb County, serving as the lead hospital for the Metropolitan Medical Strike Team (MMST), an organization that falls under the Department of Homeland Security. EAH has received federal designation as a National Disaster Medical System Hospital and has the only stationary decontamination facility in Cobb County.

Today the hospital campus includes the hospital facility, the Emory Clinic building and the Medical Arts Center, which houses internal medicine and family practice physicians as well as a variety of specialists. Some of the services you will find at EAH include emergency services, laboratory, imaging/radiology, interventional radiology, surgery, rehabilitation services, lithotripsy, sleep studies, diabetes education program, ICU, and Medical-Surgical care. In addition, EAH is the only hospital in Georgia to offer InQuickER, an innovative online ER registration system which allows patients to wait in the comfort of their home and avoid crowded waiting rooms and long waits.

The hospital is located at 3949 South Cobb Drive in Smyrna and on the Internet at www.emoryadventist.org.

❖

Emory-Adventist Hospital at Smyrna has received federal designation as a National Disaster Medical System Hospital and has the only stationary decontamination facility in Cobb County.

The Bankers Exchange LLC, a worldwide supplier of new and remanufactured ATM parts, banking equipment, supplies and services based in Smyrna, was founded in 1991 when Jim Trout saw the need within the financial services industry for a ONE STOP shop for all financial institutions, government agencies and ATM deployment companies. At the time he had worked several years in the computer industry.

The company has grown during the past two decades to become a market leader in the industry, both domestically and globally. It got its start in a 7,500 square foot garage and is now housed in a 30,000 square foot state-of-the-art facility in Highlands Park.

In 1999 the company made a major personnel move when it hired Christian Ranke. Ranke, originally from Rochester New York, relocated to Atlanta from Pordenone, Italy, where he was serving for the 31st Expeditionary Task Force/ NATO since 1995.

In 2007 the founders sold the company to Summit Equity Partners, a Georgia firm. A year later the company moved into its new headquarters in Highlands Park and Ranke was named president.

ATMatrix LLC, a wholly owned subsidiary of The Bankers Exchange, was established in 2008 for expansion into the ATM Deployment market.

"We are proud of the fact that our engineers, technicians and subject matter experts have been satisfying the needs of the financial and ATM industry since the company's inception," Ranke commented. "Our company is unique in culture, aggressive in the marketplace, and genuine in ability. I feel this current economic environment needs companies such as ours to help people remember that their work and doing a good job for the company, client, and vendor paves the way in ones personal life as well as business life."

In 2009, The Bankers Exchange was named the leader in the ATM Support Industry globally. "Our new focus is to create a simple, turnkey solution for the banking community here in Georgia. As we experience the change in generations, new services and customer feel will direct the market. We plan to create that new experience for the marketplace."

Today, The Bankers Exchange operates with less than fifty employees and has revenues of approximately $12 million a year with a forecasted growth of more than fifty percent over the next five years. The firm's customer base includes over 40,000 financial institutions nationwide as well as the leading companies in the ATM Industry.

COBB CHAMBER OF COMMERCE

For nearly seven decades the Cobb Chamber of Commerce has been a major force in working to maintain a healthy economy and way of life second to none in Cobb County.

Founded in 1942 the Chamber's mission is to strengthen the local economy, promote the community, build solid relationships and provide quality service to its members.

To be a member of the Cobb Chamber is to be a part of a strong business identity. With more than 2,500 businesses in its membership, the Chamber is the largest local organization offering access to the community and the community's movers and shakers. From First Monday Breakfasts to Business-After-Hours to Area Council meetings, Chamber gatherings offer an abundance of networking opportunities. Through its Chairman's Club, the Chamber also brings together the area's most influential leaders and decision makers.

As a participant in efforts to drive economic development the Chamber fosters a healthy business climate by working to bring in new industry while expanding opportunities for existing businesses. Among its many activities are networking events and business-focused classes such as Business University. The Chamber maintains a professional Business Resource Center staffed with outstanding and knowledgeable managers committed to the businesses of Cobb.

The Chamber works behind the scenes every day in the areas of economic development and government affairs to ensure Cobb remains a great place to live, work and play. A long-standing advocate for business, the Cobb Chamber works year round with local, state and national officials to ensure that the voice of Cobb's businesses is heard.

The Cobb Chamber provides members diverse business opportunities positively impacting their bottom line. By being a member of the Cobb Chamber means investing in the future of your business and community.

❖

Above: Chamber members gather at Washington Fly-In.

Below: Johnny H. Isakson Building, Cobb Chamber Headquarters.

The Development Authority of Cobb County is closely aligned with the Cobb Chamber of Commerce working to encourage quality growth within Cobb County while supporting economic development enhancing the respective tax base.

Under state law industrial revenue bond financing has been recognized and justified as a bona fide public purpose and has served as a legitimate incentive/instrument to locate business, retain and enhance existing infrastructure, and support economic development initiatives that are in keeping with the economic development plan of Cobb County.

The Authority works in concert with the County Commission, economic development professionals and state agencies, to ensure that projects are in best interest and support the overall growth and economic development strategies of the county.

Created by the state of Georgia in 1972, the Authority consists of seven members appointed by the Board of Commissioners, and supported by an executive director, an administrative assistant, financial/bookkeeping professional and counsel, who provide guidance pertaining to each project. Members of the Authority are committed citizens who volunteer. The Authority, to ensure balance and relevant expertise, works with the Commissioners to make sure that those who are asked to serve bring skills suited for such responsibility.

The Authority is committed to assisting companies in locating and expanding their operations. It serves as a useful vehicle in coordinating the expeditious completion of a project, in particular in relationship to local and statewide government bodies.

Working in concert, the Cobb Chamber and the Development Authority of Cobb County are in the vanguard of progress in Cobb County.

Above: Cobb Development Authority, along with local builders, aids county building boom.

Below: Kennesaw Hall is the result of Cobb Development Authority supporting county development.

First Baptist Smyrna

In his very fine 1984 centennial history of Smyrna First Baptist Church, local historian, leading citizen and longtime First Baptist Church member Harold Smith commented in the book's preface, "The First Baptist Church of Smyrna has a glorious past, a wonderful present and with God's continued leadership, will have an exciting future as it begins its second hundred years."

During the past twenty-five years Harold's prophecy of "an exciting future" has come to pass. While adhering to its Articles of Faith set forth in the Church's constitution of 1884, First Baptist has entered the modern era in the words of Pastor Steven Kimmel, "...continuously making a difference in the community and in the lives of families and individuals of all ages through the Church's many outreach programs and ministries."

Dr. Kimmel talks about some of the programs and ministries which make First Baptist relevant in today's society, while serving its varied congregation: "Every child who participates in Upward Sports basketball, football or cheerleading is a winner. Teenagers reach out to needy families at Christmas and enjoy special activities and events year-round that are designed for their high energy levels and creativity. People of all ages grow spiritually and cultivate friendships through Bible studies and spread God's love in tangible ways through mission activities in the community, our nation and around the world."

"Today the church is multi-generational and offers a blended style worship service where people come together for praise and worship, Bible study and ministry," Dr. Kimmel points out. "In addition, there are dozens of other ministries tailored to meet specific needs."

Following are some of the multiple ministries with brief descriptions provided by Dr. Kimmel:
- Music Ministry: The annual Glory of Christmas presentation features Christmas music, drama and a few special surprises as the choir, orchestra and drama team join together for an unforgettable presentation that ushers in the holiday season. Everyone from preschoolers to senior citizens can participate.
- Preschool and Children's Ministries: Sunday School and preschool and children's worship, music and mission activities. Hundreds of children enjoy the fast-paced hands-on experience of Vacation Bible School, as well as the summer camp tradition of Camp Lee.
- Student Ministry: The student ministry has special weekend retreats for spiritual growth, ski trips, and adoption of families in need for

Christmas; every Wednesday they get together at AWOL for fellowship, to hear a Christian student band and an inspirational message. Every summer student mission teams take trips to help people in the United States or abroad.

- Singles Ministry: Focuses on bringing single adults into a growing relationship with Jesus Christ.
- Adults: Bible study classes, women's and men's ministries, college and career ministry, ministries to the divorced, classes on financial management and parenting classes. Church and community members enjoy fellowship at special events.
- Senior Adults: Offering any person over age fifty-five an involvement with Church ministries.
- Partnering with a Sister Church: First Baptist partners with Crossroads Community Church in Kenner, Louisiana.
- Missions Across the Street and Around the World: Involvement with helping flood victims, volunteering at MUST Ministries, the Baptist Men cooking meals in disaster areas, or working along side a church in Moldova.
- Bible Studies: Studies and prayer groups are active almost daily, including Kay Arthur's Precept studies, Bible Study Fellowship, men's prayer group and college and career studies.
- School for Young Children: A weekday education program has been provided for preschoolers and kindergartners in the community for more than fifty years.
- Lending Helping Hands: Volunteers offer special assistance to those in the community with special needs.
- First Aid Ministry: Ministering to the physical needs of the church and community coordinated by registered nurses is the focus.
- Upward Sports Ministry: Focused on changing generations globally and recognizing that every child is a winner. More than 700 boys and girls are involved.
- Brown Elementary School Partnership: Activities include helping with fall festivals, helping children with reading and in computer labs, donating school supplies and hosting teacher appreciation lunches.

To find out more about First Baptist Dr. Kimmel urges those interested to visit the Church Internet site, www.smyrnafirst.org or call the Church office at 770-435-3231.

KENNY'S®
GREAT PIES!

When nine-year-old Kenny Burts' grandfather introduced him to that Florida delicacy, real, bona fide, Key Lime Pie, he was hooked for life. His passion for the pie as a young man, and later, his vision for its potential as the basis for a business led him to found what is today one of Smyrna's and metro Atlanta's most successful and fastest growing businesses, Kenny's® Great Pies, Inc.

A native of Atlanta, Kenny founded the company in Marietta in 1989 and relocated to Smyrna in 1992 into a leased 3,000 square foot space in an existing building.

The company's "flagship" product is that authentic key lime pie that ignited Kenny's passion when he was a child. For the first decade under the name Key Lime, Inc., the company produced key lime pies exclusively. Dedicated to making the finest, genuine tropical pies available, Kenny's began to produce its mango and lemon pies and changed the name of the company to Kenny's Great Pies. "We have a chocolate banana cream pie currently under development and an old family favorite, cherry cheese pie, which will be brought to the market soon," Kenny enthused.

"The primary purpose of Kenny's Great Pies is to produce the finest, genuine, tropical cream pies available on the market with the goal of worldwide distribution," Kenny stated. To that end, over the course of the first fourteen years the company expanded its operation and took over the entire 18,000 square foot building where it was housed, which included an essential additional tractor trailer frozen storage unit outside of the building.

It was 2004 when the Burts family purchased three acres and a 33,000 square foot building at 5200 Highlands Parkway in the Smyrna city limits. In 2006 there was an extensive upgrading of the property and a year-long renovation of the building, making it a state-of-the-art food processing facility turning out Kenny's award winning products.

"Our current production rate capabilities exceed 6,000 pies a day," Kenny points out. "We are proud of the fact our products are recognized as the 'gold standard' of quality in our industry."

"Many hours of research and extensive testing go into production to maintain high standards of quality and consistency," Kenny reiterated. "Each product is designed to be a long-term benchmark of quality for the industry."

Kenny's signature key lime pie continues to be its star product, consistently winning awards at the prestigious Great American Pie Festival in Celebration, Florida. The pie was entered in the commercial segment of the competition in 2006, 2005 and 2004, walking away each time with the blue ribbon in the "Super Gourmet Open Cream Pie" category.

❖

Right: Kenny Burts received the Co-Citizen of the Year Award by Mayor Max Bacon, 2002.

Soon after the company was founded it became a family affair when Kenny's father, Ransom Burts, became actively involved, assuming the responsibilities of vice president and finance manager. By late 1992 a partnership was formed with a private investor which helped fund the company's immediate needs and spurred substantial growth.

As the old adage goes, "the proof is in the pudding" or as in this case, the pies. In testimonials, devotees of Kenny's pies wax eloquent about the products. "Being a connoisseur of all things decadent I have to admit that Kenny's Great Pies has the BEST key lime I have ever tasted," wrote Laura S. "I also tried the new addition, the chocolate cream pie. Holy moly people!! What a delight!" she exclaimed.

Kenny's products are distributed throughout the country via nearly 100 wholesale food service companies, supported by a network of food brokers. The company works closely with its broker network. The famous Kenny's key lime pies have been served on the overseas flights of several international airlines.

Kenny was effusive in his praise of Smyrna Mayor Max Bacon, a long-time supporter of the business. "We appreciate the fact that Max has always been one of our biggest supporters and is a true ambassador for Kenny's Great Pies."

The company currently has approximately twenty-five employees and contracts additional product development personnel and advisors.

Commenting on the future Kenny said, "Our ambition is to triple in size over the course of the next few years and continue to be the world's best cream pie maker."

Additional information is available at www.kennysusa.com.

Left: On September 14, 2009, Ransom Burts was presented with the five millionth pie ever made by Kenny's Great Pies! From left to right: Jeff Cook, Scott Levasseur, Ransom Burts, Kenny Burts, and Gary Muter.

STEVENSON & PALMER ENGINEERING, INC.

❖

Above: B. T. Brown water treatment plant, Coweta County.

Below: Barnesville-Downtown Phase II TE Project.

Smyrna's Stevenson & Palmer Engineering, Inc., was a pioneer in providing environmentally sound services to clients beginning in the early 1960s when founder Earl Stevenson, Jr., would visit small cities throughout the state showing them how to provide proper sewage treatment systems for their communities. Today the firm, which has shown steady growth during the past four decades, offers a wide array of environmentally friendly engineering services to a growing list of clients throughout the state.

Stevenson, a 1953 Georgia Tech graduate in civil engineering, was a Smyrna resident when he founded the company in 1960 with urban planners John Miller and John Steinichen as Miller, Stevenson & Steinichen, Inc. The corporate headquarters was moved from Atlanta to Smyrna in 1978 where it has remained. Stevenson & Palmer, the successor to the original firm, now also has offices in Augusta and Albany.

A succession of top leaders and professionals joined the firm, contributing to its success over the years, beginning with Joe Palmer in 1980, who served as the company CEO from 1984 to 1993. Charles A. "Corkey" Welch joined the firm in 1981 and today serves as Chairman of the Board. Present President and CEO William D. White joined Stevenson & Palmer in 1989.

Commenting on the firm's commitment to clients, CEO White said, "We stay involved in every project from concept to the completion of construction. After construction we are available to assist with operation and maintenance questions as they arise. Our commitment to the client is indefinite and has extended throughout the life of the facility on many projects."

In addition to its in-house capabilities, Stevenson & Palmer maintains associate relationships with architects, engineers in other disciplines, geologists and scientists in order to respond to any need a client may have. "The firm has developed an excellent working relationship and maintains frequent contact with all regulatory agencies at the state and federal level," White emphasized. "In this way, we ensure unified and

consistent project development under our project managers regardless of the complexity of the job."

Several of our employees have experience in private industry or local government, including operations and administration. The realities of serving the public, in concert with our design experience, allows Stevenson & Palmer to understand the project needs, complete it on time and within budget," White continued. "Our projects are designed to provide the most cost-effective alternative, not necessarily the lowest construction cost, but minimal long-term maintenance and operating costs as well as a long operational life span. Our staff is capable of completing any task, regardless of size or scope; however, we appreciate the client's needs and strive to bring personal service. For over forty-eight years Stevenson & Palmer has been built on a tradition of service."

The myriad engineering consulting services offered by the firm are drinking water, wastewater treatment, water and sewer systems, inflow and infiltration studies, environmental services, utility studies, operations and permitting, surveying and mapping services, funding assistance, civil site work, downtown beautification, transportation, storm water, construction management and industrial parks.

Stevenson & Palmer is employee owned, having completed an ESOP (Employee Stock Ownership Plan) in 1995. "Our employee owners are proud of the services we provide throughout the state. Known for personal service, Stevenson &Palmer has served a number of clients continuously since our inception. The operation of three fully staffed offices in Albany, Augusta and Smyrna allows rapid response to meet clients' needs," White concluded.

The company is involved in donations and sponsorships to Georgia Municipal Association, Georgia Rural Water Association, Association of County Commissioners of Georgia and other water and wastewater organizations. Many of its employees are involved in community and civic activities, including the American Legion, Boy Scouts of America, church organizations and youth recreation organizations.

Today the company has revenues of more than five and one-half million dollars and over forty employees in its three offices statewide. Corporate headquarters is located at 2430 Herodian Way, Suite 220, in Smyrna and on the Internet at www.speng.com.

Below: City of Stockbridge elevated stage tank.

Bottom: Shenandoah WWTF Expansion, Coweta County,

RIDGEVIEW INSTITUTE

Robert M. Fink, chairman and founder of Ridgeview Institute, remembers the time thirty-three years ago when "many professionals said the facility was not needed and could not be successful." More than three decades later against all odds and because of its pursuit of quality with compassion, trust and respect, Ridgeview is an established leader in high quality mental health and addiction treatment in the Atlanta metro area.

Speaking of Ridgeview's success in 2005, its founder said, "...I did not realize the impact the development would have on my life or the lives of the more than 57,000 people eventually treated at Ridgeview." As of spring 2009, more than 65,000 individuals and their families have been treated on the Ridgeview campus.

It was during Fink's involvement with the development of Smyrna Hospital (now Emory Adventist Hospital) that he envisioned the need for a free-standing psychiatric hospital with specialty programs which would respond to mental health needs of the community.

The construction of Ridgeview was financed by tax-exempt bonds and opened on November 3, 1976, with an Adult Addiction Program, Adult Psychiatry Program and Adolescent Services Program. Each program was located in a separate cottage, which was unique at that time. In 1978 a professional office building was constructed.

The original Board of Directors included Fink, John Porterfield, Smyrna's mayor at the time, Dorothy Bacon, and Wyman Pilcher.

Present CEO, Paul Hackman, who was serving as Chief Operating Officer when Fink retired, pledged to maintain the Ridgeview standards established by his predecessors.

During 1980 the hospital operated at almost full capacity and a new adolescent cottage was completed in 1981. Within four months, the adolescent cottage was full with a waiting list.

In 1984 an extensive expansion program was pursued. An additional patient cottage, conference center and new office building were planned. Upon completion of the expansion program in 1985, Ridgeview Institute was a 200-bed psychiatric hospital located on fifty acres of land.

During the late 1980s, Ridgeview Institute became a pioneer in the treatment of adolescents suffering from addiction. In 1985 the facility purchased a school from the Cobb County School System, which was converted into an adolescent addiction day program with a significant educational component which was recognized by the Cobb County School System. The program was named ACTION with an average enrollment of approximately 100 patients. At each annual graduation ceremony, many of the adolescents shared how their lives were saved by the program. The program existed until 1984, when the insurance reimbursement rules were modified.

In the early 1990s, as managed care began to reduce the length of stay for the patients, Ridgeview began to work with managed care in an attempt to provide quality treatment with a reduced length of stay. It began to develop a day hospital to provide additional care after the discharge from inpatient treatment. Today,

Ridgeview's Day Hospital is a building dedicated to the sole purpose of outpatient treatment, which provides treatment both for those in need of a less intensive level of care or stepping down from inpatient treatment. Here patients are treated at the partial level of care which consists of treatment lasting a minimum of six hours a day, and/or intensive outpatient treatment lasting three hours a day which allows patients to work or attend school while in treatment. Many of the partial day hospitalization patients live in the Recovery Residence on campus.

Over the years Ridgeview has become a respected continuing education resource, offering approved continuing education credit for psychologists and master's level therapists throughout the greater Atlanta area. Throughout the year Ridgeview offers seminars and workshops on a broad range of mental health and addiction topics presented by nationally and regionally known speakers.

Ridgeview Institute is a distinguished training placement for the next generation of addictionologists, psychiatrists, nurses and clinicians. As such, Ridgeview works closely with area colleges and universities to offer a variety of training rotations and internships for addiction and psychiatry residents and fellows, medical students, nurses and graduate students.

Ridgeview hosts a variety of free twelve step meetings and other support groups that are open to the public. Twelve-step meetings include Alcoholics Anonymous, AlAnon, ACA/DF, Chronic Pain Anonymous, Cocaine Anonymous, Codependents Anonymous, Eating Disorders Anonymous, Emotions Anonymous, Gamblers Anonymous, Narcotics Anonymous and NarAnon. The facility also hosts groups for depression/manic depression, anorexia/bulimia and friends and family of people with eating disorders. Ridgeview Institute supports the needs of the community with over thirty-five groups a week on its campus.

Additional information is available on the Internet at www.ridgeviewinstitute.com.

GEORGIA POWER- McDONOUGH- ATKINSON

A Harvard grad and one-time cowboy and a Georgia Tech star quarterback, who is a member of its Hall of Fame, could be called the founding fathers who laid the groundwork for what was to become Georgia Power's McDonough-Atkinson Plant nestled on 357 scenic acres on the Chattahoochee River in Cobb County's Smyrna.

Georgia Power is the largest subsidiary of its parent, the Southern Company.

Henry M. Atkinson (1862-1939), a Bostonian and a banker before becoming a utility executive, and John "Jack" McDonough, a Savannah native who was president of Georgia Power (1957-1963) and lived until 1983, were of different times and eras but had the

same dedication and drive to make their company and community better places to work and live. "A Citizen wherever We Serve" is a motto that perfectly fit both of them and the company they helped nurture.

When Georgia Power decided never to solely rely on one resource for generation, it built the Atkinson plant in 1930. It was the first of its modern central generating stations using fossil fuels to produce steam rather than relying on hydro power. The company retired the plant in 2003 due to waning efficiency and availability of parts.

Construction of Plant McDonough began in 1960 and was completed in 1963. It began producing electricity with one 245-megawatt generating unit. A year later another identical unit was placed in operation, bringing the plant's total electrical output to 490 megawatts. At this time and for several years after it was the largest and most powerful generating station in the Georgia Power system and the only plant built directly adjacent to another generating facility Plant Atkinson. Today, it continues to be a mainstay in the company's fossil fuel steam electric generating plants. The average annual output of McDonough-Atkinson is a staggering four billion kilowatt hours which is enough electricity to supply more than one million homes.

Currently, 160 employees operate and maintain the plant.

McDonough-Atkinson is part of a fascinating history of electricity in the region, state and Cobb County.

It was just three years after Thomas Edison invented the light bulb in 1879 that the southeast saw the beginning of electric lighting in the region led by the Southern Company's Alabama, Georgia and Florida companies.

By 1890 hydroelectric projects were underway in Georgia and Alabama. Electric street railways, generating plants and municipal arc lighting systems also began to take shape in the major cities.

The Chattahoochee River Substation was significant in local history by providing electrical power to street cars in Atlanta from 1903 to 1946. Power for the rail bed was obtained from the water power station of Atlanta Water and Electric Power Company, which was later bought by Georgia Power. The last rail car ran in January of 1947.

Two of local history's little known stories involve Kennesaw and Austell Electric companies. Around 1910, J. G. Lewis was interested in providing electrical service for himself and a few neighbors. He purchased gas engine and dynamo equipment and then constructed a distribution system himself to lessen the cost of service. It is said he kept no records and never knew if he made or lost money. In 1927, Lewis sold to Georgia Power. Austell Electric was owned and operated by J. B. McCrary. But its date of construction and how long it

operated independently is unknown because no records were kept. Georgia Power purchased it in 1926.

Looking to the future and addressing environmental needs and concerns, there are plans to retire the two coal units at plant McDonough-Atkinson and replace them with three 840 MW gas fired combined cycle units, which will reduce emissions and meet the generation needs for Atlanta in 2011. NOx emissions and SO2 levels will be reduced by more than ninety percent and mercury emissions will essentially be eliminated, using natural gas as compared to the current emissions levels of the coal-fueled plant.

Georgia Power also committed to being good environmental stewards and installed cooling towers at the plant to reduce thermal impacts on the river. The cooling towers are currently used with coal units and will be adapted for use with the combined cycle technology which significantly reduces daily water withdrawal from the Chattahoochee River.

At Georgia Power: "Our mission is simple: to safely deliver affordable, reliable and environmentally responsible energy so every customer in every community is satisfied."

Cooper Lake Automotive

Smyrna's Cooper Lake Automotive is a family-owned and operated full service automotive shop which has been recognized as a leader in its field since it opened in 1991.

Founded by William C. Rimmer, Sr., today his son Bill, Jr., heads a group of highly skilled technicians who carry on the company's mission of providing "the very highest quality automobile repair humanly possible."

The Rimmer tradition of providing top quality auto repair service began in 1968 when William, Sr., opened the first of three service stations he owned and operated over the years, specializing in solving the problems of hard to repair trucks and cars. "We worked on vehicles that other shops couldn't repair," he said, "and we still do that today at Cooper Lake Automotive."

Speaking about those tough, early days, Rimmer, Sr., said, "We worked eighty hour weeks to get to become the successful business we are today. I did all the repair work by myself, with my wife taking the money and pumping gas."

Bill, Jr., who has more than twenty years of experience in the business, began working with his father when he was fifteen. "I have completed countless courses in automotive repair and stay as up to date as possible with continued training," he pointed out. "Our shop is still run by my father's principles and rules which have made him and us successful for almost forty years."

Cooper Lake Automotive offers full service on anything a car or light truck may need, from engines to transmissions and everything in between. "We pride ourselves on giving you the actual repairs you need quickly and accurately," Bill, Jr., emphasized.

The company can test all vehicle makes and model years that require an emission test. Cooper Lake Automotive also has all the equipment, along with the know-how, to repair any vehicle that has failed the state required emission test.

Included among the many services offered by the company are transmission work, basic tune-ups, oil changes, suspension, brakes, bumpers, check engine lights, performance upgrades, tires and a variety of other customer mechanical needs.

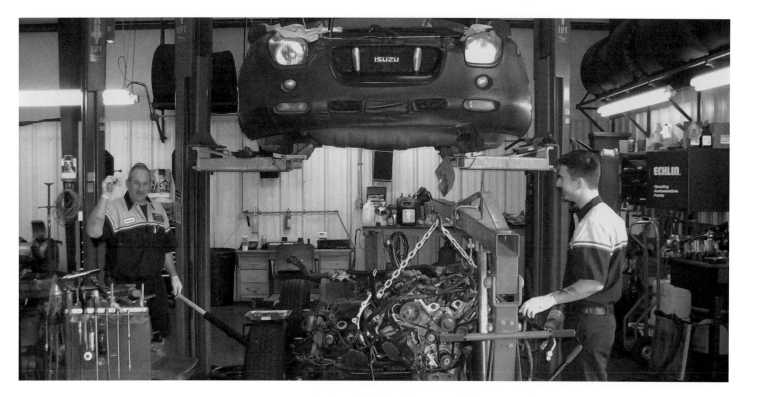

Reviews of the company posted on the Internet by customers give support to Cooper Lake Automotive's mission "…to strive to be honest…be on the cutting edge by embracing new car technologies and keeping current the equipment and tools to repair them." Here is an example: "I went to them and they fixed about five things that were wrong with my truck. They offered me the chance to see the parts and take them with me if that would make me comfortable. Six months later one of the same parts broke again. With no problem I was told to drop my truck off. I did and picked it up the next day. All was fixed and there was no charge. This is a Christian-based family that does not feel that they have to get over on people to make money. I will always take my truck back to them for any future repairs."

Located at 4738 South Cobb Drive, and on the Internet at www.cooperlakeautomotive.com, the firm has a 10,000 square foot facility with fourteen car lifts and numerous flat boys. "We employ ASE certified technicians, so if you need simple work done, such as a light bulb or major work done like an engine light, we are the place for you," Bill, Jr., elaborated. "We are happy to now allow you to make appointments online and also to allow you to look up anything you have done to your car at our shop online at any time. If you need to wait on your repair to be done we

now offer free Wi-Fi in our lobby, so bring along your laptop and surf the web while you wait. Customers may call on 770-431-1936."

Active in the community, among the many activities the company supports are sports at Campbell High School and the local Sheriffs' Association.

The company has eight highly qualified employees and does an annual gross business of around $1 million, helping bolster the Smyrna economy.

Ask-kay
Electrical
Contractors,
Inc.

❖

The old office on Ventura Road in the mid-1980s.

Smyrna's Ask-kay Electrical Contractors, Inc. has been among metro Atlanta's premier full service electrical contractors since it was incorporated by Bill Askea in 1964. Today the company is run by his son, Steve, and over the years the company's success has been due to many dedicated long term employees and several family members, including three of Bill's brothers. Steve's son, Billy, now also works for the firm.

"It was in October of 1963 when I started the business in my home on Hurt Road. I was trying to think of a name for it," Bill relates. "We were sitting around the kitchen table and my mother

(Oma Askea) came up with the name Ask-kay, which is the way we pronounce our name." The name made for a clever slogan and logo with wide practical application, including being showcased on the company's large fleet of trucks.

The company was briefly in downtown Atlanta, with the name Metro-Electric, but was moved later into two remodeled homes in Smyrna and the name change was made. Ask-kay moved into its present spacious quarters in 1983 after being in several other locations in the Smyrna area.

Located at 2970-D Ask-kay Drive on property which was developed by Bill, the company is noted for offering its services twenty-four hours a day, seven days a week, and fifty-two weeks a year. "Our employees take the utmost pride in their work," Steve emphasized. "We continually invest in state-of-the-art equipment so we can handle any situation."

"Backing up our contracting work is our acclaimed 24/7 service crew and supply vehicle fleet," Steve added. "Supporting the construction crews and service electricians is our 8,000 square foot warehouse stocked with over $200,000 of the latest electrical supplies."

Relating the history of the company and its more than four decades in business, Bill tells how it took a lot of dedication and hard work to be successful: "It was tough back when I first went into business. I had to take tests in twenty-two different cities and counties around Atlanta

just to do business," he remembers. Bill later became an expert on matters affecting local electrical contractors and he helped develop the statewide code for them. He served as National President of the Independent Electrical Contractors Association and was instrumental in developing a national apprenticeship program for electricians. More than 200,000 electricians have graduated from the program.

From 1975 until 1983 the company had an office in Hilton Head, South Carolina, and Bill passed the very difficult South Carolina test for electrical contractors the first time he took it.

Steve began working with his dad at an early age, but really was not sure he wanted to make electrical contracting a career. After making his decision to stay in the business, he took over the business in 1990 and with the help of Bill and the rest of the family took Ask-kay to another level. "Steve has really grown the business." Bill says proudly.

Over the years Ask-kay has done work for UPS, many metro schools, major commercial and industrial accounts and at one time did the electrical contracting work for approximately thirty percent of the apartments in metro Atlanta.

Both Bill and Steve have been deeply involved in civic and community affairs throughout their business careers. In what is undoubtedly a first, both have served as president of the local Rotary Club. Bill and Steve were instrumental in helping found several local banks. In fact Steve currently serves on a local bank board.

A man of deep religious faith, Bill said, "Through all of this, working with this business, I couldn't have developed the business if I hadn't had the Lord in my heart. I have stayed involved in my church work and still am today."

Ask-kay lives by its mission statement: Quality and service are our most important concerns. Information is available on the Internet at www.ask-kay.com.

August 2009, front left to right, Traci Hendricks, Cathy Popham, Steve Askea, Bill Askea, Sara Harris and Joyce Cox. Back, Billy Askea, James Thomas, Tim Askea, Vice President, Wes Askea, Lynn Newton and Garry Shipman.

SMYRNA FIRST UNITED METHODIST CHURCH

❖

Above: Smyrna First Methodist Church 1911 to 1967 located at the intersection of Atlanta Road and Church Street. The church parsonage was on the right.

PHOTOGRAPH COURTESY OF THE SMYRNA MUSEUM.

Opposite, top: Smyrna First United Methodist Church sanctuary was dedicated June 11, 1967.

Opposite, bottom: The fellowship hall and welcome center were added later.

The rich history of Smyrna First United Methodist Church began when "…a few families gathered in homes for prayer and testimony," according to the 1990 history of Methodists in Smyrna, *But Thou Art Rich*. It is recorded that worship was held in "several brush arbors" until the first brick church was built on Atlanta Road in 1911. Growing from such humble beginnings, Smyrna First United Methodist Church has become a vibrant place of worship and fellowship and is one of the largest churches in the Smyrna area.

Today more than 800 members worship each Sunday at their three worship services. Traditional worship is offered in the Sanctuary at 8:45 a.m. and 11:00 a.m. with a Praise and Worship Service offered in the Fellowship Hall at 9:00 a.m.

"We are a vibrant church with active ministries for children, families, youth and adults," Senior Pastor Steve Lyle commented. Reverend Lyle was appointed to Smyrna First UMC in June 2009 and he succeeds a long line of distinguished ministers who have served in the Smyrna First UMC pulpit. Reverend Lyle preaches at both the 9:00 a.m. and 11:00 a.m. worship services.

Among the many distinguished ministers during the church's 170-year history were Reverend Walter Crawley, (1907-1909) whose two sons became Methodist ministers; Reverend Lewis Van Landingham (1948-1952), who received a bachelors degree in philosophy from Emory and Master of Divinity degree from the Candler School of Theology; and Reverend James Scarborough (1964-1968), who shepherded the completion of a new sanctuary in 1967.

Reverend Barbara Hatchell has served as Associate Pastor since September 2000 and she preaches at the 8:45 a.m. service. She is actively involved in teaching, Lay Caregiving and missions. She was part of the team that brought the Stephen Ministry program to Smyrna First. Stephen Ministry is a confidential, Christian, one-to-one counseling and support ministry. Reverend Hatchell currently serves as Chairperson of the Atlanta-Marietta District Committee on Ordained Ministry and is a member of the North Georgia Annual Conference Board of Ordained Ministry.

Smyrna First UMC offers a myriad of varied programs for its members. They include:

- Fifteen adult Sunday School classes with additional classes throughout the week.
- Fifteen children's Sunday School classes including nursery.
- Eighteen ways to worship with music, including several choirs; ten for adults and eight for children and youth, two hand bell choirs and an orchestra.
- Special programs for Senior Adults throughout the week, including PrimeTimers, United Methodist Women circles, and United Methodist Men's Group.
- Ongoing programs for children and youth such as Children's Church, Youth ROC, Inside Out (for students/youth) and more.
- Special events throughout the year for children, older kids, and families, such as Vacation Bible School, Hands on Christmas, Easter Egg Hunt, Fall Festival and Summer Camps.
- An offering of several Bible studies and classes during the week at different times of the day which can be long or short term studies focusing on a specific Biblical concept or book of the Bible.
- Life Groups which offer a place to connect with and build relationships with other like-minded individuals who enjoy participating in similar activities or interests.

Smyrna First Methodist Church is located at 1315 Concord Road in Smyrna and on the Internet at www.smyrnafumc.org. Smyrna First UMC is always ready to welcome you. Come to see us!

CARMICHAEL FUNERAL HOME

Randy Carmichael began working in the funeral business in southwest Georgia when he was fifteen years old and today runs one of the most successful funeral home businesses in metro Atlanta with locations in Smyrna and Marietta.

Carmichael Funeral Homes, Inc., was founded in Smyrna in 1976 when Randy purchased Sanders Funeral Home, which was located in the old Rice family home on King Street. The present modern, state-of-the-art facility was built on the same site four years later in 1980. The Marietta location was opened in 1990.

The son of a minister, Randy offers this somewhat humorous and most likely apocryphal story of what prompted him to enter the funeral business: "My daddy was a Baptist preacher and I would go with him when someone would die and we would go in a car that was just about worn out and he would have a suit on that was so slick it would shine and here would come the undertaker in a good-looking suit and I knew I wanted to be an undertaker instead of a preacher," he laughs.

Although Randy is known for his sense of humor, which stands him in good stead in a serious business, he is better know for the compassionate, caring service his funeral homes offer. "One thing I am most proud of is we are the only Cobb County funeral home that is a member of Selected Independent Funeral Homes and we have been since 1984." It is an international organization of independent funeral home owners. Membership is by invitation only and there is a strict set of guidelines for admission. The organization provides training, annual conferences, and local roundtables with other independent owners to discuss issues and solutions pertaining to member independent homeowners.

Growing up in Richland, Georgia, just below Columbus, Randy worked for the local funeral home while in high school. When he graduated he continued to work in his hometown where he was making fifty dollars a week. When Castellaw Funeral Home offered him a twenty dollar a week raise and a place to stay, he moved to Smyrna.

In 1968, he went to mortuary school in Houston and graduated the following year. He

❖

Carmichael Funeral Home, Marietta.

returned to Smyrna where he went to work for Sanders Funeral Home. After serving two years in the Army, he returned to Smyrna in 1970 to work for Sanders and, in 1976, Randy purchased the Sanders operation. Four years later today's present modern mortuary was completed at the King Street site. Three sets of lead glass windows from the old Rice home place were used in the front door and large windows in the current funeral home. The lounge area of the King Street building has a collection of pictures from old Smyrna dating from the 1800s to the 1960s reproduced from the state archives. A wood and wrought iron waiting bench from the old Smyrna depot is currently used in the lounge of the Smyrna location for seating.

In 1990, Randy's reputation as one of metro Atlanta's premier funeral home operations had spread and the Marietta operation was opened at 1130 Whitlock Avenue.

Jim Carmichael, a licensed funeral director, joined his father at the King Street operation in 1998. "Dad and Ken Turner and Dickie Carter have been here the longest, since the late '60s and it is a privilege for me to work with them," Jim said.

The ever iconoclastic Carmichael points out that he is a member of the First Baptist Church of Smyrna. "But, I attend the First Methodist," he says with a mischievous grin.

Active in civic and community affairs, Randy has not only been a member of the Smyrna Rotary Club for thirty-two years, he has an enviable perfect attendance record. He served as president of the club 1985-86.

Among its civic and community contributions, Carmichael's hosts an annual Christmas dinner for senior citizens and an annual Christmas memorial service for families of the deceased at the First Baptist Church of Smyrna.

Speaking about the future, Randy said simply, "We will continue to provide the same level of caring service."

Additional information on services, grief management, and much more is available at www.carmichaelfuneralhomes.com.

Carmichael Funeral Home, Smyrna.

WELLSTAR HEALTH SYSTEM

❖

Below: WellStar Cobb Hospital.
PHOTOGRAPH COURTESY OF HAROLD SMITH.

Opposite, top: WellStar Cobb Hospital located on Austell Road near the East-West-Connector.
PHOTOGRAPH COURTESY OF HAROLD SMITH.

Opposite, bottom: One of the many WellStar facilities, conveniently located for patient and health worker, throughout the area. This one is located at 532 Concord Road in Smyrna.
PHOTOGRAPH COURTESY OF HAROLD SMITH.

The genesis of today's comprehensive WellStar Health System was around the turn of the century in 1906 when prominent Marietta doctor C. T. Nolan opened a sanitarium. Since that time WellStar, which was formed in 1992, has grown to include WellStar Cobb, Douglas and Kennestone, Paulding and Windy Hill hospitals serving five counties, Bartow, Cobb, Cherokee, Douglas and Paulding, with more than eleven thousand employees. Included in its operation is a training/office/meeting facility in Marietta, an administration building housing senior leadership, accounting and human resources, plus seventy-five WellStar physician group locations servicing the patient population in northwest Georgia.

WellStar is the area's leading and largest not-for-profit healthcare provider. "Because we are not-for-profit, maintaining such a high level of service is a constant challenge," said Gregory L. Simone, M.D., president and CEO for WellStar Health System. "With the support of community leaders and donations, the Foundation has raised over $30 million that has helped fund programs like the Open Heart Program, Cyberknife and Safe Kids as well as many other programs and improvements to WellStar."

WellStar is the largest non-academic health system in Georgia, recognized for providing comprehensive clinical services, the latest in medical technology, and an employed physicians group of more than four hundred physicians and advanced practitioners. All of the System's five hospitals have undergone major changes and upgrades over the years.

Over the past forty years, major structural changes were made to WellStar Kennestone, and currently plans are underway to renovate the existing main hospital building to include renovated surgical suites for expanded inpatient and outpatient state-of-the-art services.

During the past twenty-five years, major structural additions have been made to the WellStar Cobb facility and campus in several construction phases. Tranquility, an inpatient hospice center, was opened in 1998 and the Emergency Department underwent an expansion and renovation that opened in 2008.

The Hospital Authority of Douglas County was formed in 1946 and the present WellStar Douglas Hospital was constructed in 1974. A major structural addition was made in 1985. Major Emergency Room and Operating room renovations were made beginning in 2002.

Paulding County's Hospital Authority was established in 1954 and Paulding Memorial Hospital opened as a twenty-five bed acute care, general hospital in 1958. Since then the hospital has undergone four expansion and renovation programs, including the addition of a 136-bed medical nursing unity in 1965.

Windy Hill was originally constructed in 1973. In January of 1980 the Cobb County Kennestone Hospital Authority purchased Urban Medical Center and began operating Kennestone and Windy Hill under the umbrella of the Kennestone Regional Health Care System.

"Our mission continues to be to create and deliver high-quality hospital physician and other healthcare related services that improve the health and well-being of the individuals and communities we serve," Dr. Simone emphasized.

"To deliver world-class healthcare for a community exceeding 600,000 people, WellStar is more than 11,000 strong to meet the health demands of the community," Dr. Simone added. "The healthcare facilities and employees are equipped with the best technology, resources and education available and we are constantly seeking ways to improve care, knowing each day holds more miracles, more life, more chances, more compassion and more opportunities."

WellStar's senior leadership, Board of Trustees and Regional Health Boards constantly evaluate community healthcare needs and consider demographics, physician resources and advancements in technology to develop new services and facilities.

For more than half a century and three generations, WellStar has grown to a network securing grants and partnerships for research, training, and development. WellStar has received accolades by some of healthcare's top organizations such as the Joint Commission of Accreditation of Healthcare Organizations (JCAHO). In 2002, WellStar accepted the nation's first certification for the management of multiple chronic diseases from JCAHO, the nation's predominant standards-setting and accrediting body in healthcare. WellStar also is a destination for hospital planners and healthcare industry experts from around the world to observe family-centered healthcare in action in WellStar's celebrated maternity/neonatal intensive care units.

DICKSON SHOPPING CENTER

More than six decades ago the late T. L. Dickson, one of Cobb County's early civic and community leaders who served as a county commissioner, had a vision of creating a convenient place where people could shop. From that vision came the county's first shopping center, Dickson Shopping Center, which has served Cobb for sixty-six years and is still going strong even though it was partially destroy by fire in 1983. The Center was renovated in 2007. "It was done in the spirit of incorporating old and new Smyrna while keeping the city's essence in today's ever changing, fast-paced life style," John Dickson, T. L.'s son and present owner, said.

T. L. Dickson began business in Smyrna when he opened T. L. Dickson Grocery & Meat located just south of the present shopping center on South Cobb Drive. "People would come from miles around to buy groceries because of fair prices," John remembers. "His favorite sign read 'four pounds of hamburger for $1 and fryers for 29 cents a pound'."

The late Dickson was one of the first merchants to introduce a shopping cart for his customers' convenience.

It was because of increasing business and customer demand that his father had the idea to build a shopping center John recalls. His goal was to give his neighbors a variety of stores where they could shop. It was an immediate success.

In the beginning, along with a service station and grocery store, John and his wife, Marlene,

had an anchor store called Jolene's. Later in 1980, Marlene, along with a partner, opened Floral Creations Florist.

A very important addition to the Center was a U.S. Post Office. Other tenants added an eclectic mix to the Center: Smyrna Cleaners & Laundry, a barber shop, Colquitt Dress Shop, Butler Drugs, Cochran's Furniture, Dixie Dip Ice Cream & Sandwich Shop, Barnett Bakers, Fowlers Insurance, John Mann Men's Clothing, Lamar Shoe Store, Down to Earth Arts & Craft, TLC & Antiques, Vickery Hardware, Wayne's Five & Ten, Becky's School of Dance (which returned after being destroyed by the 1983 fire), and Harris Jewelry, one of Smyrna's oldest businesses.

The 1983 fire destroyed about half the center and Dickson and his sons, John and Lamar, made the decision not to rebuild.

Although T. L. died in 1989, his family has carried on with the same enthusiasm and dedication that he displayed throughout his lifetime.

"Our goal is for people in this area to continue to have a place where shoppers can find friendly, family service," John emphasized. "Currently, with the proposed plans the city has to rebuild the four corners of South Cobb Concord Road, we want to preserve the Center to help bring history alive once again," John pointed out.

"While progress is important for the city, we think it's nice for our neighbors to know they have an old fashioned family-run center where they can shop," he added.

In 1980, Marlene Dickson and a copartner found a great little location along Concord Road to open a flower shop and decided to call it Floral Creations Florist, Inc. They quickly outgrew the space because of the popularity and demand for floral arrangements. The following year the flower shop moved to its current location at Dickson Shopping Center.

Professional floral designer Kristin King of Floral Creations Florist won a prestigious floral award at the 2007 and 2009 annual Southeastern professional florist show. This coveted award recognizes outstanding design and arrangement, both cutting edge, as well as classic traditional design.

Floral arrangements for a wedding will enhance the mood and feel whether the bride and groom have chosen an outdoor garden wedding under arched gardenias and open roses, a 1970s wildflower and barefoot summer event by the lake, or an exquisite indoor extravaganza with lit trees and candelabras. Floral Creations designs corporate holiday parties and any social event from centerpieces on the tables to floor plant decor.

Floral Creations has a large variety of lush green and blooming plants. European Gardens are artisitically arranged to create a mini-garden effect, whether designed in a basket, ceramic or metal container that compliments any decor in the home.

Long-time residents are familiar with Floral Creations Florist's strong reputation as a solid, traditional florist with an excellent record of accomplishment, accountability, and quality and customer service. The florist is located at 3308 South Cobb Drive at the corner of Concord Road in the Dickson Shopping Center and on the Internet at www.floralcreationsflorist.com. Come and visit, or browse, because walking into the

shop brings you back to a time when people stopped to smell the roses. As the oldest founded flower shop in Smyrna, Floral Creations strives to offer the freshest flowers to their customers that they purchase from all areas of the world. They want to be recognized as the florist that offers the most friendly and neighborly service with a smile!

HARRIS JEWELRY COMPANY

❖

Maxine and J. D. Harris.

The late Jack (J. D.) Harris fulfilled a lifelong dream when he opened Smyrna's Harris Jewelry Company in 1961 in Dickson Shopping Center. He discovered he had a talent for the trade when he attended watch and jewelry repair classes in Texas shortly after being honorably discharged from the Navy after World War II in 1946.

"Daddy wanted to make an honest living doing something he loved by offering his customers the best quality for the best price," his daughter, Brenda Haney, fondly recalls. "He always treated others the way he wanted to be treated."

His wife, Maxine, was his partner, doing the bookkeeping, buying and selling watches and jewelry. She passed away in 1998 after an extended illness. J. D. continued to run the store and worked every day until his death in February 2009. In April of 2009 his grandson, Steven Barrer took over the business to carry on the legacy of his grandfather.

"The company was so successful because it was founded and operated based on Daddy's and Mother's strong Christian values," Brenda commented. "They were generous, compassionate, forgiving and loving people."

BECKY JONES SCHOOL OF DANCE

✦

Above: Founder and owner Becky Jones.

Right: Janet Jones, Kristi Rice, Lisa Young, Wendy Smith, Kim Henderson and Susan Surber.

Becky Jones who began dancing at the tender age of six and performed recitals at Atlanta's venerable old Roxy Theatre has spent a lifetime pursuing her love of dance by teaching young dancers.

A native of Atlanta it was 1972 when she opened the Becky Jones School of Dance in the lower level of the Jones' split level home. The school was an immediate success and quickly needed room to grow. She opened her first commercial studio in Smyrna's Dickson Shopping Center, but soon after the studio and shops were destroyed by fire. At the time the *Atlanta Journal Constitution* ran an article about Becky's determination to continue the school.

The School moved across Concord Road and stayed in that location until January 2008 when it relocated back to Dickson Shopping Center due to a redevelopment project.

Becky Jones School of Dance offers tap, ballet, jazz, lyrical, pointe, hip-hop, clogging, gymnastics, and pom. All classes participate in an annual recital.

The School is celebrating its thirty-seventh year in business and Becky says, "I have no plans to stop doing the thing I love."

Atlanta had just won the 1996 Olympic bid and Sanquinetta Dover decided it was a good time to fulfill a lifelong dream of being an entrepreneur. Taking advantage of the economic boom created by the Olympics, she founded DoverStaffing, Inc., which now, after more than a decade, is one of metro Atlanta's most successful temporary staffing service companies, placing candidates in a variety of industries, disciplines, and professions.

DoverStaffing serves myriad industries including healthcare, banking, federal, state, and local governments, distribution, education, telecommunications, construction, transportation, customer care, and manufacturing. Over the years, the company has provided numerous job opportunities to many individuals throughout metro Atlanta, Georgia, and the United States, aiding the development of the local, state, and national economies.

A graduate of the Tuck School of Business Executive Education Program at Dartmouth College, President and CEO Sanquinetta Dover founded the company with no outside financial backing, but with a lot of religious faith and faith in her own God-given abilities.

Initially, Dover ran the company from a home office. She would meet clients at various public places such as Wendy's and McDonalds to take job applications and interview candidates.

Today, DoverStaffing is headquartered at 4499 South Cobb Drive in Smyrna with satellite offices in Atlanta and Decatur. The firm has five highly-trained staff members and employs hundreds of individuals.

Looking to the future, the company is poised for expansion. As a client of the Georgia Minority Business Enterprise Center at Georgia Tech, Dover has implemented key strategies to propel DoverStaffing to the next level. She has expanded into new markets, created new services, and has founded the Dover Training Institute, a nonprofit organization created to help underserved populations become well-equipped to meet workplace challenges.

"Our mission is to attract, develop, motivate and retain qualified staff to meet our clients' staffing needs in the ever-changing workplace," says Dover. "Our company's sustainability is a result of its fundamental core values of which exemplary customer service and quality head the list. Through our win-win-win philosophy, we promote a flourishing working environment for our clients, employees, and the company."

CAYCE FOODS

Christopher and Yvonne Ogbuefi were working professionals, he as a Civil Engineer and she as a Registered Nurse. At times they thought they may have made the wrong decision to quit their professional jobs to run a food business full time.

In 1991 they purchased Mom & Pop Family Food Store in Smyrna. They continued to work fulltime and manage the business full time. They worked from paycheck to paycheck, sixteen hours a day, seven days a week. In the late 1990s, they made another huge decision to pursue the selling of international foods within their small convenient store. Both decisions proved to be a success.

After eighteen years of business, Cayce Foods is a vibrant successful international food store specializing in many different kinds of food from various countries such as Nigeria, Norway, Australia, Kenya, Malaysia, and Cameroon. "We also sell CDs and DVDs depicting the life styles of people in their native environment," Yvonne points out.

In 2004 they purchased over one and one-half acres in front of their original location at 1687 Roswell Street on which to build a new headquarters for Cayce Foods. Getting the proper zoning was not easy, but with the help of former city Councilman Bill Scoggins, Johnny Wilson, a prominent City of Smyrna resident, and Engineer Etoke Atabang they were able to get the proper zoning needed for the new construction.

"We are located in an area of Smyrna where there hasn't been much development and the city of Smyrna has been very supportive of our plans to build a new facility," Yvonne said.

"We are currently providing products to retail stores in metro Atlanta and wholesale service to customers across the United States, Canada, Japan and the Bahamas," Christopher pointed out. "We plan to extend our product line of foods to other ethnic groups as well in our new location."

Over the years the business has prospered and sales have more than doubled. "We now sell thousands of items retail and wholesale," Yvonne said. "We are still a small business, but with a large business vision."

Christopher and Yvonne credit the success of their business to dedicated loyal customers, good products, good customer service, business integrity and a new vision always on the horizon.

Above: Present location Mom & Pop Family Food Store, dba Cayce Foods, Inc., at 1687 Roswell Street.

Below: Roswell Plaza Phase I. Future location at 1680 Roswell Street.

In 1980, Post Properties, under the guidance of John Williams, purchased a large tract of land in Smyrna and decided to develop a large multifamily community.

The Arbors was the first neighborhood in what was then known as Post Village. During the next several years four more neighborhoods were constructed. Each community has their own unique characteristics and floor plans. Once completed, there were 1,738 apartment homes on 115 acres. In the early years each neighborhood operated independently but the addition of a central Leasing Center in 1998 enabled all of the communities to be operated at one central location. This community was not only the largest apartment community in the southeast but had many more amenities for residents than most communities offered. The property boasts 7 pools, 11 tennis courts, 5 car wash areas, 6 laundry centers, a Resident Business Center, a cardio-vascular room and activity center. The Village at Lake Park has been the recipient of many awards due to the exceptional landscape plan.

In 1999 a state-of-the-art 11,000 square foot Athletic Club that provides residents many fitness options was constructed within the community. In addition to this facility the property abuts the Poplar Creek Nature Preserve and a 2.5 mile jogging trail weaves through the community and the preserve ending at the clock tower on Cobb Parkway. The clock tower has long been identified with the Village and is used as a point of reference when locals are asked for any directions along Cobb Parkway. The number of people that have resided at the Village during its twenty-five year history could populate a small city. Everyone either knows someone who has lived at the Village at one time or has lived there themselves. The close proximity to all major highways, cultural and entertainment venues, shopping centers and downtown Atlanta make the Village an ideal location for the universities and major employers in the area.

Post Properties sold the community in 2005 to RREEF and the community became known as the Village at Lake Park. Today the property still boasts the same upscale amenities and lush landscaping. The location is still a favorite for newcomers to the area as well as long time Smyrna residents.

COMMERCIAL SIGNS

Smyrna's largest and longest operating sign shop grew from a humble beginning in a parents' basement. In 1986, while attending Kennesaw State University, Jeff Kendrick combined ambition and his experience working at another sign company to found Commercial Signs, Inc.

After four years of promising growth and encouragement from his late grandfather, Al Hudgins, Jeff moved into a 2000 square foot building at 3548 Atlanta Road. For the first few years the company was a typical shop and only produced small signs and banners. However, as business grew so did Commercial Signs' capabilities. In 1995 a second building was built and dedicated to manufacturing lighted signs. More recently, in 2000, another building was added to accommodate larger signs and pushed the manufacturing facilities to over 10,000 square feet. The original structures now house the corporate offices and a state-of-the-art graphics department. During this time the firm went from being a local company to servicing national accounts and producing signs for Wal-Mart, Lowes and Target. Today's clients include Ace Hardware, Benjamin Moore Paints and Northwest Exterminating.

"Since the company started we have been dedicated to serving the Smyrna community, Metro Atlanta and southeast regional clients as a full service sign provider," Jeff commented. "Over the years we purposely maintained a small organizational structure and this strategy has been elemental to our success and also fosters a relaxed working environment for our valued employees."

One such employee is Derrick McCravy who has worked in various capacities since 1992 and is now in sales. Speaking of his staff, Jeff states, "Our reputation in the sign industry for honesty and integrity is a key reason for employee retention and the fact that Atlanta's best sign professionals migrate to Commercial Signs."

Another key to success is that all work is done in-house rather than being outsourced to other manufacturers or installers. This insures quality control from start to finish. Customers are encouraged to visit the facility to see their sign in production and meet with the owner and employees.

"We can accommodate any size project and are committed to creating unique signage that helps our customers make a great first impression," Jeff added.

When reference was made to "redneck Smyrna" in an article about the Atlanta area which appeared in *National Geographic* during 1988, the unflattering description hit the collective face of local civic pride like a bucketful of freezing water. Said publication would become an impetus of sorts for sweeping modernization that would literally transform the landscape of midtown Smyrna. It was, as one veteran council member and life-long Smyrna resident succinctly stated, a catalyst.

The City's leaders understood that the nondescript conglomeration of smallish postwar period houses and commercial structures which, perhaps too optimistically, was then called "downtown Smyrna" held no appeal to local residents or to anyone else. But what type of development might draw citizens together as a community in the center of town? The city council members needed to look no further than their own constituents for answers. It was discovered that citizen wish lists almost invariably included a new library or a community center. The City's leadership decided to build both in what would become the nucleus of a new central business district. With decisive action, a brisk pace and considerable citizen support, the city council embarked on an ambitious program to revitalize Smyrna. In just three short years, a new Community Center and City Library were received with overwhelming enthusiasm by local residents and many others—this

accomplishment would garner the City Innovations Achievement Award from the Georgia Municipal Association in 1990. A new Village Green area was included in the project which quickly became a venue for concerts and other activities which appeal to a broad cross section of the citizenry. At long last, the citizens of Smyrna had a downtown area in which they could take pride and assemble as a community.

Capitalizing on their successes, and ever-attentive to the desires of their constituents, the City's leadership realized another concept synthesized from citizen input and expert consultation when the Market Village was constructed in 2002. What had been projected to require three decades to achieve was completed in fourteen years. Representatives from local governments across the nation have visited Smyrna to observe the positive impact of redevelopment on a municipality and to solicit the guidance of the city council in such matters. Mayor Max Bacon, Smyrna's voluble and forthright chief executive for over twenty years, summed it all up this way: "We accepted the challenge of the '90s. We are proud of the City's history and eagerly face her future."

HALPERN ENTERPRISES, INC.

❖

Above: The proposed redevelopment of Belmont.

Below: Belmont Hills Shopping Center. c. 1954.

Halpern Enterprises, Inc., was founded more than five decades ago by the late Bernard Halpern, who immigrated to Atlanta in 1938, at the age of sixteen, from his native Poland. Bernard worked as a retail grocer before entering the real estate business; the company he created has been a leader in the shopping center industry for over half a century.

Smyrna's Belmont Hills has long been one of the crown jewels in the Halpern portfolio. When Belmont opened for business in 1954, it was one of the largest shopping centers in the southeastern United States. The Halpern family purchased the property in 1967 and expanded it to almost 500,000 square feet making Belmont Hills a local showplace and regional shopping destination. Many of the great American retailers of that era had stores at Belmont, including Kroger, A&P, W. T. Grant, Sears, and JCPenney.

For more than four decades, Belmont provided a thriving, vibrant shopping venue for the citizens of Smyrna and surrounding communities. In 1986 the center was totally renovated and was the first recipient of Smyrna's newly-established "Clean and Beautiful Award."

Over time, Belmont Hills and the surrounding residential neighborhoods experienced a variety of market and demographic changes. Following the creation, during the 1990s, of the downtown Smyrna government complex

two blocks to the south along Atlanta Road, Belmont itself became a natural candidate for redevelopment.

The city of Smyrna worked closely with Halpern Enterprises to create a new vision for the nearly fifty acre property, which included a mixed-use community featuring retail shops, restaurants, professional offices, and residential units, all located in an open, pedestrian friendly environment containing public plazas and abundant green space.

Headquartered in northeast Atlanta, Halpern Enterprises owns more than 3.4 million square feet of leasable space in thirty-three retail properties. The company manages its centers with a long-term perspective, taking a "hands-on" approach that helps to ensure the continuing success of each property. With leasing, management, and maintenance staff assigned to each shopping center, Halpern sees to it that all tenants receive personal attention and unusually high value for their rental dollar.

Halpern Enterprises remains a family owned and operated business. The founder's son, Jack, currently serves as chairman, and his sister, Carolyn Halpern Oppenheimer, as vice president.

Halpern Enterprises is committed to giving back to the communities in which it does business, and its principals and employees are involved in numerous volunteer and civic endeavors. The company's owners have also extended their philanthropic activities and reach through creation of the Halpern-Oppenheimer Family Foundation, which annually contributes financial support to a wide variety of charitable causes.

Building upon the legacy created by the company's founder, Chairman Jack Halpern summarizes Halpern Enterprises' long-term vision as follows: "We strive to be a positive force—a caring, committed partner—in each community where we do business."

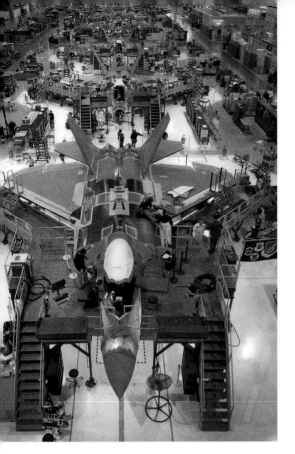

LOCKHEED MARTIN AERONAUTICS COMPANY

Lockheed Martin Aeronautics Company is an industry leader in the design, development, systems integration, production and support of advanced military aircraft for the United States and its allies.

The Marietta site is one of the company's three main production facilities and has been in operation under the Lockheed or Lockheed Martin name since January 1951.

Since reopening Air Force Plant 6, employees in Marietta have built nearly 3,300 advanced aircraft and modified nearly 7,500. The Marietta operation was originally built in 1942-43 for licensed production of B-29 Superfortress heavy bombers. The plant sat idle from 1945 until 1951 when Lockheed reopened the plant to refurbish B-29s for the Korean War.

The plant has been an integral part of the nation's military might since it opened, building B-47 bombers, C-130 Hercules transport, C-141 StarLifter strategic transport and the JetStar executive transport. The C-130 production line is the longest continuously active military assembly line in history.

Lockheed Martin Aeronautics Company is the third largest employer in Cobb County, with around 7,000 employees, and it has an estimated economic impact on the county of nearly $40 million annually. The company promotes volunteerism, provides financial support and donates other resources to support nonprofit organizations throughout the Atlanta area.

The F-22, the world's most advanced fighter, is now operational with the U.S. Air Force. The C-130J is a complete reinvention of the venerable Hercules transport. The Hercules will continue to be the plant's bread and butter for many years.

The C-5, one of the world's largest aircraft, has approximately eighty percent of its useful life left, and the Marietta workforce has embarked on two efforts to keep the C-5 fleet flying for another forty years. The P-3 is the world's standard in maritime patrol aircraft. In 2008 the Marietta facility established production of replacement wings for the P-3.

The Marietta plant is the only military aircraft start-to-finish assembly plant in the southeast, and it is among the few factories building aircraft of any type in the United States. The facility is truly a national resource.

C. J. FOUTS

❖

C. J. Fouts.

C. J. Fouts was a pioneer in business and community development in Smyrna, owning and operating key businesses in the city for more than fifty years while making contributions to civic affairs during that time.

In 1952, C. J. and his brother, Jerry, founded Fouts Brothers. Their first business was a Sinclair Service Station. In the early 1960s they opened a wrecker service and auto parts store. In 1969 the ever entrepreneurial C. J. took a chance on selling a Japanese car, Datsun, made by Nissan, which turned into a successful twenty-four year partnership with Nissan. Never satisfied, a truck dealership was opened in the mid 1980s. Today the business consists of truck equipment sales, a van body manufacturer and a fire apparatus manufacturer with sales throughout the United States.

Shortly before C. J.'s death in June 2006, he was honored by Smyrna Mayor Max Bacon, United States Representative Phil Gingrey and the Smyrna City Council for his civic contributions as an active and original member of the Smyrna Downtown Development Authority and for holding one of the longest active business licenses in the city. Today, at the site of the original business a plaque reads: "The City of Smyrna recognizes the civic contributions of C. J. Fouts as an original and continuously active member of the Downtown Development Authority. This site is the location of Fouts Brothers Sinclair Service Station where C. J. and his brother Jerry established their first business in 1952. Fouts has owned and operated businesses in Smyrna for fifty years and continues to maintain the city's longest active business license."

C. J.'s legacy lives on today through his sons Barry and Tim who still operate the day to day business. They carry the same vision and hope for this business that C. J. did, displaying that vision when they hired C. J.'s grandson, Scott Edens, as general manager.

The Smyrna Historical & Genealogical Society was chartered as a not-for-profit organization under Georgia laws on May 17, 1985. The incorporators were former Smyrna Mayor Harold Smith, his wife Betty, Emmett Yancey and attorney George Carreker.

The purposes were to establish a membership organization and a museum for collecting and preserving photographs, documents and other memorabilia relative to the City of Smyrna and Cobb County. The first membership meeting was held March 27, 1986, at King Springs Park (now Tolleson Park) with eighteen people in attendance. The Societies first issue of *Lives & Times* was published in March 1986.

Five years later, the Smyrna Museum was opened on Saturday, April 25, 1992. The original location was 2858 King Street in a building constructed by the Smyrna Jaycees for the Smyrna Health Clinic.

Historical Society members, city officials and other Smyrna residents were saddened on September 20, 1993, when museum co-founder Betty Smith died of cancer. Several hundred people attended an open house when the Museum was dedicated to Betty's memory in services conducted by Mayor Max Bacon, Councilman Bill Scoggins and Councilman Pete Wood. During ceremonies Mayor Bacon said the current museum building would be demolished as a part of the redevelopment program of downtown and provisions would be made for a new museum.

Several months later, Mayor Bacon revealed plans for the future Smyrna Museum. A replica of the 1905 Western and Atlantic (NC & St. L. and L & N) railroad station that was demolished in the late 1950s would be constructed near its original location. It became the new home of the Historical Society and Museum and is located in the heart of Smyrna. The grand opening for the Historical Society and Museum as well as the new Welcome Center was held on April 25, 1999. Hundreds of citizens, and national, local and state officials attended the ceremony.

In its eleventh year, the Museum houses thousands of photographs, documents, publications and memorabilia dating to the 1830s. It serves the community by providing educational programs and various publications. A meeting room and research facilities are available to schools, civic and service organizations. It is operated by volunteers from the Historical Society, Golden K Kiwanis Club and many individuals who have an interest in preserving history and contributing service to the community.

The Smyrna Historical & Genealogical Society is located at 2861 Atlanta Road and on the Internet at www.smyrnahistory.org.

❖

Left: The original location was 2858 King Street. The building was constructed by the Smyrna Jaycees in 1967 for the Smyrna Health Clinic. The clinic had previously been in a small Justice of the Peace Courthouse that was slated for demolition for another city facility. The Health Clinic moved to a new location at 3830 South Cobb Drive.

Below: The first membership meeting was held March 27, 1986, at King Springs Park (now Tolleson Park) with eighteen people in attendance. Left to right: Emmett Yancey, Jane Yancey, Carolyn Amburn, Jean Bennett, Judith Lowry, Jeane Travis, Mayor Max Bacon, Corrine Hosch, Joan Bennett, Bobbie Shirley, Doris Morris, Tarver Shirley, Betty Smith, Bill Hamilton, George Carreker and Harold Smith.

CONCORD BODY SHOP

While working with Central Chevrolet in Atlanta's upscale Buckhead community in the late 1950s, Cecil Pickens decided it was time to take his talents for doing auto body and paint work to open his own business.

❖

Above: Front of Concord Body Shop at 802 Smyrna Hill Drive, present location since 1975.

Right: Owner and President, Cecil Pickens.

Below: Cecil Pickens inspects a job.

In 1960 he and his wife, Merlene, and one employee, Ethan "Junior" Rainwater, opened Concord Body Shop at the corner of Concord and South Cobb Drive in a rented three car garage. Business was good and it was not long before Cecil decided to build a new shop at 812 Smyrna Hill Drive. The Body Shop moved in 1962 to a new building in what is now Adams Car Center. After thirteen years at the location,

Concord made its final move to its present location at Smyrna Hill Drive in 1975. It is on the property which was the old home place of pioneer Smyrna residents Gilbert Pickens and Wilson Farmer.

Concord takes pride in being Smyrna's oldest and "Best" local body shop, having offered quality service for forty-five years. "We are proud to have maintained solid relationships with our customers and proud to help get their vehicles back on the road," Cecil commented. "Our goal is to return a vehicle back to the customer in quality condition, satisfaction guaranteed."

The company now has twelve employees and James Pickens, Cecil's son, is shop manager.

Among the many services offered are complete body work, collision related wheel alignments, collision related steering suspension frame straightening, theft and vandalism restoration, classic car restoration and repair, and expert color matching.

"These are just a few areas of our expertise," James points out. "We are a premier collision repair center and our facility is equipped with the best tools and state-of-the-art equipment."

Concord Body Shop has a long history of community involvement. Among the activities it supports are Special Olympics and many area Little League teams.

SPONSORS

For more information about the following publications or about publishing your own book, please call
Historical Publishing Network at 800-749-9790 or visit www.lammertinc.com.

Albemarle & Charlottesville:
An Illustrated History of the First 150 Years
Black Gold: The Story of Texas Oil & Gas
Garland: A Contemporary History
Historic Abilene: An Illustrated History
Historic Alamance County: An Illustrated History
Historic Albuquerque: An Illustrated History
Historic Amarillo: An Illustrated History
Historic Anchorage: An Illustrated History
Historic Austin: An Illustrated History
Historic Baldwin County: A Bicentennial History
Historic Baton Rouge: An Illustrated History
Historic Beaufort County: An Illustrated History
Historic Beaumont: An Illustrated History
Historic Bexar County: An Illustrated History
Historic Birmingham: An Illustrated History
Historic Brazoria County: An Illustrated History
Historic Brownsville: An Illustrated History
Historic Charlotte:
An Illustrated History of Charlotte and Mecklenburg County
Historic Chautauqua County: A Bicentennial History
Historic Cheyenne: A History of the Magic City
Historic Clayton County: An Illustrated History
Historic Comal County: An Illustrated History
Historic Corpus Christi: An Illustrated History
Historic DeKalb County: An Illustrated History
Historic Denton County: An Illustrated History
Historic Edmond: An Illustrated History
Historic El Paso: An Illustrated History
Historic Erie County: An Illustrated History
Historic Fayette County: An Illustrated History
Historic Fairbanks: An Illustrated History
Historic Gainesville & Hall County: An Illustrated History
Historic Greene County: An Illustrated History
Historic Gregg County: An Illustrated History
Historic Hampton Roads: Where America Began
Historic Hancock County: An Illustrated History
Historic Henry County: An Illustrated History
Historic Hood County: An Illustrated History
Historic Houston: An Illustrated History
Historic Hunt County: An Illustrated History
Historic Illinois: An Illustrated History
Historic Kern County:
An Illustrated History of Bakersfield and Kern County
Historic Lafayette:
An Illustrated History of Lafayette & Lafayette Parish
Historic Laredo:
An Illustrated History of Laredo & Webb County
Historic Lee County: The Story of Fort Myers & Lee County
Historic Louisiana: An Illustrated History
Historic Mansfield: A Bicentennial History
Historic McLennan County: An Illustrated History

Historic Midland: An Illustrated History
Historic Montgomery County:
An Illustrated History of Montgomery County, Texas
Historic Ocala: The Story of Ocala & Marion County
Historic Oklahoma: An Illustrated History
Historic Oklahoma County: An Illustrated History
Historic Omaha:
An Illustrated History of Omaha and Douglas County
Historic Orange County: An Illustrated History
Historic Osceola County: An Illustrated History
Historic Ouachita Parish: An Illustrated History
Historic Paris and Lamar County: An Illustrated History
Historic Pasadena: An Illustrated History
Historic Passaic County: An Illustrated History
Historic Pennsylvania An Illustrated History
Historic Philadelphia: An Illustrated History
Historic Prescott:
An Illustrated History of Prescott & Yavapai County
Historic Richardson: An Illustrated History
Historic Rio Grande Valley: An Illustrated History
Historic Rogers County: An Illustrated History
Historic Santa Barbara: An Illustrated History
Historic Scottsdale: A Life from the Land
Historic Shelby County: An Illustrated History
Historic Shreveport-Bossier:
An Illustrated History of Shreveport & Bossier City
Historic South Carolina: An Illustrated History
Historic Smith County: An Illustrated History
Historic Temple: An Illustrated History
Historic Texarkana: An Illustrated History
Historic Texas: An Illustrated History
Historic Victoria: An Illustrated History
Historic Tulsa: An Illustrated History
Historic Wake County: An Illustrated History
Historic Warren County: An Illustrated History
Historic Williamson County: An Illustrated History
Historic Wilmington & The Lower Cape Fear:
An Illustrated History
Historic York County: An Illustrated History
Iron, Wood & Water: An Illustrated History of Lake Oswego
Jefferson Parish: Rich Heritage, Promising Future
Miami's Historic Neighborhoods: A History of Community
Old Orange County Courthouse: A Centennial History
Plano: An Illustrated Chronicle
The New Frontier:
A Contemporary History of Fort Worth & Tarrant County
San Antonio, City Exceptional
The San Gabriel Valley: A 21st Century Portrait
The Spirit of Collin County
Valley Places, Valley Faces
Water, Rails & Oil: Historic Mid & South Jefferson County